VIETNAM
and Other American Fantasies

OTHER BOOKS BY H. BRUCE FRANKLIN

The Wake of the Gods: Melville's Mythology

Future Perfect: American Science Fiction of the Nineteenth Century

Who Should Run the Universities? (with John A. Howard)

From the Movement: Toward Revolution

Herman Melville's Mardi (edition)

Herman Melville's The Confidence Man (edition)

Back Where You Came From

The Scarlet Letter *and Hawthorne's Critical Writings* (edition)

Prison Literature in America: The Victim as Criminal and Artist

Countdown to Midnight

American Prisoners and Ex-prisoners: An Annotated Bibliography

Robert A. Heinlein: America as Science Fiction

Vietnam and America: A Documented History
(with Marvin Gettleman, Jane Franklin, and Marilyn Young)

War Stars: The Superweapon and the American Imagination

M.I.A. or Mythmaking in America

The Vietnam War in American Stories, Songs, and Poems

Prison Writing in Twentieth-Century America

and Other American Fantasies

VIETNAM

H. Bruce Franklin

UNIVERSITY OF MASSACHUSETTS PRESS

Amherst

LC 00-030275
ISBN 1-55849-332-8 (pbk. : alk. paper)
Designed by Richard Hendel
Set in New Baskerville and Gill types by Keystone
    Typesetting, Inc.
Printed and bound by Thomson-Shore, Inc.

Library of Congress Cataloging-in-Publication Data
Franklin, H. Bruce (Howard Bruce), 1934–
Vietnam and other American fantasies /
H. Bruce Franklin.
    p. cm.
Includes bibliographical references and index.
ISBN 1-55849-279-8 (cloth : alk. paper)
1. Vietnamese Conflict, 1961–1975 — Public opinion —
United States.   2. Vietnamese Conflict, 1961–1975 —
Influence.   3. United States — Civilization — 1970–
I. Title.
DS559.62.U6 F73 2000
959.704'31 — dc21   00-030275

British Library Cataloguing in Publication data
are available.

A volume in the series Culture, Politics, and the Cold War.

For my grandchildren

Emma Lourdes Amelia Franklin

Gregory Saboya Franklin

Samantha Michelle Franklin

James Bruce Franklin

Maya Louise Saboya Franklin

Alexandra Rosalie Franklin

The Trustees were really angry about my

having wobbled the students' faith in the

intelligence and decency of their country's

leadership by telling them the truth about

the Vietnam War.

Kurt Vonnegut Jr., *Hocus Pocus,* 1990

CONTENTS

ACKNOWLEDGMENTS

Because I have been working on this book for a long time, parts of it have been published in earlier forms as they shaped themselves. I wish to express my gratitude to the editors and publishers of the following:

An earlier version of chapter 1 appeared in the *Georgia Review* 48 (Spring 1994); Susan Jeffords and Lauren Rabinovitz, eds., *Seeing Through the Media: The Persian Gulf War* (New Brunswick: Rutgers University Press, 1994); and Linda H. Peterson, John C. Brereton, and Joan E. Hartman, eds., *The Norton Reader,* 9th edition, and *The Norton Reader,* shorter 9th edition (New York: W. W. Norton, 1996). An earlier version of chapter 4 appeared in Mary Susannah Robbins, ed., *Against the Vietnam War: Writings by Activists* (Syracuse: Syracuse University Press, 1999). Parts of chapter 5 are adapted from my essay "1968: The Vision of the Movement and the Alternative Press," in Michael Klein, ed., *The Vietnam Era: Media and Popular Culture in the U.S. and Vietnam* (London: Pluto Press, 1990). Parts of chapter 7 appeared in *Science-Fiction Studies* 21 (March 1994); *Locus* (October 1994); and *Film & History* 24 (February–May 1995). Earlier versions of chapter 8 appeared in *Science-Fiction Studies* 17 (November 1990); Glenwood Irons, ed., *Gender, Language, and Myth* (Toronto: University of Toronto Press, 1992); and Brett Cooke, George Slusser, and Jaume Marti-Olivella, eds., *The Fantastic Other: An Interface of Perspectives* (Amsterdam: Editions Rodopi, 1998). Parts of chapter 9 are taken from *M.I.A. or Mythmaking in America,* revised and enlarged edition (New Brunswick: Rutgers University Press, 1993).

"Making the Children Behave" and excerpt from "POW/MIA" are reprinted from *Beautiful Wreckage: New and Selected Poems* by W. D. Ehrhart (Easthampton, Mass.: Adastra Press, 1999). Copyright © 1999 by W. D. Ehrhart. Used by permission of the author.

Steve Hassett, "And what would you do, ma." Copyright © 1976 by Steve Hassett. Reprinted by permission of the author.

Excerpt from Bruce Weigl, "Song of Napalm." Copyright © 1988 by Bruce Weigl. Used by permission of the author.

Excerpt from Joe McDonald, "I-Feel-Like-I'm-Fixin'-to-Die Rag." Copyright © 1965, renewed 1993 by Alkatraz Corner Music/BMI. Used by permission.

xii   Photograph of General Loan executing prisoner. Copyright © 1968 by AP/Wide World. Used by permission of AP/Wide World.

The book has benefited from exceptionally insightful critiques by Chris Appy and Marilyn Young. Clark Dougan has given splendid editorial guidance, and the manuscript has benefited greatly from the copyediting of Amanda Heller. My greatest debts are to Jane Morgan Franklin, who helped inspire the book, enriched it with her own knowledge and four decades of antiwar activism, participated in each stage of composition, and contributed in more ways than can ever be acknowledged.

H. B. F.

VIETNAM

and Other American Fantasies

On "Differing Perceptions of Reality"

During the ill-fated invasion of Laos in early 1971, workers at the Stanford Computer Center discovered that the main university computer was running a program code-named Gamut-H, a Stanford-designed plan for a U.S. air, sea, and land invasion of North Vietnam. In the ensuing protests against the university's deep and protracted involvement in the Vietnam War, I gave speeches that led to my being fired, despite my academic tenure, for "urging and inciting disruption of campus activities." Without reopening all the issues of that time and place, I do want to highlight an interesting aspect of the case, one of central relevance to the present book.[1]

Although the Advisory Board that acted as judge and jury in the case acknowledged "Professor Franklin's exceptional competence as a scholar and teacher," it ruled that dismissal, rather than any lesser sanction, was the only practical punishment for words that I had spoken in public (the three acts for which I was found "guilty" were two public speeches and a verbal protest to the police against their declaration that an

entirely peaceful gathering outside the Computer Center was an unlawful assembly). In the published version of its ruling, the board explained the basis of its decision in a section titled "Differing Perceptions of Reality," where the following was presented as proof that my
"perception of reality . . . differs drastically from the consensus in the
university": "In his opening argument Professor Franklin proclaimed
deep convictions about the evils of American foreign and domestic
policy and about the inevitable influences of our socio-economic system in shaping that policy. Essential to this perception is a mistrust of
the allegedly intricate interrelationship between the economic power
of American's [*sic*] 'ruling class' and the maintenance of policies that
are imperialistic abroad and oppressive at home."[2] Arguing that this
perception of reality was too "deeply-held" to be changed by any
punishment (or at least by any they could administer), the majority of
the board members then offered the following logic for my dismissal as
the only viable solution to the problem:

> We are highly dubious whether *rehabilitation* is a useful concept in
> this case. . . . "Rehabilitation" might appear to Professor Franklin as
> a highly unfair mandate to change his convictions. Barring a dra-
> matic change in perception he is unlikely to change his conduct;
> thus "rehabilitation" is likely to fail, whatever the sanction.[3]

Given its premises, this is a compelling argument (and its forecast,
I'm happy to report, has turned out to be accurate). The main issues
about appropriate responses to America's war in Vietnam did then —
and still do — swirl around "differing perceptions of reality." Rehabilitation does not seem to be a useful concept either in my individual case
or for those millions of other Americans whose perception of reality
then or now "differs drastically from the consensus" presumed to dominate Stanford University in the early 1970s. After all, what can possibly
be done to convince such abnormal people that in reality America's
socioeconomic system does *not* shape foreign and domestic policy, that
America has no "ruling class," and if it does, there is certainly *not* any
"intricate interrelationship between the economic power" of this class
and "the maintenance of policies that are imperialistic abroad and
oppressive at home"? No, such deviants are so out of touch with reality,
so imprisoned by their own fantasies, that questions need to be implied
about their sanity. After all, truly rational people — such as the majority of the Stanford faculty and administration — understood that the

Vietnam War was just a mistake, or series of mistakes, made by well-intentioned, fallible men governing a representative democracy.

But suppose that this "consensus" perception of reality is itself a fantasy. Suppose that this fantasy, perhaps interwoven with other fantasies, had something to do with making it possible for the United States to initiate and perpetuate for decades that disastrous war in Vietnam, Laos, and Cambodia—as well as various kinds of subsequent warfare, including bombings or invasions, in Grenada, Panama, Libya, Nicaragua, El Salvador, Iraq, Somalia, Haiti, Sudan, Afghanistan, and Yugoslavia. Further, suppose that the Vietnam War itself would induce profound transformations in American culture and life, including the normal range of "perceptions of reality." And then suppose that these transformations would spawn forms of official, cultural, and psychological denial so extreme that fantasy would become the norm in perceiving the reality of something called "Vietnam"—no longer really a country or even a war but a "syndrome."

Rehabilitation might then indeed become a useful concept—for American society. If so, the necessary therapy would have to include some confrontation with the fantasies that made the war possible as well as those myths, celluloid images, and other delusory fictions about "Vietnam" that in the subsequent decades have come to replace historical and experiential reality. That confrontation is one of the main purposes of this book.

But not all fantasies are delusory. After all, as a teacher of literature I spend much of my life promoting the value of some other kinds of fantasy, those that purportedly put us in touch, not out of touch, with reality. Such fantasies express what Tim O'Brien calls the "story-truth" that allows us to comprehend "happening-truth."

The Vietnam War has created and continues to create an astonishing body of imaginative literature, much of it written by veterans of the war, full of invaluable, often painful, insights into the kinds of fantasies that have obscured or deformed our understanding of America's effects on Vietnam and Vietnam's effects on America. This intensely purposeful literature of experience and discovery tends to run counter to some high fashions in contemporary literary theory and practice. One of the most knowledgeable critics of American Vietnam War literature, Philip Beidler (himself a Vietnam combat veteran), has argued that its "impassioned intensity" and "profound experiential authority" suggest how the nation's literature could be rescued from the epidemic

4 of texts that are mainly about themselves and that are largely unreadable except by a literary coterie.[4] Although I have dealt with this literature more extensively in my anthology *The Vietnam War in American Stories, Songs, and Poems,* I have chosen in the present volume to delve deeper into genres, such as science fiction, that most obviously utilize fantasy as a route to "happening-truth."

There is now fairly widespread acknowledgment that the Vietnam War shattered many of the traditional narratives central to formerly prevailing visions of the United States and its history. Some people regret this and seek to restore old narratives that they consider essential to a unifying national identity, but their mighty efforts are unlikely to put Humpty Dumpty back together again. Others see this shattering as a liberation from dangerous illusions, a wake-up call that forced millions of Americans toward more truthful and beneficial narratives about American history and culture. There is a third view, one that has gained considerable influence in intellectual circles, that sees any "master narrative" or "meta-narrative" — or, for that matter, any coherently structured narrative — as a socially constructed fantasy that radically falsifies the fragmentary, conflicted, and de-centered character of social experience. Although in this book I do not engage in overt arguments about narrative theory, I do operate from a theoretical position that highly values narratives, especially coherently structured narratives — including some forms of fantasy — as crucial to comprehending, within our human limits, human reality.

CHAPTER ONE

From Realism to Virtual Reality

IMAGES OF AMERICA'S WARS

The industrial revolution was only about one century old when modern technological warfare burst upon the world in the U.S. Civil War. Of course during that century human progress had already been manifested in the continually increasing deadliness and range of weapons, not to mention other potential military benefits of industrial capitalism. But it was the Civil War that actually demonstrated industrialism's ability to produce carnage and devastation on an unprecedented scale, thus foreshadowing a future more and more dominated by what we have come to call technowar. Immense armies were now transported by railroad, coordinated by telegraph, and equipped with an ever-evolving arsenal of mass-produced weapons designed by scientists and engineers. The new machines of war — such as the repeating rifle, the primitive machine gun, the submarine, and the steam-powered ironclad warship — were forged by other machines. Industrial organization was essential not only in the factories where the war machines were manufactured but also on the battlefields and waters where these machines destroyed one another and slaughtered people.

Prior to the Civil War, visual images of America's wars were, almost without exception, expressions of romanticism and nationalism. Paintings, lithographs, woodcuts, and statues displayed a glorious saga of thrilling American heroism from the Revolution through the Mexican War.[1] Drawing on their imagination, artists could picture action-filled scenes of heroic events, such as that great icon of American nationalism, Emmanuel Leutze's 1851 painting *Washington Crossing the Delaware*.[2] (The most highly charged symbols in this oil painting by that German romantic are pure fiction: the Stars and Stripes was not carried into battle until the nineteenth century, Washington would hardly have been standing upright in a tiny storm-tossed boat, and there were no ice chunks in the river that night.)

Literature, however, was the only art form capable of projecting the action of warfare as temporal flow and movement. Using words as a medium, writers had few limitations on how they chose to paint this action, and their visions had long covered a wide spectrum. One of the Civil War's most distinctively modern images was expressed by Herman Melville in his poem "A Utilitarian View of the Monitor's Fight." Melville sees the triumph of "plain mechanic power" placing war "Where War belongs— / Among the trades and artisans," depriving it of "passion": "all went on by crank, / Pivot, and screw, / And calculations of caloric." Since "warriors / Are now but operatives," he hopes that "War's made / Less grand than Peace."[3]

The most profoundly deglamorizing images of the Civil War, however, were produced not by literature but directly by technology itself. The industrial processes and scientific knowledge that created techno-war had also brought forth a new means of perceiving its devastation. Industrial chemicals, manufactured metal plates, lenses, mirrors, bellows, and actuating mechanisms—all were essential to the new art and craft of photography. [Thus the Civil War was the first truly modern war not only in how it was fought but also in how it was imaged.] Images of warfare introduced by photography now threatened to undermine or even replace the romantic images of warfare projected by earlier visual arts.

Scores of commercial photographers, seeking authenticity and profits, followed the Union armies into battle. Although evidently more than a million photographs of the Civil War were taken, hardly any show actual combat or other exciting action typical of the earlier paint-

"A Harvest of Death, Gettysburg," 1863 photograph by Timothy O'Sullivan.

ings.[4] The photographers' need to stay close to their cumbersome horse-drawn laboratory wagons usually kept them from the thick of battle, and the collodion wet-plate process, which demanded long exposures, forced them to focus on scenes of stillness rather than action. Among all human subjects, those who stayed most perfectly still for the camera were the dead. Hence Civil War photography, dominated by images of death, inaugurated a grim, profoundly antiromantic realism.

Perhaps the most widely reproduced photo from the war, Timothy O'Sullivan's "A Harvest of Death, Gettysburg," is filled with the corpses of Confederate soldiers, rotting after lying two days in the rain. Stripped of their shoes and with their pockets turned inside out, the bodies stretch into the distance beyond the central figure, whose mouth gapes gruesomely.

The first of such new images of war were displayed for sale to the public by Mathew Brady at his Broadway gallery in October 1862. Brady titled his show "The Dead of Antietam." The *New York Times* responded with an awed editorial:

> The living that throng Broadway care little perhaps for the Dead at Antietam, but we fancy they would jostle less carelessly down the great thoroughfare . . . were a few dripping bodies, fresh from the field, laid along the pavement. . . .

Mr. Brady has done something to bring home to us the terrible reality and earnestness of war. If he has not brought bodies and laid them in our dooryards and along the streets, he has done something very like it. At the door of his gallery hangs a little placard, "The Dead of Antietam." Crowds of people are constantly going up the stairs; follow them, and you find them bending over photographic views of that fearful battle-field, taken immediately after the action. . . . You will see hushed, reverend groups standing around these weird copies of carnage, bending down to look in the pale faces of the dead, chained by the strange spell that dwells in dead men's eyes.[5]

Oliver Wendell Holmes went further in explicating the meaning of the exhibition, which gave "some conception of what a repulsive, brutal, sickening, hideous thing it is, this dashing together of two frantic mobs to which we give the name of armies." Here, he wrote, was the reality of war: "Let him who wishes to know what war is look at this series of illustrations. These wrecks of manhood thrown together in careless heaps or ranged in ghastly rows for burial were alive but yesterday."[6]

Yet three decades after the end of the Civil War, the surging forces of militarism and imperialism were reimaging the conflict as a glorious episode in America's history. The disgust, shame, guilt, and deep national divisions that had continued after this war—just like those a century later that continued after the Vietnam War—were being buried under an avalanche of jingoist culture, the equivalent of contemporary Ramboism, even down to the cult of muscularism promulgated by Teddy Roosevelt.

It was in this historical context that Stephen Crane used realism, then flourishing as a literary mode, to assault just such treacherous views of war. As Amy Kaplan has shown, *The Red Badge of Courage,* generally viewed as the great classic novel of the Civil War, can be read much more meaningfully as Crane's response to the romantic militarism that was attempting to erase from the nation's memory the horrifying lessons taught by the war's realities.[7] Crane, not subject to the technological limitations of the slow black and white photographs that had brought home glimpses of the war's sordid repulsiveness, was able to portray the animal frenzy that masqueraded as heroic combat and even to add color and tiny moving details to his pictures of the dead: "The corpse was dressed in a uniform that once had been blue but was now faded to a melancholy shade of green. The eyes, staring at the youth, had changed to the dull hue to be seen on the side of a dead fish. The mouth was opened. Its red had changed to an appalling yellow. Over the grey skin of the face ran little ants. One was trundling some sort of a bundle along the upper lip."[8]

Other literary reactions to the new militarism looked even farther backward to project images of a future dominated by war. Melville's *Billy Budd,* completed in 1891, envisions this triumph of war in the aftermath of the American Revolution on the aptly named British warship HMS *Bellipotent,* where the best of humanity is hanged by the logic of war, the common people are turned into automatons "dispersed to the places allotted them when not at the guns," and the final image is of a sterile, lifeless, inorganic mass of "smooth white marble."[9]

In *A Connecticut Yankee in King Arthur's Court,* published in 1889, Mark Twain recapitulates the development of industrial capitalism and extrapolates its future in a vision of apocalyptic technowar. Hank Morgan and his young disciples of technowar have run "secret wires" to dynamite deposits under all their "vast factories, mills, workshops, magazines, etc." and connected them to a single command button so that nothing can stop them "when we want to blow up our civilization."[10] When Hank does initiate this instantaneous push-button war, "in that explosion all our noble civilization-factories went up in the air and disappeared from the earth" (476).

Beyond an electrified fence, the technowarriors have prepared a forty-foot-wide belt of land mines. The first wave of thousands of knights triggers a twentieth-century-style explosion: "As to destruction of life, it was amazing. Moreover, it was beyond estimate. Of course we could not *count* the dead, because they did not exist as individuals, but merely as homogeneous protoplasm, with alloys of iron and buttons" (478). After Hank and his boys trap the rest of the feudal army inside their electric fence, Hank electrocutes the first batch, a flood is released on the survivors, and the boys man machine guns that "vomit death" into their ranks: "Within ten short minutes after we had opened fire, armed resistance was totally annihilated. . . . Twenty-five thousand men lay dead around us" (486). That number of dead exactly matches the total casualties in America's costliest day of war, the battle of Antietam, and thus recalls Brady's exhibition, "The Dead of Antietam." Twain's vision is even more horrific, for the victors themselves are conquered by "the poisonous air bred by those dead thousands" (487). All that remains of this first experiment in industrialized warfare is a desolate landscape pockmarked by craters and covered with unburied rotting corpses.

Twain's vision of the future implicit in industrial capitalism began to materialize in the First World War, when armies slaughtered one another on an unprecedented scale, sections of Europe were turned into a wasteland, and weapons of mass destruction first seemed capable of actually destroying civilization. Meanwhile, the scientific, engineering, and organizational progress that had produced the modern machine gun, long-range artillery, poison gas, and fleets of submarines and warplanes had also created a new image-making technology that broke through the limits of still photography. Just as the Civil War was the first to be extensively photographed, the War to End All Wars was the first to be extensively imaged in motion pictures.[11]

World War I of course generated millions of still photographs, many showing scenes at least as ghastly as the corpse-strewn battlefields of the Civil War, and now there was also authentic documentary film of live action. But for various reasons the most influential photographic images from World War I, though realistic in appearance, displayed not reality but fantasy. Filmmakers who wished to record actual combat were severely restricted by the various governments and military authorities. At the same time, powerful forces were making a historic discovery: the tremendous potential of movies for propaganda and for profits. The hallmark image-making of the twentieth century had arrived.

In the United States, the most important photographic images were movies designed to inflame the nation, first to enter the war, and then to wage it with unquestioning zeal. Probably the most influential was *The Battle Cry of Peace,* a 1915 smash hit that played a crucial role in rousing the public to war against Germany by showing realistic scenes of the invasion and devastation of America by a rapacious Germanic army. Once the United States entered the war, the American public got to view an endless series of feature films, such as *To Hell with the Kaiser, The Kaiser, the Beast of Berlin,* and *The Claws of the Hun,* each outdoing its predecessor in picturing German bestiality. Erich von Stroheim's career began with his portrayal of the archetypal sadistic German officer in films such as *The Unbeliever* and *Heart of Humanity,* where in his lust to rape innocent young women he murders anyone who gets in the way, even the crying baby of one intended victim. This genre is surveyed by Larry Wayne Ward, who describes the 1918 Warner Brothers hit *My Four Years in Germany,* which opens with a title card that tells the audience they are seeing "Fact Not Fiction":

After the brutal conquest of Belgium, German troops are shown slaughtering innocent refugees and tormenting prisoners of war. Near the end of the film one of the German officials boasts that "America Won't Fight," a title which dissolves into newsreel footage of President Wilson and marching American soldiers. Soon American troops are seen fighting their way across the European battlefields. As he bayonets another German soldier, a young American doughboy turns to his companions and says, "I promised Dad I'd get six."[12]

Before the end of World War I, the motion picture had already proved to be a more effective vehicle for romanticizing and popularizing war than the antebellum school of heroic painting which had been partly debunked by Civil War photography. Indeed, the audiences that thronged to *My Four Years in Germany* frequently burned effigies of the kaiser outside the theaters and in some cases turned into angry mobs that had to be dispersed by police.[13]

To restore the glamour of preindustrial war, however, it would not be sufficient to glorify just the men fighting on the ground or even the aviators supposedly dueling like medieval knights high above the battlefield. What was necessary to reverse Melville's "utilitarian" view of industrial warfare was to romanticize the machines of war themselves.

The airplane was potentially an ideal vehicle for this romance. But photographic technology would have to go a bit further to bring home the thrills generated by destruction from the sky, because it needed to be seen from the sky, not from the ground, where its reality was anything but glamorous. The central figure in America's romance with warplanes, as I have discussed at length in *War Stars: The Superweapon and the American Imagination,* was Billy Mitchell, who also showed America and the world how to integrate media imagery with technowar.

In 1921 Mitchell staged a historic event, using bombers to sink captured German warships and turning the action into a media bonanza. His goal was to hit the American public with immediate nationwide images of the airplane's triumph over the warship. The audacity of this enterprise in 1921 was remarkable. There were no satellites to relay images, and no television; in fact, the first experimental radio broadcast station had begun operation only in November 1920.

Back in 1919, Mitchell had given the young photographer George Goddard his own laboratory, where, with assistance from Eastman

Kodak, Goddard developed high-resolution aerial photography. As soon as Mitchell won the opportunity to bomb ships, he put Goddard in command of a key unit: a team of aerial photographers provided with eighteen airplanes and a dirigible. Mitchell's instructions were unambiguous: "I want newsreels of those sinking ships in every theater in the country, just as soon as we can get 'em there." This demanded more than mere picture-taking. With his flair for public relations, Mitchell explained to Goddard: "Most of all I need you to handle the newsreel and movie people. They're temperamental, and we've got to get all we can out of them."[14] Goddard solved unprecedented logistical problems, flying the film to Bolling Field in the District of Columbia for pickup by the newsreel people, who would take it to New York for development and national distribution. The sinking of each ship, artfully filmed by relays of Goddard's planes, was screened the very next day in big-city theaters across the country.

This spectacular media coup implanted potent images of the warplane in the public mind. Mitchell himself became a national hero overnight as millions watched the death throes of great warships on newsreel screens. He was a prophet. The battleship was doomed. The airplane would rule the world. And America was now much closer to the 1990s' media conception of the Gulf War than to Melville's "Utilitarian View of the Monitor's Fight." Melville's vision of technowar as lacking "passion" was becoming antiquated, for what could be more thrilling—even erotic—than aerial war machines? The evidence is strewn throughout modern American culture: the warplane models assembled by millions of boys and young men during World War II; the thousands of magazines and books filled with glossy photographs of warplanes that some find as stimulating as those in "men's" magazines; and Hollywood's own warplane romances, such as *Top Gun,* one of the most popular movies of the 1980s, or its 1955 progenitor *Strategic Air Command,* in which Jimmy Stewart's response to his first sight of a B-47 nuclear bomber is, "She's the most beautiful thing I've ever seen in my life."

One of the warplane's great advantages as a vehicle of romance is its distance from its victims. From the aircraft's perspective, even the most grotesque slaughter it inflicts is sufficiently removed so that it can be imaged aesthetically. The aesthetics of aerial bombing in World War II were prefigured in 1937 by Mussolini's son Vittorio, whose ecstatic experience of bombing undefended Ethiopian villages was expressed in his simile of his victims "bursting out like a rose after I had landed a bomb in the middle of them."[15] These aesthetics were consummated at the end of World War II by the mushroom clouds that rose over Hiroshima and Nagasaki.

Bracketed by these images, the aerial bombing of World War II has been most insightfully explored in *Catch-22* by Joseph Heller, a bombardier with sixty combat missions. The novel envisions the political and cultural triumph of fascism through the very means used to defeat it militarily. The turning point in Heller's work is the annihilation of an insignificant antifascist Italian mountain village; this event allows fascist forces, embodied by U.S. Air Corps officers, to gain total control.[16] The sole purpose of the American bombing of the village is image-making.

General Peckem, the power-mad officer who designs the raid, privately admits that bombing this "tiny undefended village, reducing the whole community to rubble" is "entirely unnecessary," but it will allow him to extend his power over the bombing squadrons. He has convinced them that he will measure their success by "a neat aerial photograph" of their "*bomb pattern* — a term I dreamed up," he confides, that "means nothing." The crews are then briefed on the purpose of their raid: "Colonel Cathcart wants to come out of this mission with a good clean aerial photograph he won't be ashamed to send through channels. Don't forget that General Peckem will be here for the full briefing, and you know how he feels about bomb patterns."[17]

Of course, pictures of bomb patterns were not the most influential American photographic image-making in World War II. The still photos published in *Life* magazine alone could be the subject of several dissertations, and World War II feature movies about strategic bombing have been discussed at length, by me and many others. Indeed, in 1945 one might have wondered how the camera could possibly play a more important role in war.

The answer came in Vietnam, the first war to be televised directly into tens of millions of homes.[18] TV's glimpses of the war's reality were so horrendous and so influential that these images have been scapegoated as one of the main causes of the United States' defeat. Indeed, the Civil War still photographs of corpses seem tame compared to the Vietnam War's on-screen killings, as well as live action footage of the bulldozing of human carcasses into mass graves, the napalming of children, and the ravaging of villages by American soldiers.

Appalling as these public images were, however, few had meanings as loathsome as those of the pictures that serve as the central metaphor of Stephen Wright's novel *Meditations in Green*. The hero of the novel has the same job that the author had in Vietnam: he works as a photo analyst in an intelligence unit whose mission is to aid the genocidal bombing, the torture and assassination program labeled Operation Phoenix, and Operation Ranch Hand (the ecocidal defoliation campaign using the toxic herbicides Agent Orange, Agent White, Agent Blue, and Agent Purple). The official name for his job is "image interpreter."[19] He scrutinizes reconnaissance films to find evidence of life so that it can be eliminated. Not just humans are targets to be erased by the bombing; even trees become the enemy. Anyone in the unit who has qualms about this genocide and ecocide is defined — in a revealing term — as a "smudge," thereby becoming something else to be eliminated. The perfect image, it is thus implied, should have nothing left of the human or the natural. From the air, the unit's own base looks like "a concentration camp or a movie lot" (199). The climax of the novel occurs when the base is devastated by an enemy attack intercut with scenes from *Night of the Living Dead,* that ghoulish 1968 vision of America which is being screened during the attack as entertainment for the American torturers, bombers, and image interpreters.

One of the most shocking, influential, and enduring single images from the Vietnam War exploded into the consciousness of millions of Americans in February 1968 when they actually watched, within the comfort of their own homes, as the chief of the Saigon national police executed a manacled NLF* prisoner. In a perfectly framed sequence, the notorious General Nguyen Ngoc Loan unholsters a snub-nosed revolver and places its muzzle to the prisoner's right temple. The prisoner's head jolts, a sudden spurt of blood gushes straight out of his right temple, and he collapses in death. The next morning, newspaper readers were confronted with AP photographer Eddie Adams's potent stills of the execution. The grim ironies of the scene were accentuated by the cultural significance of the weapon itself, a revolver, a somewhat archaic handgun symbolic of the American West.

Precisely one decade later, this image, with its roles now reversed, was transmuted into the dominant metaphor of a lavishly financed Hollywood production crucial to reimaging the history of the Vietnam War: *The Deer Hunter.* After being designated the best English-language

*National Liberation Front, correct term for "Viet Cong," a derogatory epithet roughly translated as "Viet Commies." The NLF, though Communist-led, was a broad coalition of forces opposed to U.S. and U.S.-backed forces in the southern half of Vietnam.

General Nguyen Ngoc Loan, head of South Vietnam's police and intelligence, executing a prisoner in 1968, photograph by Eddie Adams.

film of 1978 by the New York Film Critics Circle, this celluloid displacement of reality with illusion was sanctified by four Academy Awards, capped by Best Picture — an award presented appropriately enough by John Wayne, the World War II draft dodger who received a Congressional Gold Medal for playing a warrior hero in the movies. *The Deer Hunter* succeeded not only in reversing key images of the war but also in helping to canonize U.S. prisoners of war as the most significant symbols of American manhood for the 1980s, 1990s, and beyond.

The reimaging was blatant, though most critics at the time seemed oblivious to it. The basic technique was to take images of the war that had become deeply embedded in America's consciousness and change them into their opposites. For example, in the film's first scene in Vietnam, a uniformed soldier throws a grenade into an underground village shelter harboring women and children, and then with his automatic rifle mows down a woman and her baby. Although the scene resembles the familiar TV sequence of GIs in Vietnamese villages, as well as *Life*'s photographs of the My Lai massacre, the soldier turns out to be not American but North Vietnamese. He is then killed by a lone guerrilla — who is not a "Viet Cong" but our Special Forces hero, played by Robert De Niro. Later, when two men plummet from a heli-

FROM REALISM TO VIRTUAL REALITY

In The Deer Hunter *(1978), General Loan's revolver becomes a North Vietnamese officer's revolver, and his NLF prisoner is replaced by U.S. prisoners forced to play Russian roulette.*

copter, the images replicate a telephotographic sequence once seen by millions of Americans that showed a Vietnamese prisoner being hurled from an American helicopter to make other prisoners talk;[20] but in the movie the falling men are American POWs attempting to escape their murderous North Vietnamese captors.

The structuring metaphor of the film is the game of Russian roulette the sadistic Asian communist guards force their prisoners to play. The crucial torture scene consists of sequence after sequence of images replicating and replacing that infamous historical sequence in which General Loan placed a revolver to the right temple of his NLF prisoner and killed him with a single shot. In the movie the American captives are kept in tiger cages, another image that reverses reality; the actual tiger cages, also overseen by General Loan, were used by the Saigon government to torture thousands of Vietnamese political prisoners. The movie shows American prisoner after prisoner being hauled out of the tiger cages and forced by the demonic North Vietnamese officer in charge, who always stands to the prisoner's right and our left, to place a revolver to his own right temple. Then the image is framed to eliminate the connection between the prisoner's body and the arm holding the

P.O.W.: The Escape *(1986) transforms General Loan's execution of an NLF prisoner into a North Vietnamese prison commander's murder of a U.S. prisoner.*

revolver, thus bringing the image closer to the famous execution image. One sequence even replicates the blood spurting out of the victim's right temple.

The Deer Hunter's manipulation of this particular image to reverse the roles of victim and victimizer was used again and again by other vehicles of the militarization of American culture in the 1980s, from movies to comic books. Take, for example, *P.O.W.: The Escape,* an overtly militaristic 1986 POW rescue movie inspired by *Rambo* and starring David Carradine as superhero. The bestiality of the Asian communists is here embodied by a North Vietnamese prison camp commander who executes an American prisoner with a revolver shot to the right temple in a tableau modeled even more precisely than *The Deer Hunter*'s on the original execution of the NLF prisoner in Saigon. Then, just in case viewers missed it, this scene is replayed later as the movie's only flashback.

The brazen reversal of this image was a spectacular success, as I discovered while giving lectures about it on college campuses in 1992. I would begin by projecting a slide of the original AP photo. Then I would ask, "How many people here are familiar with this image?" Almost every hand would go up. Then I would ask, "What is this a picture of?" Almost invariably, at least three fourths of those who had raised their hands would declare that it was a picture of a "a North Vietnamese officer" or "a communist officer" executing "a civilian" or "a prisoner" or "a South Vietnamese."

Meanwhile, however, the militarization of American culture was going even further in manipulating the original image of that high South Vietnamese official executing an unarmed captive, shifting the role of the most heartless shooters from North Vietnamese communists to the photographers themselves. For example, the cover story of the November 1988 issue of the popular comic book *The 'Nam* portrays the photojournalists, both still photographers and TV cameramen, as the real enemies because they had placed the image on the "front page of every newspaper in the states!" The cover literally reverses the original image by showing the execution scene from a position behind the participants. This offers a frontal view of the photographer, whose deadly camera conceals his face and occupies the exact center of the picture. The prisoner appears merely as an arm, a shoulder, and a sliver of a body on the left. The only face shown belongs to the chief of the security police, who displays the righteous — even heroic — indignation that has led him to carry out this justifiable revenge against the treacherous actions of the "Viet Cong" pictured in the story. The climactic image is a full page in which the execution scene appears as a reflection in the gigantic lens of the camera above the leering mouth of the photographer, from which comes a bubble with his greedy words, "Keep shooting! Just keep shooting!" "Shooting" a picture here has become synonymous with murder and treason.

In the next panel, two GIs register their shock — not at the execution, but at a TV cameraman focusing on the dead body: "Front page of every newspaper in the States!" "Geez . . . " One can hardly imagine a more complete reversal of the acclaim accorded to those Civil War photographers for bringing the reality of war and death home to the American people.

The logic of this comic book militarism is inescapable: photographers should be allowed to show the public only what the military deems suitable. It is the logic that has been put into practice for each of America's wars since Vietnam. Nonmilitary photographers and indeed all journalists were simply banished from the entire war zone during the 1983 U.S. invasion of Grenada. Partly as a result of this exclusion, the major media accepted a pool system for the 1989 invasion of Panama — and meekly went along with the military's keeping even these selected journalists confined to a U.S. base throughout most of the conflict.[21] Attempting to report directly on the action, a Spanish photographer was killed and a British journalist wounded when caught

Cover story of the November 1988 issue of The 'Nam *glorifies General Loan and makes the photographer into the villain.*

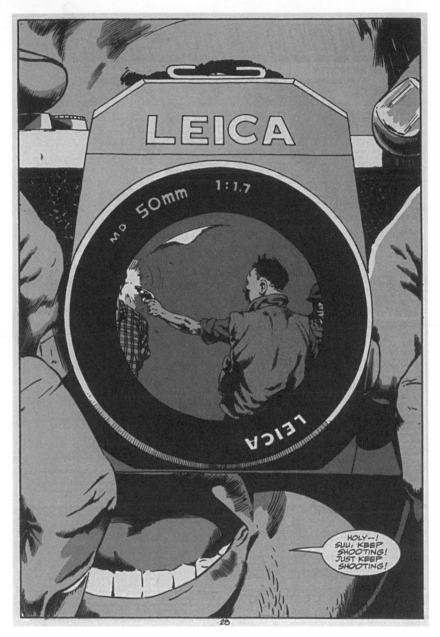

The 'Nam *images the photographer as the shooter and the camera as the most destructive weapon.*

G.I.s spell out The 'Nam*'s message about photographs and TV.*

in "friendly" cross fire between U.S. soldiers removing them from the scene and a U.S. armored personnel carrier.[22]

The almost complete absence of photographic images was quite convenient for the Grenada and Panama invasions, which were carried out so swiftly and with such minimal military risk that the government did not bother to seek prior congressional or public approval. And for the first several days after U.S. troops had been dispatched to confront Iraq in August 1990, Secretary of Defense Dick Cheney refused to allow journalists to accompany them.[23] The Pentagon seemed to be operating under the belief that photographic and televised images had helped bring about the U.S. defeat in Vietnam. But for the Gulf War, with its long buildup until Washington launched its assault in January, its potential for significant casualties, and its intended international and domestic political purposes, *some* effective images had to be engineered.

To control these images, the U.S. government set up pools of selected reporters and photographers, confined them to certain locations, required them to have military escorts when gathering news, established stringent guidelines limiting what could be reported or photographed, and subjected all written copy, photographs, and videotape to strict censorship.[24] Most of those admitted to the pools represented the same newspapers and TV networks that were simultaneously mounting a major campaign to build support for the war.[25] Journalists were forced to depend on military briefings, where they were often fed deliberately falsified information. Immediately after the ground offensive began, all press briefings and pool reports were indefinitely suspended. In a most revealing negation of the achievement of Civil War photography, with its shocking disclosure of the reality of death, the Pentagon banned the press entirely from Dover Air Force Base during the arrival of the bodies of those killed in the war. Responding to an ACLU legal argument that it was attempting to shield the public from disturbing images, the Pentagon replied that it was merely protecting the privacy of grieving relatives.[26]

Although the media were largely denied access to the battlefields, the Gulf War nevertheless gained the reputation of the first "real-time" television war, and the images projected into American homes helped to incite the most passionate war fever since World War II.[27] These screened images ranged from the most traditional to the most innovative modes of picturing America's wars.

Even the antiquated icon of the heroic commanding general, miss-

Technowar triumphs in TV sequence of a smart bomb destroying an Iraqi building.

ing from public consciousness for about forty years, was given new life. Though hardly as striking a figure as the commander in Leutze's *Washington Crossing the Delaware* or the posed picture of General Douglas MacArthur returning to the Philippines during World War II, a public idol took shape in the corpulent form of General Norman Schwarzkopf in his fatigues, boots, and jaunty cap.

The preeminent public relations firm Hill and Knowlton, working closely with the governments of Kuwait and the United States, staged a brilliant propaganda campaign including thirty video releases distributed free to television stations. Its most audacious and successful concoction was an elaborate but entirely phony scenario of Iraqi soldiers dumping Kuwaiti babies out of hospital incubators, a story first told to the Congressional Human Rights hearings (which Hill and Knowlton helped to organize) by an unidentified "eyewitness" (actually the daughter of the Kuwaiti ambassador to the United States).[28]

But the most potent images combined techniques pioneered by Billy Mitchell with General Peckem's quest for aerial photos of perfect bomb patterns, the medium of television, and the technological capabilities of the weapons themselves. After all, since one of the main goals of the war makers was to create the impression of a "clean" technowar — a war almost devoid of human suffering and death, conducted with surgical precision by wondrous mechanisms — why not project the war from the point of view of the weapons? And so the most thrilling images were transmitted directly by the laser guidance systems of missiles and by those brilliant creations, "smart" bombs. Fascinated, tens of millions of excited Americans stared at their screens, sharing the experience of these missiles and bombs unerringly guided by the wonders of American technology to a target identified by a narrator as an important military installation. A generation raised in video arcades and on Nintendo could hardly be more satisfied. The target got closer and closer, larger and larger. And then everything ended with the explosion. There were no bloated human bodies, as in the photographs of the battlefields of Antietam and Gettysburg. There was none of the agony of the burned and wounded glimpsed on television relays from Vietnam. There was just nothing at all. In this magnificent triumph of technowar, America's images of its wars had seemingly reached perfection.

"They were only war casualties," he said. "It was a pity, but you can't always hit your target. Anyway, they died in the right cause."
Graham Greene, *The Quiet American,* 1955

"We didn't know who we were till we got here. We thought we were something else."
Robert Stone, *Dog Soldiers,* 1974

Plausibility of Denial

Denial has been, in every sense, the term necessary to fathom the depths of deception and delusion essential to America's war in Vietnam.

When the men in the White House and Pentagon decided in 1945 to support France's attempt to recolonize Vietnam, they tried from the very beginning to keep their actions secret. When they decided to send Americans to fight in Vietnam, they conspired at first to wage war covertly, later to conceal how the war was being conducted, and finally to expunge the memory of the entire affair or bury it under mounds of false images. Indeed, the key phrase in their top secret 1963 plan for covert actions leading to full-scale war (National Security Action Memorandum 273) was "plausibility of denial."[1]

Moreover, U.S. policy toward Vietnam was based on a total denial of Vietnamese history and culture. After mid-1954 that policy also depended on a denial of the Geneva Accords, the origin and character of Ngo Dinh Diem's dictatorship in Saigon, the indigenous roots of the revolution against his regime, and the identity of the forces on all sides of the conflict. And from late 1963 to the present, the nature and outcome of U.S. combat have been denied in manifold ways.

One meaning of "denial" is *claiming* that something is not true or does not exist. For example, President John F. Kennedy denied any involvement in the 1963 coup he had personally approved against Diem. When Kennedy himself was assassinated three weeks after Diem was killed in this coup, one of the first acts of his successor, Lyndon Johnson, was secretly to authorize a campaign of air, sea, and land attacks against the north as a prelude to a full-scale U.S. war in Vietnam. Part of the written plan called for an assessment of whether the American people would believe the president and the Pentagon when they denied doing what they were doing. That was the section titled "Plausibility of Denial."

Another meaning of "denial" is *believing* that something is not true or does not exist despite convincing evidence to the contrary. This is a psychological condition, and it can become a chronic disease of an individual or even of a culture. The various forms of denial of the Vietnam War and of the people, history, culture, and even the very nation of Vietnam have spread wide and deep in American politics, psychology, and culture.

The presidential inauguration that takes place every four years in the United States is an important symbolic event, a moment when the newly elected president addresses the burning issues of the time, defines the goals and agenda of the new administration, and attempts to inspire the nation. Yet throughout the decades when the United States was waging war in Vietnam, even during the years when the war had become an agonizing national crisis, no incoming president uttered the word "Vietnam" in his inaugural address.[2]

The first inaugural address to mention the word "Vietnam" came in 1981, when Ronald Reagan included "a place called Vietnam" in a list of battlefields where Americans had fought in the twentieth century. Then at last in 1989, a newly elected president used the taboo word to tell the nation what to do about the Vietnam War: forget it.

It was George Bush, vice-president under Reagan from 1981 to 1989, the years when the history of the Vietnam War was being radically rewritten and reimaged, who broke the silence with these words: "The final lesson of Vietnam is that no great nation can long afford to be sundered by a memory." President Bush's usage of the term reflected what had become standard in American speech. "Vietnam" was no longer a country or even "a place called Vietnam," as his predecessor had put it. It had become a war, an American war. Or maybe not even a war. It had become an American tragedy, an event that had divided and wounded America. The grotesque title of one widely adopted history textbook reveals far more than intended: *Vietnam: An American Ordeal*.[3]

Bush's inaugural speech blamed "Vietnam" for the "divisiveness," the "hard looks" in Congress, the challenging of "each other's motives," and the fact that "our great parties have too often been far apart and untrusting of each other." "It has been this way since Vietnam," he lamented.

Two years later, gloating over what seemed America's glorious defeat of Iraq, President Bush jubilantly proclaimed to a nation festooned in jingoistic yellow ribbons, "By God, we've kicked the Vietnam syndrome once and for all!"[4] Kicked? Syndrome? Had "Vietnam" by then become America's addiction? Its pathology?

Bush was reluctantly recognizing that despite all attempts to forget the war, America in some ways was indeed addicted to the "Vietnam syndrome." Where amnesia has not worked to deny the Vietnam War, fantasies have been conceived to obscure the realities. Ironically enough, sixteen months after claiming to have cured us of our Vietnam disease, the president himself fell victim to the most pervasive of these fantasies — the POW/MIA myth — when he was shown on national television shouting, "Shut up and sit down!" at MIA family members heckling him during the July 1992 annual convention of the National League of Families of American Prisoners and Missing in Southeast Asia.

THE DOMINANT FANTASIES

The representation of the Vietnam War still dominant in America at the beginning of the twenty-first century is based on a series of fantasies originally constructed from 1954 through the 1970s and then elaborated and embellished during the 1980s and 1990s, especially under the Reagan (1981–1989) and Bush (1989–1993) administrations. Among these fantasies are the following falsehoods, accepted as true by most Americans — or rather by most Americans other than those who simply prefer not to know anything about the war:

1. Before the United States became involved, there were two separate nations called South Vietnam and North Vietnam.
2. South Vietnam was a democracy with an elected government.

3. South Vietnam was being invaded by North Vietnam, a communist dictatorship.

4. This invasion was being supported by China and the Soviet Union as part of a communist attempt to take over the world.

5. In response to this invasion, the United States provided economic and military aid to South Vietnam.

6. Then in 1964 North Vietnam attacked U.S. destroyers in the international waters of the Gulf of Tonkin, and the United States responded with a brief retaliation.

7. North Vietnam then attacked U.S. advisers in South Vietnam, and the United States responded in 1965 by sending in ground troops and bombing North Vietnam.

8. The 1968 Tet offensive by the "Viet Cong" and North Vietnam was really a military victory for the United States, but it was turned into a political defeat by the news media and politicians.

9. The United States lost the war because "we weren't allowed to win" and "we were fighting with one hand tied behind our back"; that is, the military was unduly restrained by politicians, the news media, and the antiwar movement.

10. The United States may have lost the war but it never lost any battle during the war.

11. The United States didn't lose the war; the bombing of Hanoi in December 1972 forced North Vietnam to accept Washington's peace terms.

12. Before the Vietnam War, the United States had never lost a war.

13. When American veterans came home from the war, they were routinely spat upon and abused by antiwar activists.

14. After the war, North Vietnam secretly kept hundreds or maybe even thousands of American prisoners of war, to be used as slave laborers or hostages or "bargaining chips" or sources of technological information about U.S. aircraft or simply victims to be tortured.

An extraordinary example of the denial of historical reality came from President Reagan in 1982:

If I recall correctly, when France gave up Indochina as a colony, the leading nations of the world met in Geneva with regard to help-ing those colonies become independent nations. And since North and South Vietnam had been, previous to colonization, two separate countries, provisions were made that these two countries could by a vote of all their people together, decide whether they wanted to be one country or not.

And there wasn't anything surreptitious about it, that when Ho Chi Minh refused to participate in such an election — and there was provision that people of both countries could cross the border and live in the other country if they wanted to. And when they began leaving by the thousands and thousands from North Vietnam to live in South Vietnam, Ho Chi Minh closed the border and again violated that part of the agreement.

And openly, our country sent military advisers there to help a country which had been a colony have such things as a national security force, an army, you might say, or a military to defend itself. And they were doing this, if I recall correctly, also in civilian clothes, no weapons, until they began being blown up where they lived and walking down the street by people riding by on bicycles and throwing pipe bombs at them. And then they were permitted to carry sidearms or wear uniforms. But it was totally a program until John F. Kennedy — when these attacks and forays became so great that John F. Kennedy authorized the sending in of a division of Marines. And that was the first move toward combat troops in Vietnam.[5]

This rewriting of history was fundamental to Reagan's definition of the war as "a noble cause," a phrase he first presented along with another new term — the "Vietnam syndrome" — in a 1980 campaign speech to the Veterans of Foreign Wars.[6]

Astonishingly, not a single sentence in Reagan's pseudohistory is accurate or truthful. Vietnam was at the time of the Geneva Conference a single nation, as recognized then by all attending nations and delegations (and as finally acknowledged by the United States in the Paris Peace Accords of 1973). The main negotiating parties were France and the Democratic Republic of Vietnam (DRV), which arrived at a military agreement calling for a disengagement and separation of their respective *armies* at the seventeenth parallel, to be followed by national elections within eighteen months. At the conclusion of the conference, every attending nation — except for the United States and a French puppet regime claiming to be the legitimate government of Vietnam — signed a declaration recognizing the "independence, unity, and territorial integrity" of Vietnam and stating flatly:

The Conference recognizes that the essential purpose of the agreement relating to Vietnam is to settle military questions with a view to ending hostilities and that the military demarcation line is provisional and should not in any way be interpreted as constituting a political or territorial boundary.[7]

The DRV continued to demand the promised elections, which were blocked because the Pentagon, President Dwight Eisenhower, and a Saigon regime installed by the United States during the Geneva Conference believed that Ho Chi Minh would win an overwhelming majority of any vote.[8] As an official U.S. publication put it in 1961: "It was the Communists' calculation that nationwide elections scheduled in the Accords for 1956 would turn all of South Vietnam over to them. . . . The authorities in South Vietnam refused to fall into this well-laid trap."[9] Ho Chi Minh did not close the "border"; it was the Saigon regime that, according to the Defense Department's own top secret history, turned the provisional military demarcation line into "one of the most restricted boundaries in the world," even refusing to allow postal service across the seventeenth parallel among family members.[10] It was the United States that began armed hostilities, including terror bombings by covert combat teams within weeks of the signing of the Geneva Accords.[11] By 1961, the United States had entire combat units fighting in Vietnam; for example, the historian David Marr describes his own participation in a 1961 search-and-destroy mission as one of "550 marines making up the first marine helicopter squadron" sent to Vietnam.[12] The first "division of Marines" sent openly was authorized by President Lyndon Johnson in 1965.

Admittedly, one of the more original features of Reagan's history, that Vietnam had been two countries named "North Vietnam" and "South Vietnam" *prior* to the Geneva Conference, is only a minor embellishment on Washington's official version of the history of the war, which maintained, in the face of all evidence, that the Geneva Accords had created two such nations. Indeed, it was this blatant falsehood that functioned for two decades as the main official justification for U.S. "support" of the government that it had created in Saigon, ranging from covert operations through full-scale American war. And insofar as that fantasy legitimized the war, the war was fought to maintain that fantasy.

When substantive negotiations to end the war finally began in 1969, the National Liberation Front put forward a ten-point negotiating position. The first point was a verbatim restatement of what had been agreed on at Geneva fifteen years earlier: "To respect the people's fundamental national rights, i.e., independence, sovereignty, unity and territorial integrity, as recognized by the 1954 Geneva Agreements on Vietnam." The Nixon administration responded with an eight-point negotiating position that referred to "North Vietnam" and "South Vietnam" as two separate countries while equating "North Vietnamese" and U.S. alike as "non–South Vietnamese forces." After four more years of war, the Nixon administration capitulated and accepted, word for word, almost the entire NLF negotiating position, including its first point, which was incorporated into Article I of the Paris Peace Accords:

> The United States and all other countries respect the independence, sovereignty, unity, and territorial integrity of Viet-Nam as recognized by the 1954 Geneva Agreements on Viet-Nam.

In that document, the United States also officially accepted the definition of its own forces, but not those of the Hanoi government, as "foreign."[13]

Nevertheless, in the decades since the war, the fiction of two Vietnamese nations established by the Geneva Accords in 1954 and lasting until "South Vietnam" was finally conquered by "North Vietnam" has become virtually unchallenged in American memory. But this fantasy makes it impossible to comprehend not just the political history of the war but also the military history. Even Robert McNamara, secretary of defense during the crucial 1961–1968 period, has finally been forced to acknowledge the following: that the insurgency against Diem's dictatorship began as spontaneous rebellions, mainly in the 1957–1959 period; that these rebellions were opposed, not fomented, by the Hanoi government; that only after the unbridled terror unleashed by Diem's Law 10/59 did Hanoi reluctantly accede to the organizing of armed struggle and give its blessing to the formation of the National Liberation Front; that northerners in the Hanoi government tended to be quite cautious about aiding the struggle in the south, while southerners (including Communist Party Secretary Le Duan) tended to be more militant in their support; that Hanoi sent troops from the north into the south only after the United States began bombing the north; and that many of these troops were southerners who had gone north to receive training and arms.[14]

In the years since Reagan presented his pseudohistory, the actual history of U.S. warfare in Vietnam has been buried under layer after layer of falsification, fabrication, illusion, and myth. But perhaps the most treacherous fantasy is the artfully retouched image of the war that simply erases the Vietnamese from the picture altogether. The cultural march from demonization of the Vietnamese in the late 1970s to eradication in the 1990s was graphically displayed by Hollywood. Whereas the Academy Award for the Best Picture of 1978 went to *The Deer Hunter,* with its meticulously reversed images of victims and victimizers, the winner of the Academy Award for the Best Picture of 1994 was *Forrest Gump,* which projects Vietnam as merely an uninhabited jungle that for inscrutable reasons shoots at American soldiers.

A more sophisticated and subtle denial of the actuality of the Vietnamese people and the Vietnam War comes in a package labeled "unreal," "unknowable," "incomprehensible," "crazy," or "alien." Assuming an American definition of "we" as descendants of European immigrants for whom all peoples of color are alien, and drawing on Anglo-American conceptions of "the East" as "inscrutable," this package also fits neatly into fashionable late twentieth-century theories that rejected coherent and consistent narratives as anachronistic in the epoch of "postmodernism."

As Jim Neilson has cogently argued in *Warring Fictions: Cultural Politics and the Vietnam War Narrative,* the widespread *intellectual* perception of the Vietnam experience as too alien to be comprehended has helped to establish a canon of Vietnam War literature that enshrines indeterminacy, incoherence, ambiguities, strangeness, and unknowability, with critics exalting Michael Herr's *Dispatches* as the quintessential truth about the war: "In their appreciation of *Dispatches,* however, critics ignore Herr's almost complete erasure of Vietnam. And they seem completely unaware of the mystification involved in identifying Vietnam as an irrational place beyond the grasp of logic. Herr's account seems almost to take place within a psychic rather than a real landscape. In *Dispatches* the Vietnamese are mere shadows in Herr's psychic drama, hobgoblins in America's bad trip."[15] Although many of the cultural critics who have canonized this literature consider themselves antiestablishment or even radical, as Neilson argues, "this view of the war as unknowable reinforces an ideologically useful historical ignorance and confusion." After all, as James Wilson pointed out in 1982, glorifying the literature of "cultural confusion" merely reinforces the government's decades of "official fiction" that "made the war unintelligible, but for politically intelligible reasons."[16]

When those men in the White House and the Pentagon decided to wage war in Vietnam, they probably never gave a thought to the literature that might result—or any other cultural consequences. This literature has turned out to be the second of the two great Vietnam War achievements in which Americans can legitimately take pride—the first being the antiwar movement, discussed in the next two chapters. The immense output of Vietnam War poetry and prose already constitutes the most impressive body of national literature associated with any war and shows no signs of diminishing. And its most devastating assaults on official and cultural denial have come from veterans of the war, the foremost creators of this literature.

For example, take the work of W. D. Ehrhart, one of the finest poets to emerge from the war, the leading anthologist of Vietnam War poetry, and the author of three powerful memoirs relating the history of the war to his own experience before, during, and after his two tours as a marine in Vietnam, where he was wounded in the 1968 battle to recapture the city of Hue. In his 1975 poem "Making the Children Behave," it takes Ehrhart precisely forty-eight words to demonstrate that all those perceptions of Vietnam and the Vietnamese as alien, unreal, and unknowable actually invert reality while revealing the opposite of what they profess:

> Do they think of me now
> in those strange Asian villages
> where nothing ever seemed
> quite human
> but myself
> and my few grim friends
> moving through them
> hunched
> in lines?
>
> When they tell stories to their children
> of the evil
> that awaits misbehavior,
> is it me they conjure?[17]

The poem consists of two questions—without answers. Ehrhart wonders what—or even if—"they" think about "me." In the first stanza, he recalls a time when "they" seemed to be the aliens, "strange," not "quite human." But as he looks back, he actually begins to suggest a vision of himself and his "few grim friends" as the "hunched" aliens, moving "in lines." Then in the second stanza, in an extraordinary act of imaginative displacement, he sees himself as he might appear through the eyes of the Other. The most suitable role he can imagine is the bogeyman, the hobgoblin who kidnaps and murders children, a mythical being conjured up in stories to make children "behave." The power of these final lines comes from his awareness that whatever those Vietnamese villagers think of him, Ehrhart thinks of himself in Vietnam as an evil alien who actually did murder children.

Is "murder" too strong a word? Not according to Ehrhart. In his breathtaking memoir *Passing Time,* which ranges from his enlistment in the marines as a gung-ho seventeen-year-old high school student to his cataclysmic postwar confrontation with American history, he describes the impact of reading the Defense Department's own top secret history of the war when it was leaked to the press in 1971. The pages of the *Pentagon Papers* turned into "a journey through an unholy house of horrors where all one's worst fears and darkest nightmares had suddenly become reality, hard, cold, and immutable; where all of the ugliest questions that had first arisen in the ricefields and jungles of Vietnam had suddenly been answered in the starkest and most unmerciful terms," all driving to one inescapable conclusion: "A mistake? Vietnam a mistake? My God, it had been a calculated deliberate attempt to hammer the world by brute force into the shape perceived by vain, duplicitous power brokers. And the depths to which they had sunk, dragging us all down with them, were almost unfathomable. . . . For such men I had become a murderer."[18]

Murderer? That's the key question in Tim O'Brien's 1994 novel *In the Lake of the Woods,* which probes through the deepest layers of denial that have falsified the Vietnam War. O'Brien challenges readers to swim through treacherous vortices churned by the confluence of the Vietnam War, the meaning of fiction, and the role of denial in the lives of individuals and the American nation. He provided a most useful navigational aid for this chilling journey in the form of a companion piece, a painfully revealing memoir entitled "The Vietnam in Me" published as the cover story of the October 2, 1994 *New York Times Magazine,* a month before the publication date of the novel.

Because O'Brien spins a complex dialectic between what he calls "story-truth" and "happening-truth," many critics have interpreted his fiction as validating their own view of the Vietnam War as unknowable or crazy or "unreal." O'Brien himself has attacked such interpretations for promoting the phony idea that "we're all innocent by reason of insanity; the war was crazy, and therefore we're innocent": "For me, Vietnam wasn't an unreal experience, it wasn't absurd. It was a cold-blooded, calculated war."[19]

For O'Brien, denial is an excruciatingly personal part of the Vietnam War. Unlike Ehrhart, who as a high school student wrote an editorial about the nobility of going to Vietnam to fight for "freedom,"[20] O'Brien already knew better, as he explains in "The Vietnam in Me." He wrote "earnest editorials" against the war for his college newspaper and rang doorbells for peace candidate Eugene McCarthy in 1968. But he then marched off to fight in the very war he considered "probably evil."[21] So from his first book, the somewhat fictionalized autobiography *If I Die in a Combat Zone* (1973), right on through *In the Lake of the Woods,* denial — both personal and national — has been a central theme for O'Brien.

The most revealing chapter in *If I Die in a Combat Zone,* titled "Escape," exposes the core of his own denial. Recognizing that if he kills people in a war he knows to be immoral he will be jeopardizing his very "soul," he decides that his only moral choice is to desert. But he discovers that he lacks the courage. He lets himself be sent off to Vietnam, he confesses, because "I was a coward."[22]

This confession — that cowardice kept him from making the moral choice of running away rather than becoming a killer — appears again and again in O'Brien's writings, sometimes elaborately sublimated, sometimes candidly blunt. It is central to his 1978 novel *Going After Cacciato,* winner of the 1979 National Book Award and often hailed as the great American Vietnam War novel, a book about soldiers who are trying to run away from the war, in body and in mind. In the climax of an escapist fantasy, the protagonist announces to the world: "I am afraid of running away. . . . I fear what might be thought of me by those I love. . . . I fear the loss of my own reputation. . . . I fear being thought of as a coward. I fear that even more than cowardice itself."[23]

In *The Things They Carried,* O'Brien's award-winning 1990 collection of somewhat autobiographical Vietnam stories (labeled "A Work of Fiction"), "Tim O'Brien" tells "one story I've never told before," the story of his life's crucial event, which takes place on the Rainy River between Minnesota and Canada. "For more than twenty years," he reveals, "I've had to live with . . . the shame" of the moment when, just yards from Canada, he didn't flee the draft because "I did not want people to think badly of me." "My conscience told me to run," he confesses, but "I was ashamed of my conscience, ashamed to be doing the right thing." The final words of "On the Rainy River" are: "I was a coward. I went to the war."[24] In the 1994 *New York Times Magazine* memoir, he repeats: "I was a coward. I went to Vietnam" (52). Therefore each thing he did in Vietnam "was an act of the purest self-hatred and self-betrayal" (53).

This awareness generates for O'Brien a tortured dialectic of concealment and exposure, which in turn spins the dazzlingly intricate webs of imagination and memory that constitute his fiction. In these webs, imagined acts of escape are often the desired alternative to the remembered acts of slaughter. One needs to know all this to understand the deepest meanings of *In the Lake of the Woods*.

The reality of the Vietnam War, which can be denied but not escaped, underlies every page of the novel. The main action takes place in late 1986, when that reality had been nearly buried under Ramboism and national amnesia. It is set near the mouth of the Rainy River — where O'Brien had located his own fateful choice — on the Minnesota edge of the Lake of the Woods, whose labyrinthine shoreline of 25,000 miles extends deep into the Canadian wilderness. Vietnam veteran and would-be U.S. senator John Wade has just suffered a humiliating defeat in the primary election when it was revealed that he had taken part in the 1968 My Lai massacre and then altered his service record to conceal his participation. He and his wife, Kathy, from whom he had also hidden his dreadful secret, have fled to a remote cabin, where they are futilely attempting to resurrect their relationship and their lives, built, as they now both know, on layers of concealment, illusion, and lies. On the seventh night, Kathy vanishes along with the only boat at the cabin. More than a month later, John borrows another small boat, ostensibly to search for her, heads into the remote recesses of the lake, and also disappears.

On one level, the book is a mystery story, with multiple solutions. What happened to Kathy Wade? Did she wander off and die accidentally? Did she deliberately flee, either alone or with a lover? Is she still lost in the wilderness? Did she and John conspire to disappear together and begin a new life? Or did John murder her? All of these are presented as possibilities, but the novel is not quite as indeterminate or unresolved as it may seem. Some of the hypotheses could not have happened, others may possibly have happened, and one evidently did happen. But how do fictional events "happen"? After all, don't they take place entirely in the imagination of author and reader? Don't fictional characters themselves exist only in the minds of people who create or translate the verbal symbols of which they are composed? O'Brien thrusts into this paradox and into the center of his fictional mystery the most terrifying facts of American personal and historical experience in Vietnam.

The purported author of *In the Lake of the Woods* is a Vietnam veteran whose own experience closely resembles that of Tim O'Brien. For this fictitious character, the book is not a novel at all but a profoundly disturbing investigation and exploration of a real-life mystery, the disappearance of a flesh-and-blood woman named Kathy Wade. The investigation takes him deeply into the life of John Wade, whose experience in Vietnam and afterward closely resembles his own. The trail leads him into the midst of the hideous massacre at My Lai, and thence to the significance of My Lai not just in the history of the Vietnam War but also in the history of the American nation back to its origin in continental genocide.

Twenty percent of the book consists of seven chapters titled "Evidence," including 133 footnotes from this ostensible author. The first of these chapters consists of pure fiction: exhibits from fictional events and documents; statements from fictional characters; interviews with people who are quite real to this author, but who are fictitious beings. As the novel takes us deeper into its troubled waters, however, actual historical materials, including quotations from articles and books such as a Lyndon Johnson biography and Richard Nixon's *Six Crises,* begin to take over these "Evidence" chapters. And as the massacre at My Lai moves ever closer to the core of the novel, both the fictional and actual authors become real historians, reporting on their own research at the site of the atrocity and inserting passages of testimony from the trial of Lieutenant William Calley and other materials about the event, accurately footnoted to their sources: *Report of the Department of the Army, Review of the Preliminary Investigation into the My Lai Incident,* Volume I, Department of the Army, 1970; Richard Hammer, *The Court-Martial of Lt. Calley* (New York: Coward, McCann & Geoghegan, 1971); Michael Bilton and Kevin Sim, *Four Hours in My Lai* (New York: Viking, 1992). The fictitious author only gradually reveals his identity as a Vietnam veteran who (like O'Brien) fought in My Lai's province of Quang Ngai, has his own dreadful secrets about what he did there, and wrote this book to exorcise "the long decades of silence and lies and secrecy": "To give me back my vanished life."[25]

This fictional character who writes the book ends by suggesting that we readers can choose to believe whichever solution we wish to the mystery of what happened to Kathy Wade. Each possibility is dramatized in one of the eight chapters titled "Hypothesis," where it is liberally sprinkled with "maybe" and "perhaps," emphasizing its fictive nature. Except for one, every hypothesis contains details that are inconsistent with the main narrative. For example, the first two hypotheses, that she drove off with a secret lover or simply got lost in the woods near the cabin, do not account for the fact that the boat is missing from the boathouse. The next hypothesis, that she was zooming across the lake at such high speed that she was hurled from the boat, is contradicted by the fact that the boat was powered by an old 1.6 horsepower outboard motor. And so on. The one hypothesis that does not contain contradictions is also the only one filled with details consistent with the main fictive narrative. And it is also the only one that makes the horrors of My Lai, and its denial, relevant to the horror and denial at the center of John Wade's life and relation to Kathy.

Indeed, every other hypothesis involves some form of escape from the hideous event that did happen, an event recalled in fragments that float to the surface in the chapters named "What He Remembered," "How the Night Passed," and "What He Did Next," titles indicating actuality that can be remembered — or denied. Although John apparently cannot remember whether or not he murdered his wife, enough details bubble up from the depths of his memory — not his imagination — to allow readers to reconstruct the gruesome scene. Unless, O'Brien suggests, readers would rather indulge in elaborate fantasies of denial.

On the night of Kathy's disappearance, John got out of bed in a murderous rage, poured a kettle of boiling water on each houseplant in the cabin, and then poured another kettle of boiling water on Kathy's face. Fragments of her screaming death agony, buried deep under strata of denial, later keep erupting from Wade's memory. He next concealed the crime by carefully weighting both her body and the boat and then burying them at the bottom of the lake. He thus reenacts once again the murder committed at My Lai and his attempts to expunge all records — and memory — of this act that was too awful to be possible.

My Lai, in Wade's mind, has become just a nightmare of "impossible events": "This could not have happened. Therefore it did not." (109) The most grisly detail of Kathy's death, repeated several times in the novel, evokes the same response:

Puffs of steam rose from the sockets of her eyes.
Impossible, of course. (84)

But My Lai did happen, as we know. Or do we? That is the most troubling question posed by the novel, which includes page after page of the actual testimony and other evidence of the massacre, which was not an aberration but a sample of how the United States conducted its genocidal warfare against the people of Vietnam.[26] As Jonathan Schell revealed even before the My Lai massacre, 70 percent of the villages of this entire region had already been annihilated by the fall of 1967; Schell also documented, from written materials and interviews, the fact that this was part of an official policy of terrorizing and massacring all civilians deemed sympathetic to the insurgents.[27] At My Lai, American soldiers did not just slaughter as many as five hundred unarmed people. They also sodomized young girls, raped women in front of their children, bayoneted children in front of their mothers, and used babies for target practice. Does John Wade's frenzied murder of the houseplants seem "impossible"? Then, suggests O'Brien, so must Lieutenant Calley's actions at My Lai: "He reloaded and shot the grass and a palm tree and then the earth again. 'Grease the place,' he said. 'Kill it.'" (103) This was, after all, the U.S. strategy for much of Vietnam, especially My Lai's province of Quang Ngai, as O'Brien, citing Schell and his own experience, reminds us in "The Vietnam in Me":

In the years preceding the murders at My Lai, more than 70 percent of the villages in this province had been destroyed by air strikes, artillery fire, Zippo lighters, napalm, white phosphorus, bulldozers, gunships and other such means. . . . Back in 1969, the wreckage was all around us. . . . Wreckage was the rule. Brutality was S.O.P. Scalded children, pistol-whipped women, burning hootches, free-fire zones, body counts, indiscriminate bombing and harassment fire, villages in ash, M-60 machine guns hosing down dark green tree lines and any human life behind them. (53)

In Vietnam, John Wade was so adept at making things disappear that he acquired the nickname "Sorcerer." He had perfected his magic expertise as a young boy, when he needed to build means of denial about his own identity as the son of an alcoholic father who committed suicide. Performing his magic tricks before a mirror, John had learned how to construct mirrors inside his own mind to deflect reality and to hide behind. Wade is a magician, a master of illusion. And so is O'Brien, who is such a wizard of narrative that he can make the most implausible fantasies seem believable. But this does not mean that in *In the Lake of the Woods* the products of imagination have the same ontological status as actual material events. Magic, O'Brien recognizes, is an art of illusion.

Of course imaginary events are also *real*. Although Wade's murder of his wife, just like the fantasies of escape offered as alternatives to it, is a fiction that takes place only in a novel, each scenario, whether remembered or merely imagined, has the reality offered by fiction—what O'Brien calls "story-truth."

Inverting the conventions of the mystery novel, O'Brien opts to leave the mystery to be solved by the reader's imagination. We are free to choose any of the hypotheses, even one that contradicts the evidence, which itself is fictional. Of course that freedom is also something of a trap, because our choice may be more revealing than a Rorschach test.

Not everything, however, is fiction. There is another kind of reality—what he calls "happening-truth"—such as the 1968 events at My Lai and O'Brien's own experience around My Lai the following year. Because John Wade, Kathy, and the "actual" and "imagined" events of that night all exist entirely in words and in the imagination of O'Brien and his readers, the fictive murder may or may not have "actually" occurred. But there is literally a world of difference between this act of the imagination and what happened in Vietnam. In that actuality, as O'Brien tells us over and over again, he himself, like his fictive John Wade and the American nation he represents, committed acts so horrible that they continually evoke denial.

And then there is the actual political world of 1980s and 1990s America, in which Wade's fictional senate campaign is firmly located. In that political world, it is not what Wade *did* in Vietnam that devastates his candidacy and thus destroys his life, but rather his concealment and falsification—that is, words, verbal constructs, *fictions*. As his cynical campaign manager points out, a different verbal construct could have turned Wade's participation in My Lai into a political advantage: "All you had to do was *say* something. Could've made it work for us. Whole different spiel." After all, he sardonically quips, "A village is a terrible thing to waste" (202). Indeed, "The Battle Hymn of Lt. Calley," a 1971 song celebrating the man who led the massacre, sold more than a million copies, and there are now men sitting in the U.S. Senate who killed many more Vietnamese civilians in fact than John Wade did in fiction. In O'Brien's 1994 novel, Kathy and John Wade vanish in late 1986. It was just over two years later in the actual world of American politics that President George Bush told us in his inaugural address how to make Vietnam vanish: "The final lesson of Vietnam is that no great nation can long afford to be sundered by a memory."

LEGACIES OF DENIAL

If America's war in Vietnam is not too ambiguous, "crazy," indeterminate, incoherent, or "unreal" to be comprehended, then what narrative structure best tells the story? Every narrative has a beginning, which determines and is determined by the shape and meaning of the whole story. So each story that purports to tell the true history entails an answer to the deceptively simple-sounding question "When did the Vietnam War begin?"

The three main competing American stories of the Vietnam War can be titled "A Noble Cause," "Quagmire," and "Imperialism."

The first, summed up in President Reagan's capsule concoction, begins sometime after 1954, when a country named "North Vietnam" attempted to take over another country named "South Vietnam." According to this story, the U.S. military "came home without a victory not because they'd been defeated, but because they had been denied permission to win," a doctrine Reagan reiterated from beginning to end of his two terms as president.[28] So the explicit moral of "A Noble Cause" is plain: "If I had to come out with one thing learned, I would have to say that never again must a government of the United States ask young men to go out and fight and die for a cause that we're unwilling to win. That was the great tragedy — that was the great disgrace, to me, of Vietnam — that they were fed into this meatgrinder, and yet, no one had any intention of allowing victory."[29]

While the war was going on, Reagan unambiguously defined what he meant by victory, and his definition suggests why the history of Vietnam, indeed the very existence of the Vietnamese people, is irrelevant to the "noble cause" story: "It's silly talking about how many years we will have to spend in the jungles of Vietnam when we could pave the whole country and put parking stripes on it and still be home by Christmas."[30] If turning all of Vietnam into an uninhabited parking lot can represent "victory," then the "noble cause" story can incorporate thousands of My Lais, not to mention the erasure of the Vietnamese from postwar American memory.

There is also a corollary to the moral of the "noble cause" story. If not one of the American Presidents for two decades — Eisenhower, Kennedy, Johnson, and Nixon — ever "had any intention of allowing victory," then Americans must choose a different kind of leader in order to avoid any similar "tragedy" and "disgrace" in the future. The nation must also transform its attitudes toward the military and "victory." This message closely resembles the underlying argument of volume one of Adolf Hitler's *Mein Kampf,* which blames the "liberal press," "thoughtless women," and the "half-heartedness and weakness" of cowardly politicians for preventing "the army's heroism" from achieving German victory in World War I.[31]

The "Quagmire" story, originally told by David Halberstam, also begins in 1954, when "a reluctant United States" chose to "back" Ngo Dinh Diem because "it was a time of human bankruptcy in South Vietnam and Diem was the one straw for a grasping America"; and so "we found ourselves caught in a limited, ineffective and almost certainly doomed holding action." Then come years of errors, misunderstanding, and confusion as America lurches and wallows deeper and deeper into the mire of Vietnam. The moral of the "Quagmire" story is this: "The lesson to be learned from Vietnam is that we must get in earlier, be shrewder and force the other side to practice the self-deception."[32]

The "Imperialism" story begins in 1945, when America's economic and political leaders committed the nation to buttressing, maintaining, and becoming the dominant power within the "Free World," that is, a global Anglo-European-American imperial system that had controlled the planet's economy for about a century. Weakened by World War II and menaced by anticolonial and anticapitalist movements throughout Asia and Africa, the old colonial system faced its most direct challenge in Vietnam, the first European colony to emerge from the war with a claim of independence, a national government, and its own army. The "Imperialism" story is the only one that adequately accounts for America's half century of military, political, and economic warfare against Vietnam and hostility toward every other colony and former colony that has resisted the "New World Order" or "globalization."

Perhaps the best source for the "Imperialism" story is the *Pentagon Papers,* the government's own top secret history of the Vietnam War. Senator Mike Gravel, who made these documents public by reading

> The Pentagon Papers show that we have created, in the last quarter of a century, a new culture, a national security culture. . . . The Pentagon Papers reveal the inner workings of a government bureaucracy set up to defend this country, but now out of control, managing an international empire by garrisoning American troops around the world. It created an artificial client state in South Vietnam, lamented its unpopularity among its own people, eventually encouraged the overthrow of that government, and then supported a series of military dictators. . . . The elaborate secrecy precautions, the carefully contrived subterfuges, the precisely orchestrated press leaks, were intended not to deceive "the other side," but to keep the American public in the dark.

As Senator Gravel noted, only a person who "has failed to read the Pentagon Papers" can believe in "our good intentions" or that we were fighting for "freedom and liberty in Southeast Asia."[33]

These three stories, so mutually contradictory in most respects, do have one striking feature in common: in each story, the United States government that conducted the war is at best an untrustworthy character. In "A Noble Cause," the government is a coward and a weakling. In "Quagmire," the government is a well-intentioned but self-deceived incompetent. In "Imperialism," the government is a ruthless agent of power and dominion.

When and why did this distrust of the U.S. government become rampant? It is easy to determine *when:* during the Vietnam War. The way may also have something to do with *why.* The American people's opinion of their government underwent a dizzying reversal, chronicled in a poll taken every two years since 1958 by the University of Michigan's Center for Political Studies (see table 1). In 1958, on the eve of direct U.S. military involvement in Vietnam, over three fourths (76.3 percent) of the American people believed that the government was run for the benefit of all, while only 17.6 percent believed that it was run by a few big interests. In 1964, as thousands of American "advisers" were engaged in combat, and after the Gulf of Tonkin incidents, 64 percent still believed that the government was run for the benefit of all, while the number who believed that it was run by a few big interests had jumped to 28.6 percent. This shift continued inexorably. Just before the 1972 elections, for the first time a plurality (48.8 percent) believed

TABLE 1. Government run by few big interests or for benefit of all? (1958–1972)

Question: "Would you say the government is pretty much run by a few big interests looking out for themselves or that it is run for the benefit of all the people?"

	1958*	1964	1966	1968	1970	1972 (Pre-election)	1972 (Post-election)
Few big interests	17.6%	28.6%	33.3%	39.5%	40.8%	48.8%	53.3%
For benefit of all	76.3	64.0	53.2	51.2	50.1	43.7	37.7
Other, depends	1.0	4.0	6.3	4.8	5.0	2.5	2.5
Don't know	5.1	3.5	7.2	4.5	4.1	5.1	6.5

Source: University of Michigan, Center for Political Studies, election surveys.[34]
*Question in 1958 was: "Do you think that the high-up people in government give everyone a fair break whether they are big shots or just ordinary people, or do you think some of them pay more attention to what the big interests want?"

TABLE 2. Is the government run for the benefit of all? (1974–1996)

Question: "Would you say the government is pretty much run by a few big interests looking out for themselves or that it is run for the benefit of all the people?"

	1974	1976	1978	1980	1982	1984	1986	1988	1990	1992	1994	1996
Few big interests	66%	66%	67%	70%	61%	55%	—	64%	71%	75%	76%	70%
Benefit of all	25	24	24	21	29	39	—	31	24	20	19	27
Don't know, depends	9	10	9	9	10	6	—	5	5	4	5	3

Source: The National Election Studies, Center for Political Studies, University of Michigan. Electronic resources from the NES World Wide Web site (www.umich.edu/~nes). Table generated May 10, 1998.

that the government was run by a few big interests, while only 43.7 percent still maintained the prewar faith. Then within a few months the numbers shifted even more dramatically. By late 1972, well over half of those polled believed that the government was run by a few big interests, and just slightly over one third (37.7 percent) still thought that the government was run for the benefit of all. So during the years of active U.S. warfare in Vietnam, the almost unchallenged prewar belief that America was truly a representative democracy had evidently become the opinion of a relatively small minority of Americans.

This reversal in Americans' view of their government became even more overwhelming as the Saigon regime — established, financed, armed, and controlled by Washington — was utterly destroyed between 1973 and April 1975. Even before they watched on TV the panic-stricken collapse of the Saigon army and the frenzied helicopter airlift from the abandoned U.S. embassy in Saigon, two thirds of Americans had already decided that their government was run by a few big interests (see Table 2). The change in opinion has not turned out to be temporary. By 1994, 76 percent expressed this profound distrust of the government, while a mere 19 percent still clung to the belief that they lived in a representative democracy.

It is of course impossible to determine precisely how much the Vietnam War itself directly contributed to changing Americans' attitudes toward their government. Economic and social problems also played a role, as did a series of political events from the assassination of John F. Kennedy to Richard Nixon's Watergate felonies; but none of these problems and events were unrelated to the war. It is safe to say, however, that before the Vietnam War Americans trusted their government and after the war they did not. Can one imagine, for example, members of *any* postwar movement singing these words from a popular prewar civil rights song: "The Government is behind us, we shall not be moved"?

No, today all across the political spectrum there is general agreement that the government is not to be trusted. So one consequence of decades of official denial is the common belief that whatever the government denies may be true, and the more the government denies, the more likely it is deceiving. This may be the most conspicuous, and probably the least unhealthy, legacy of denial.

bags of "dog shit" on returning veterans and telephoned bereaved parents to gloat over the deaths of their sons in Vietnam.

While this reimaging was being perpetrated, the history of the antiwar movement was being rewritten to make it seem some bizarre anomaly that mysteriously sprang from nowhere and then disappeared, leaving hardly a trace. It was, so the story goes, a phenomenon of that strange period known, somewhat inaccurately, as "the sixties."

When did Americans actually begin to oppose U.S. warfare against Vietnam? As soon as the first U.S. act of war was committed. And when was that? In 1965, when President Lyndon Johnson ordered the marines to land at Da Nang and began the nonstop bombing of North Vietnam? In 1964, when Johnson launched "retaliatory" bombing of North Vietnam after a series of covert U.S. air, sea, and land attacks? In 1963, when nineteen thousand U.S. combat troops were participating in the conflict and Washington arranged the overthrow of the puppet ruler it had installed in Saigon in 1954? In 1961, when President John F. Kennedy began Operation Hades, a large-scale campaign of chemical warfare? In 1954, when U.S. combat teams organized covert warfare to support the man Washington had selected to rule South Vietnam? Americans did oppose all of these acts of war, but the first American opposition came as soon as Washington began warfare against the Vietnamese people by equipping and transporting a foreign army to invade their country—in 1945.

Those Americans who knew anything about Vietnam during World War II knew that the United States had been allied with the Viet Minh, the Vietnamese liberation movement led by Ho Chi Minh, and had actually provided some arms to their guerrilla forces commanded by Vo Nguyen Giap. American fliers rescued by Giap's guerrillas testified to the rural population's enthusiasm for both the Viet Minh and America, which they saw as the champion of democracy, antifascism, and anti-imperialism.[2] American officials and officers who had contact with Ho and the Viet Minh were virtually unanimous in their support and admiration.[3] The admiration was mutual. In September 1945 the Viet Minh issued the Vietnamese Declaration of Independence, which began with a long quotation from the U.S. Declaration of Independence, proclaiming the establishment of the Democratic Republic of Vietnam.[4] The regional leaders of the OSS (predecessor of the CIA) and U.S. military forces joined in the celebration, with General Philip Gallagher, chief of the U.S. Military Advisory and Assistance Group (USMAAG), singing the Viet Minh's national anthem on Hanoi radio.[5]

But in the following two months the United States committed its first act of warfare against the Democratic Republic of Vietnam. At least eight and possibly twelve U.S. troopships were diverted from their task of bringing American troops home from World War II and instead began transporting U.S.-armed French troops and Foreign Legionnaires from France to recolonize Vietnam. The enlisted crewmen of these ships, all members of the U.S. Merchant Marine, immediately began organized protests. On November 2, all eighty-eight noncommissioned crew members of the *Pachaug Victory* drew up a protest letter they sent to the War Shipping Administration in Washington. Later that month, the crew of the *Winchester Victory* sent this cablegram to President Harry Truman and Senator Robert Wagner of New York: "We, the unlicensed personnel [i.e., non-officers] of the S. S. Winchester Victory, vigorously protest the use of this and other American vessels for carrying foreign combat troops to foreign soil for the purpose of engaging in hostilities to further the imperialist policies of foreign governments when there are American troops waiting to come home. Request immediate congressional investigation of this matter." On arriving in Vietnam, where they were shocked to be saluted by Japanese soldiers recently rearmed by the British to suppress the Vietnamese, the entire crews of four troopships met together in Saigon and drew up a resolution condemning the U.S. government for using American ships to transport troops "to subjugate the native population" of Vietnam.[6]

The full-scale invasion of Vietnam by French forces, once again equipped and ferried by the United States, began in 1946. An American movement against the war started to coalesce as soon as significant numbers of Americans realized that Washington was supporting France's war against the Democratic Republic of Vietnam (DRV).

For example, on September 23, 1947, a large meeting hall in New York was filled for a "Celebration of the Second Anniversary of the Independence of the Republic of Viet-Nam," an event organized by the Viet Nam American Friendship Association. Chairman Robert Delson prophetically saw what would be at stake in Vietnam for several decades: "the founding of the newest Republic in the world — the Democratic Republic of Viet Nam, . . . an event which history may well record as sounding the deathknell of the colonial system." Speaker after speaker rose to denounce the war being waged to annihilate this republic. And as six-time presidential candidate Norman Thomas explained to the assembly, "It is only by direct and indirect aid . . . from the United States that colonial imperialism can be maintained in the modern world."[7]

As Washington's active support of the French war kept increasing, so did opposition to this creeping escalation by the Truman and Eisenhower administrations. The opposition came from across the entire political spectrum — right-wing Republicans, liberal Democrats, socialists, communists, women's and veterans' organizations, and many others. This growing dissension between the White House and the American people reached a climax just as the French were being militarily defeated in the spring of 1954.

Speaking to the American Society of Newspaper Editors on April 16, Vice President Richard Nixon declared that because "the Vietnamese lack the ability to conduct a war or govern themselves," U.S. military intervention might be imminent: "It is hoped the United States will not have to send troops there, but if the government cannot avoid it, the Administration must face up to the situation and dispatch forces."[8] This speech was widely interpreted as a trial balloon launched by the White House. Reaction to what some called the "Nixon War" was swift, broad, and impassioned.[9]

Thousands of letters and telegrams opposing U.S. intervention deluged the White House. An American Legion division with 78,000 members demanded that "the United States should refrain from dispatching any of its Armed Forces to participate as combatants in the fighting in Indochina or in southeast Asia."[10] There were public outcries against "colonialism" and "imperialism." Senators from both parties rose to denounce any contemplation of sending U.S. soldiers to Indochina. The Monday after Nixon's Saturday speech, for example, Democratic Senator Ed Johnson of Colorado declared on the Senate floor: "I am against sending American GI's into the mud and muck of Indochina on a blood-letting spree to perpetuate colonialism and white man's exploitation in Asia."[11]

By mid-May, a Gallup poll revealed that 68 percent of those surveyed were against sending U.S. troops to Indochina.[12] Nevertheless, the Eisenhower administration was already actively shifting from supporting the French to replacing them. The same month marked the fall of the French bastion at Dien Bien Phu, the opening of the Geneva Conference to end the French war, and the selection by Washington of Ngo Dinh Diem to be the U.S. puppet ruler of "the State of Vietnam."

May was also the month when these words appeared in an eye-opening essay by Paul Sweezy and Leo Huberman titled "What Every American Should Know about Indo-China":

> The American people, by and large, are against colonialism and aggression, and believe in the right of every country to manage its own affairs free from outside interference.
>
> Rarely have these simple principles been so clearly and grossly violated as in present United States policy towards Indo-China. . . . [I]f we send American forces into Indo-China, as [Secretary of State John Foster] Dulles and other high government spokesmen have repeatedly threatened to do in the last two months, we shall be guilty of aggression. . . .
>
> Are we going to take the position that anti-Communism justifies anything, including colonialism, interference in the affairs of other countries, and aggression? That way, let us be perfectly clear about it, lies war and more war leading ultimately to full-scale national disaster.

This analysis, which looks uncannily accurate from the vantage point of the twenty-first century, concluded with a prophetic call for action: "There never has been and never will be a clearer test case than Indo-China. The time for decision is now. Let everyone who cares about the future of our country stand up and speak out today. Tomorrow may be too late."[13] Within two weeks of the publication of this prediction, a clandestine U.S. military team arrived in Vietnam to conduct covert warfare throughout the country, including sabotage in Hanoi.[14]

One of the most widespread fantasies about the Vietnam War blames the antiwar movement for losing the war by not supporting the government, thus forcing the military to "fight with one arm tied behind its back." But this stands reality on its head. Right from the beginning, the government understood that the American people did not and would not support a war in Vietnam. Therefore, when Washington decided to replace France in the war against the DRV, it necessarily committed itself to a covert war, a policy based on deception, sneaking around, hiding its actions from the American people. Each administration, from Eisenhower through Kennedy and Johnson to Nixon, was aware that whenever bits and pieces of the truth about this war leaked out, opposition to the war would build. Every administration was also aware that each escalation of the war would intensify the forms of opposition. It was the U.S. government that thus created the internal nemesis of its own war. Eventually that nemesis of necessity would also emerge inside the army and navy fighting that war.

Looking back to the 1945–1954 period, one may be jolted to hear 53
words like "imperialism" and "colonialism" and "white man's exploitation" in the mouths of merchant seamen and U.S. senators. Such words
would not be applied very frequently to our government in subsequent
decades, at least by white Americans, except for a brief period in the
late 1960s and early 1970s. Even then, they were hazardous to use. In
that period, whenever the word "imperialism" came out of my own
mouth during antiwar speeches, I could actually see people tuning me
out. So I started asking: "What happened when I said 'imperialism'?
Did a little alarm go off inside your head, warning you against listening
to anyone who used that word? How did that alarm get inside your
head?" Then I would note that during the impassioned national debate
of the 1890s about whether the United States should become an imperialist power, both sides used the term—and the debate was won in
1898 by those who proudly called themselves imperialists.

The years when the United States was steadily escalating its military
presence and combat role in Vietnam—1954 to 1963—were also years
when fundamental critiques of U.S. foreign policy had become marginalized. Outspoken domestic opposition to Cold War assumptions had
been eviscerated by the purges, witch-hunts, and everyday repression
(misleadingly labeled "McCarthyism") conducted under the Truman
and Eisenhower administrations. The main targets of that repression
had been carefully selected to include anyone in a position to commu-
nicate radically dissenting ideas to a large audience: teachers, union
leaders, screenwriters, movie directors, radio and print journalists. So
by the early 1960s, the aftershocks of that earlier political hammering,
combined with the stifling of foreign policy debate by "bipartisanship"
between the two ruling political parties and supersaturation in Cold
War culture, had stripped the American people of any dissenting political consciousness or even a vocabulary capable of accurately describing
global political reality. Those 1940s and 1950s views of U.S. Indochina
policy as imperialist had been forced deep underground, not to re-
emerge until the zenith of the antiwar movement in 1968. By then,
most participants regarded such views as brand-new discoveries.

Although that 1954 call to the American people to "speak out"
against U.S. war in Indochina before it was "too late" to avert "full-scale
national disaster" may have been forgotten by 1963, its message was
repeated by many in the ensuing decade. Indeed, these were the feelings of ever-growing numbers of Americans. And for most of this period, the main form of antiwar action was to "speak out"—in the form

THE ANTIWAR MOVEMENT

of letters to editors, appeals to Congress, articles and books, petitions and advertisements, sermons and teach-ins, banners and picket signs, leaflets and graffiti, resolutions and demands, referenda and slogans.

By 1963, the basis of a broad popular movement against the war was forming. The American people had seen on television huge demonstrations in Saigon, with Buddhist nuns and priests setting themselves afire, in protest against Ngo Dinh Diem's brutal regime. Many thousands of U.S. soldiers, sailors, and airmen were already involved in the fighting. Operation Hades, that chemical warfare campaign begun in 1961, though renamed Operation Ranch Hand and passed off as a harmless defoliation program involving innocuous weedkillers, was already arousing anxiety. Then in November 1963, three weeks before the assassination of John F. Kennedy, came the assassination of Diem and the takeover of the Saigon government by generals on the U.S. payroll — generals, ironically enough, mainly from the northern half of Vietnam.

The first nationwide action in the United States against the war in Vietnam came the following year. It took the form of campaigning for the 1964 presidential candidate who pledged over and over again, "I shall never send American boys to Vietnam to do the job that Asian boys should do" — President Lyndon Johnson, who defeated war hawk Barry Goldwater in an unprecedented landslide. Not until 1971 and the release of the *Pentagon Papers* would Americans learn that within forty-eight hours of assuming the presidency in November 1963, Johnson had signed National Security Action Memorandum 273 (NSAM 273) implementing a secret plan for a full-scale U.S. war to be covered by "the plausibility of denial."[15]

When the bombing of North Vietnam began in February 1965, less than three weeks after Johnson's inauguration as elected president, and the first acknowledged American combat troops went ashore in March, the antiwar movement appeared for the first time as a national phenomenon distinct from electoral politics. The first teach-ins materialized in March 1965.

As the antiwar movement was becoming a mass movement in 1965, it was fundamentally aimed at achieving peace through education, and it was based on what now seem incredibly naive assumptions about the causes and purposes of the war. We tend to forget that this phase of the antiwar movement began as an attempt to *educate* the government and the nation. Most of us opposed to the war in those relatively early days naively believed — and this is embarrassing to confess — that the government had somehow blundered into the war, maybe because our leaders were simply ignorant about Vietnamese history. Perhaps they didn't remember the events of 1940 to 1954. Maybe they hadn't read the Geneva Agreements. So if we had teach-ins and wrote letters to editors and Congress and the president, the government would say, "Gosh! We didn't realize that Vietnam was a single nation. Did the Geneva Agreements really say that? And we had told Ho Chi Minh we'd probably support his claims for Vietnamese independence? Golly gee, we had better put a stop to this foolish war."

Experience was the great teacher for those who were trying to teach, a lesson lost in the miasma of so-called theory that helped to paralyze activism in the 1990s. Teaching the Vietnam War during the 1960s and early 1970s meant giving speeches at teach-ins and rallies, getting on talk shows, writing pamphlets, articles, and books, painting banners, picket signs, and graffiti, circulating petitions and leaflets, coining slogans, marching, sitting-in, demonstrating at army bases, lobbying Congress, testifying before war crimes hearings and congressional investigations, researching corporate and university complicity, harboring deserters, organizing strikes, heckling generals and politicians, blocking induction centers and napalm plants, and going to prison for defying the draft. It is hard to convey the emotions that inspired these actions. Probably the most widely shared was outrage, a feeling that many came to consider outdated in the cool 1990s.

While the repression of the late 1940s and 1950s helped create the embarrassing naïveté and innocence of the early 1960s, these very qualities fueled the movement's fervor. People believed that the government would respond to them because they believed in American democracy and rectitude. Then, when the government did respond — with disinformation and new waves of repression — the fervor turned to rage.

Back in December 1964 an obscure little organization called Students for a Democratic Society (SDS) had issued a call for people to go to Washington on April 17, 1965, to march against the war. Only a few thousand were expected. But when the march took place, it turned out to be the largest antiwar demonstration so far in Washington's history — 25,000 people, most neatly dressed in jackets and ties or skirts and dresses.

What seemed at the time very large demonstrations continued throughout 1965, with 15,000 marching in Berkeley on October 15, 20,000 marching in Manhattan the same day, and 25,000 marching again in Washington on November 27. These early crowds would have been imperceptible in such later giant protests as the April 1967 New York demonstration of 300,000 to 500,000 people or among the half million or more who converged on Washington in November 1969 and again in the spring of 1971. In the nationwide antiwar Moratorium of October 15, 1969, millions of Americans—at least ten times the half million then stationed in Indochina—demonstrated against the war.

Demonstrations were one form of the attempt to go beyond mere words. Other forms appeared as early as 1965. Many of the activists were veterans of the civil rights movement, who now began to apply its use of civil disobedience and moral witness. That summer, the Vietnam Day Committee in northern California attempted to block munitions trains by lying on the tracks; hundreds of people were arrested for civil disobedience in Washington; and public burnings of draft cards began. Moral witness was taken to its ultimate by Norman Morrison, a thirty-two-year-old Quaker who drenched himself with gasoline and set himself on fire outside the Pentagon; pacifist Roger La Porte, who immolated himself at the United Nations; and eighty-two-year-old Alice Herz, who burned herself to death in Detroit to protest against the Vietnam War. By 1971 civil disobedience was so widespread that the number *arrested* in that spring demonstration in Washington—14,000—would have been considered a good-size march in 1965.

Whether the majority of Americans at any point supported the government's policies in Vietnam (or even knew what they were) is a matter of debate. Certainly most Americans never supported the war strongly enough to agree to pay for it with increased taxes, or even to demonstrate for it in significant numbers, much less to go willingly to fight in it. Nor were they ever willing to vote for any national candidate who pledged to fight until "victory." In fact, every nominee for president of both major parties after the 1960 elections through the end of the war, except for Barry Goldwater in 1964, ran as some kind of self-professed peace candidate.

Who opposed the war? Contrary to the impression promulgated by the media then and overwhelmingly prevalent today, opposition to the war was not concentrated among affluent college students. In fact, opposition to the war was *inversely* proportional to both wealth and education. Blue-collar workers generally considered themselves "doves" and tended to favor withdrawal from Vietnam, whereas those who considered themselves "hawks" and supported participation in the war were concentrated among the college-educated, high-income strata.[16]

For example, a Gallup poll in January 1971 showed that 60 percent of those with a college education favored withdrawal of U.S. troops from Vietnam, 75 percent of those with a high school education favored withdrawal, and 80 percent of those with only a grade school education favored withdrawal.[17] In *Lies My Teacher Told Me,* James Loewen reports a revealing experiment he conducted repeatedly in the 1990s. When he asks audiences to estimate the educational level of those who favored U.S. withdrawal back in 1971, by an almost ten-to-one margin they believe that college-educated people would have been the most antiwar. In fact, they estimate that 90 percent of those with a college education would have favored withdrawal, scaling down to 60 percent of those with a grade school education.[18]

Opposition to the war was especially intense among people of color, though they tended not to participate heavily in the demonstrations called by student and pacifist organizations. One reason for their caution was that people of color often had to pay a heavy price for protesting the war. For speaking out in 1966 against drafting black men to fight in Vietnam, Julian Bond was denied his seat in the Georgia legislature. World Heavyweight Boxing Champion Muhammad Ali was stripped of his title and criminally prosecuted for draft resistance. When 25,000 Mexican-Americans staged the Chicano Moratorium, the largest antiwar demonstration held in Los Angeles, the police attacked not just with clubs but with guns, killing three, including popular television news director and *Los Angeles Times* reporter Rubén Salazar.[19]

Certainly the campus antiwar movement was spectacular. The teach-ins of spring 1965 swept hundreds of campuses and involved probably hundreds of thousands of students. By the late 1960s, millions of students were intermittently involved in antiwar activities ranging from petitions and candlelight marches to burning down ROTC buildings and going to prison for draft resistance. In May 1970 the invasion of Cambodia was met by the largest student protest movement in American history, a strike that led to the shutdown of hundreds of campuses, as well as the gunning down of students by national guardsmen at Kent State University in Ohio (where four were killed and nine wounded) and by state troopers at Jackson State in Mississippi (where two were killed and at least twelve wounded).[20]

There are three principal misconceptions about the college movement. First, it was not motivated by students' selfish desires to avoid the draft, which was relatively easy for most college men to do and automatic for all women. In fact, one of the earliest militant activities

58   on campus was physical disruption of the Selective Service test that granted draft deferments to college students; the student demonstrators thus jeopardized their own deferments while protesting against them as privileges unfair to young men unable to attend college (they also risked punishment by the college authorities and sometimes physical attacks by men taking the tests). Second, most college students were not affluent (indeed, most came from the working class), and some of the largest and most militant demonstrations were at public universities that could hardly be labeled sanctuaries of the rich, such as Kent State, San Francisco State, and the state universities of Michigan, Maryland, and Wisconsin. Third, although college antiwar activism did hamper those in Washington who were trying to conduct the war without hindrance, the most decisive opposition to the war came ultimately not from the campuses but from within the cities and the army itself.

To understand the antiwar movement, one must perceive its relations with that other powerful mass movement hamstringing the Pentagon: the uprising of the African American people. The civil rights movement of the 1950s and early 1960s had certainly not achieved economic progress for the majority of African Americans, whose conditions were made even worse as the war brought conscription and inflation to the inner cities and the poorest regions of the rural South. The civil rights movement, in fact, hardly outlived its crescendo, the huge 1963 march on Washington climaxed by Martin Luther King, Jr.'s, "I Have a Dream" speech. The most memorable event of Mississippi Freedom Summer in 1964 proved to be the white terrorist murder of James Chaney, Andrew Goodman, and Michael Schwerner. That summer — also the summer of the Gulf of Tonkin incidents — a different form of social action arrived as rebellions erupted in several urban ghettos, the most serious since the World War II riots in Harlem, Detroit, and Los Angeles. Rioting spread in the summer of 1965, and by 1966 the pattern of "long, hot summers" seemed to be intensifying each year. In April 1967, Martin Luther King linked the ghetto violence directly to the war in Vietnam, declaring, "I could never again raise my voice against the violence of the oppressed in the ghettos without having first spoken clearly to the greatest purveyor of violence in the world today — my own government."[2] The 1967 summer uprisings reached new heights, especially in blue-collar cities such as Newark and Detroit. Then in April 1968, Martin Luther King was assassinated. During the week that followed, rebellions broke out simultaneously in more than a hundred U.S. cities. Coupled with the Tet offensive, which several weeks earlier had hit over a hundred cities and towns in South Vietnam, this climax of the urban revolts would prove to be a decisive event in the history of the Vietnam War.

The African American movement had been helping to energize the antiwar movement at least since 1965, when a number of leading black activists and organizations condemned the war as an assault on another people of color while articulating an anti-imperialist consciousness that would not be common in the broader antiwar movement until 1968.[22] In January 1965, the month before he was assassinated, Malcolm X denounced the Vietnam War, placed Africans and African Americans on the same side as "those little rice farmers" who had defeated French colonialism, and predicted a similar defeat for "Sam."[23] That July the Mississippi Freedom Democratic Party called on African Americans not to participate in the Vietnam War and implied that their war was closer to home: "No one has a right to ask us to risk our lives and kill other Colored People in Santo Domingo and Vietnam, so that the White American can get richer. We will be looked upon as traitors by all the Colored People of the world if the Negro people continue to fight and die without a cause."[24] In January 1966 the Student Nonviolent Coordinating Committee (SNCC) explained why it was taking a stand against the Vietnam War: "We believe the United States government has been deceptive in claims of concern for the freedom of the Vietnamese people, just as the government has been deceptive in claiming concern for the freedom of the colored people in such other countries as the Dominican Republic, the Congo, South Africa, Rhodesia and in the United States itself."[25] Stokely Carmichael in 1966 was the main speaker at the first rally against napalm (see chapter 4). In 1968, dozens of black soldiers, many of them Vietnam veterans, were arrested and court-martialed for refusing to mobilize against antiwar demonstrators outside the Chicago Amphitheatre during the Democratic convention (see chapter 5). What made the convergence of the black and antiwar movements explosively dangerous for those trying to maintain order and sustain the war was the disintegrating and volatile situation within the armed forces, as pointed out by an alarming article published in the January 1970 *Naval War College Review*.[26]

Very little awareness of resistance to the war inside the military survives today. But without this awareness, it is impossible to understand not just the antiwar movement but also the military history of the war from 1968 to 1973, not to mention the end of the draft and the creation of a permanent "volunteer" army to fight America's subsequent wars.

To begin to get some sense of the relative scale and effects of civilian and active-duty war resistance, compare the widely publicized activity of draft avoidance with some little-known facts about desertion (a serious military crime defined by being away without leave more than thirty days and having the intention never to return). Although draft evasion and refusal certainly posed problems for the war effort, desertion was much more common and far more threatening.

The number of draft evaders and resisters was dwarfed by the number of deserters from the active-duty armed forces. During the 1971 fiscal year alone, 98,324 servicemen deserted, an astonishing rate of 142.2 for every 1,000 men on duty.[27] Revealing statistics flashed to light briefly as President Gerald Ford was pondering the amnesty he declared in September 1974 (at the same time he also pardoned ex-President Nixon for all federal crimes he may have committed while in office). According to the Department of Defense, there were 503,926 "incidents of desertion" between July 1, 1966, and December 31, 1973.[28] From 1963 through 1973 (a period almost half again as long), only 13,518 men were prosecuted for draft evasion or resistance. The admitted total of deserters still officially "at large" at the time was 28,661 — six and a half times the 4,400 draft evaders or resisters still "at large."[29] These numbers only begin to tell the story.

Some of the deserters became politically active in other countries, including Germany, Sweden, Canada, the Soviet Union, Japan, England, Switzerland, the Netherlands, and France. An underground railroad, or rather searoad, was created from Asia to Europe.[30] By early 1967 a network of deserters and civilian supporters had built an underground organization in western Europe whose activities soon included establishing sanctuaries, obtaining work permits, leafleting U.S. military bases, helping to publish GI newspapers, and building an antiwar infrastructure inside the army known as RITA (Resistance Inside the Army).[31] Members of the deserter movement were active in the huge antiwar rebellion of April 1967 that temporarily seized control of much of Paris, and the deserter infrastructure played a significant role in the near-revolution that shook France in May 1968.[32] In England, organized deserters helped spark activities such as a 1971 antiwar demonstration by more than a thousand active-duty servicemen.[33]

As a militant antiwar movement erupted on army and navy bases across the United States, civilians and veterans rushed to provide support. Antiwar coffeehouses became centers of organization for active-duty servicepeople near dozens of bases. Lawyers offered free legal

services to the thousands of GIs being prosecuted for antiwar activities.
Pete Seeger, Barbara Dane, Country Joe McDonald, Jane Fonda, Joan Baez, and many other performers brought antiwar shows to throngs of cheering soldiers and sailors who joined in the singing.[34]

Thousands of veterans who had fought in Vietnam moved to the forefront of the antiwar movement after they returned to the United States, and they—together with thousands of active-duty GIs—soon began to play a crucial role in the domestic movement.[35] Dozens of teach-ins on college campuses were led by Vietnam veterans, who spoke at hundreds of rallies.[36] More and more demonstrations were led by large contingents of veterans and active-duty servicepeople, who often participated under risk of grave punishment. The vanguard of that Washington demonstration by half a million people in the spring of 1971 was a contingent of a thousand Vietnam veterans, many in wheelchairs and on crutches, who then conducted "a limited incursion into the country of Congress" which they called Dewey Canyon III (Dewey Canyon I was a 1969 covert "incursion" into Laos; Dewey Canyon II was the disastrous February 1971 invasion of Laos). About eight hundred marched up to a barricade hastily erected to keep them away from the Capitol and hurled back their Purple Hearts, Bronze Stars, Silver Stars, and campaign ribbons at the government that had bestowed them.

Anyone who still envisions the antiwar movement according to the caricatures in this chapter's opening paragraph should see the 1971 NewsReel documentary film *Only the Beginning,* which opens and closes with footage of Dewey Canyon III.[37] One after another, these decorated Vietnam combat veterans make brief statements as they rid themselves of their badges of honor. One "spec. 4 retired" hobbles on a cane to the microphone and angrily growls, "I'm taking in nine Purple Hearts, Distinguished Service Cross, Silver Star, Bronze Star, Army Commendation, and a lot of other shit." This is 1971, and these veterans are leading the transformation of the antiwar movement into an anti-imperialist or even revolutionary movement. When some raise a clenched fist and shout, "Power to the People!" hundreds of others echo their words in a roar. A much-decorated African American explains that he is "returning all medals given me by the power structure with genocidal policies against nonwhite peoples of the world." The final image is of a white veteran pointing toward the Capitol and grimly stating, "We don't want to fight anymore, but if we have to fight again it will be to take these steps."

Having experienced the close relations among veterans, active-duty servicepeople, and civilians in the antiwar movement, many participants were flabbergasted to hear it asserted, years after the war was over, that veterans were customarily and frequently spat upon by antiwar demonstrators. I have yet to meet a single person in the antiwar movement who saw or knew of any such incident. As the Vietnam veteran and sociologist Jerry Lembcke has demonstrated in his invaluable 1998 book *The Spitting Image: Myth, Memory, and the Legacy of Vietnam,* the vast majority of returning veterans characterized their reception as friendly. There is no contemporaneous evidence of any antiwar activists spitting on veterans. The first allegations of such behavior did not appear until the late 1970s. The spat-upon veteran then became a mythic figure used to build support for military fervor and, later on, the Gulf War, but the myth has become so powerful that many veterans have now come to believe, despite all evidence to the contrary, that it actually happened to them personally.[38]

Of course it is possible that isolated instances may have occurred. But if antiwar activists were frequently spitting on veterans or otherwise abusing them, why has nobody ever produced even the tiniest scrap of contemporaneous evidence? According to the myth, spitting on veterans was a regular custom as they arrived from Vietnam at the San Francisco and Los Angeles airports. We are supposed to believe that these men just back from combat then meekly walked away without attacking or even reporting their persecutors, and that nobody else, including airport security officers, ever noticed what was going on. For there is not one press report, airport security report, police report, court record, diary entry, video shot, or photograph of a single incident at these airports or anywhere else.

How then to explain the belief now held by many veterans that they were indeed spat upon as they arrived from Vietnam at the San Francisco and Los Angeles airports? The answer lies in the transformative power of collective national myth over individual memory. The myth is so strong that it has even determined their memory of where they arrived, for they were flown back not to these civilian airports but to military bases closed to outsiders.[39] Before the myth arose, years after the war, the only veterans who ever reported or who were observed being spat on were antiwar veterans — by prowar partisans. And a 1975 survey revealed that 75 percent of Vietnam veterans were opposed to the war.[40]

Especially after the 1968 Tet offensive, antiwar sentiment spread widely among the combat troops in Vietnam, where peace symbols and antiwar salutes became commonplace. Some units even organized their own antiwar demonstrations to link up with the movement at home. For example, to join the November 1969 antiwar Mobilization, a unit stationed at Pleiku fasted against the war and boycotted the Thanksgiving Day dinner. Of the 141 soldiers classified below the rank of specialist fifth class, only eight showed up for the traditional meal; this "John Turkey Movement" spread to units all over Vietnam.[41] When Bob Hope introduced General Creighton Abrams, commander of all U.S. forces in Vietnam, to the 30,000 troops assembled for a Christmas show at the sprawling Long Binh base, the entire throng leaped to their feet and held their hands high in the "V" salute of the peace movement.[42] But the main activities of antiwar U.S. servicepeople in Vietnam were not peaceful demonstrations.

An ongoing dilemma for the antiwar movement back home was the difficulty of finding ways to move beyond verbal protest and symbolic acts to deeds that would actually interfere with the conduct of the war. The soldiers in Vietnam had no such problem. Individual acts of rebellion, ranging from desertion and sabotage to injuring and even killing officers who ordered hazardous search-and-destroy missions, merged into mutinies and large-scale resistance.[43]

As early as the spring of 1967, sporadic small-scale mutinies were being reported in the French press but not in the U.S. media — except for the movement's own press (see chapter 5). The most serious occurred on April 14 at the base of Dau Tieng (east of Tay Ninh, north of Cu Chi), when a unit of the Third Brigade of the Fourth Infantry Division defied orders to proceed on a search-and-destroy mission near where another unit had been badly cut up. The commanding officer ordered other soldiers to fire on the rebels, who returned the fire. One report indicated dozens of men killed or wounded and three helicopters destroyed. The base was sealed off and no outside personnel were admitted for three days.[44]

Combat refusal and outright mutinies spread rapidly after the Tet offensive in 1968. But news about this form of growing GI resistance was kept rather efficiently from most of the American public until August 1969, when correspondents reported firsthand on the unanimous battlefield refusal of a badly mauled infantry company to go back into combat.[45] During the next two years, the press published numerous reports of entire units refusing direct combat orders, and the public actually got to see two incidents of rebellion on network television.[46]

Resistance took another form so widespread that it brought a new word into the English language: "fragging." Originally taking its name from fragmentation grenades but soon applied to any means of killing commissioned or noncommissioned officers, fragging developed its own generally understood customs, usages, and ethos. Officers who aggressively risked or otherwise offended their men were customarily warned once or twice by a nonlethal grenade before being attacked with a booby-trapped or hurled grenade. By mid-1972, the Pentagon was officially acknowledging 551 incidents of fragging with explosive devices, which had left 86 dead and more than 700 wounded.[47] These figures were no doubt understated, and they did not include a common and less conspicuous method of killing unpopular officers: rifle fire, often in the midst of combat.[48]

In June 1971 the *Armed Forces Journal* ran an article by Colonel Robert Heinl titled "The Collapse of the Armed Forces," which asserted: "By every conceivable indicator, our army that now remains in Vietnam is in a state approaching collapse, with individual units avoiding or having refused combat, murdering their officers and noncommissioned officers, drug-ridden, and dispirited where not near mutinous."[49] The main concern now was not so much the fighting capabilities of the remaining ground army, which was only one third the size it had been before its forced withdrawal began in mid-1969, but the ability of the armed forces in general to remain viable as the "near mutinous" resistance spread and intensified.

The Nixon administration tacitly recognized that the U.S. armed forces could not win a ground war in Vietnam. With his policy of "Vietnamization," Richard Nixon began belatedly moving toward fulfilling Lyndon Johnson's 1964 electoral promise not to use "American boys to do the job Asian boys should do," but only because now the American "boys" in the field were plainly unwilling and unable to do the job. By mid-1972, U.S. combat forces in Vietnam had been reduced to almost the same size as when Johnson made that promise.

Meanwhile, the United States poured even more massive amounts of money and arms into South Vietnam, giving the Saigon government overwhelming superiority in numbers, firepower, and modern weapons, including the world's fourth-largest air force. But in the spring of 1972, "Vietnamization" took a body blow when the DRV launched a major offensive that routed Saigon's army, despite all its numerical and technological advantages, and captured large sections of South Vietnam. All that saved Saigon's forces from total collapse was U.S. airpower.

This was a critical period during the negotiations that had been going on in public since early 1968 and in secret since 1969. Washington had to retain some kind of military credibility to have any leverage in these negotiations. But with no reliable army on the ground, U.S. strategy was forced to shift almost entirely to aerial technowar. One main component was to be a flotilla of Seventh Fleet aircraft carriers (twice as many as in 1971) massed in the Gulf of Tonkin, bringing warplanes closer than the fighter-bombers based in Thailand and the B-52s on Guam to targets all along the narrow land of Vietnam. This strategy was torpedoed by a massive antiwar movement among the sailors, who combined escalating protests and rebellions with a widespread campaign of sabotage.

The actions of these sailors cannot be written off the way some revisionist historians have tried to explain away the fraggings, sabotage, and mutinies of the ground troops as merely attempts at self-preservation. The sailors could not be motivated by any desire to avoid wounds or death because their ships were not in any danger of enemy attack. So what were their motives? Many of them shared the same revulsion that had inspired those first antiwar actions by hundreds of merchant seamen in 1945, a revulsion now immeasurably intensified by the kind of war being waged by the United States against the people of Vietnam.

In 1970 and 1971 ships had been sporadically forced out of action by outbreaks and even sabotage by crew members. Occasional inconspicuous newspaper articles allowed perceptive members of the general public to get inklings of what was happening to the fleet. An early example was the destroyer *Richard B. Anderson*, which was kept from sailing to Vietnam for eight weeks when crew members deliberately wrecked an engine.[50] Toward the end of 1971, the sailors' antiwar activities coalesced into a coherent movement called SOS (Stop Our Ships/Support Our Sailors) that emerged on three of the gigantic aircraft carriers crucial to the Tonkin Gulf strategy: the USS *Constellation*, the USS *Coral Sea*, and the USS *Kitty Hawk*. (One early act was a petition by 1,500 crew members of the *Constellation* demanding that Jane Fonda's antiwar show be allowed to perform on board.) On these three ships alone that fall, thousands of crew members signed antiwar petitions, published onboard antiwar newspapers, and supported the dozens of crew members who refused to board for Vietnam duty.[51]

In March 1972 the aircraft carrier USS *Midway* received orders to leave San Francisco Bay for Vietnam. A wave of protests and sabotage swept the ship, hitting the press when dissident crewmen deliberately spilled three thousand gallons of oil into the bay.[52] In June the attack carrier USS *Ranger* was ordered to sail from San Diego to Vietnam. The Naval Investigative Service reported a large-scale clandestine movement among the crew and at least twenty acts of physical sabotage, culminating in the destruction of the main reduction gear of an engine; repairs forced a four-and-a-half-month delay in the ship's sailing.[53] In July the aircraft carrier USS *Forrestal* was prevented from sailing by a major fire deliberately set by crewmen, which caused millions of dollars of damage to the captain's and admiral's quarters of the ship.[54] In September and October the crew of the *Coral Sea*, which had been publishing the antiwar newspaper *We Are Everywhere* for a year, staged renewed protests against the war, with over a thousand crewmen signing a petition to "Stop Our Ship." It was forced to return to San Francisco Bay, where crew members held a national press conference and helped organize support rallies and other demonstrations. Almost a hundred crew members, including several officers, refused Vietnam service and jumped ship in California and Hawaii.[55] In September crew members of the aircraft carrier USS *Ticonderoga* organized their own "Stop It Now" movement, and navy intelligence tried unsuccessfully to break up the SOS movement on the showpiece carrier USS *Enterprise*, home of the antiwar paper *SOS Enterprise Ledger*.[56] A bloody September battle between groups of marines on the amphibious landing ship USS *Sumter* in the Gulf of Tonkin off Vietnam was not made public until the following January.[57]

One of the most serious outbreaks took place in October on the *Kitty Hawk*, where organized antiwar activities (including publication of the antiwar paper *Kitty Litter*) had continued during its eight-month tour off Vietnam. When the ship was ordered to return to Vietnam from Subic Bay instead of continuing its voyage home, African American members of the crew led a major rebellion, fought hand-to-hand battles with the marines sent to break up their meeting, and reduced the ship to a chaos of internal fighting for several hours. Four days later, fighting spread to the *Kitty Hawk*'s oiler, the USS *Hassayampa*. The *Kitty Hawk* was forced to retire to San Diego, whence it sailed to San Francisco in early January, where it underwent a "six-month refitting job."[58] The sailors' movement had thus removed this major aircraft carrier from the war.

Especially damaging were the synergistic effects of the protests, sabotage, and rebellions on the aircraft carriers central to Pentagon strategy. For example, when the House Armed Services Committee investigated the hundreds of reports of "successful acts of sabotage," one conclusion reached in their report was that the rebellion on the *Kitty Hawk* had been precipitated by the orders to return to Vietnam, orders mandated because two other aircraft carriers had been disabled: "This rescheduling apparently was due to the incidents of sabotage aboard her sister ships *U.S.S. Ranger* and *U.S.S. Forrestal.*"[59]

In October and early November, incidents of sabotage and an open revolt brewing on the *Constellation* forced it to return to San Diego, where 130 sailors prevented the ship's departure for two months by refusing to reboard and staging a militant demonstration onshore, resulting in their discharge from the crew. The media called this a "racial outbreak," but the picture in the *San Francisco Chronicle*, captioned "The dissident sailors raised their fists in the black power salute," shows mainly white sailors with upraised arms and clenched fists.[60] When I went to speak in San Diego on November 10, I found five aircraft carriers tied up, all forced out of combat in the Gulf of Tonkin by their crews, each of which was publishing an antiwar — and increasingly revolutionary — newspaper on board. That night I addressed hundreds of these crew members in San Diego antiwar movement centers, where men from the different aircraft carriers and their attendant vessels were getting together to build a fleet-wide organization.

In December the *Ranger*, all repaired now, finally made it to the Gulf of Tonkin, where it was immediately disabled by a deliberately set fire. The navy admitted that this was the sixth major disaster on a Seventh Fleet carrier since October 1. Meanwhile, the internally embattled *Constellation* was not even able to sail from San Diego for Vietnam until January 5, 1973, three weeks before the signing of the Paris Peace Accords; the rebellious crewmen had in effect permanently removed another major aircraft carrier from the war.[61] Not since Pearl Harbor had the U.S. Navy been so crippled, and then the damage had been done by an enemy that could be defeated in combat.

In October 1972, Washington finally accepted the basic peace terms put forth by the other side back in May 1969, including the immediate withdrawal of all U.S. military forces and bases, but then reneged when the Saigon government, recognizing that it could not survive without massive U.S. military protection, refused to acquiesce. On December 18, Nixon launched Linebacker II, better known as the Christmas bombing, a twelve-day all-out bombardment of Hanoi, Haiphong, and other areas of North Vietnam, intended to force the DRV to accept major changes in the draft pact. Giant B-52 bombers flew 729 sorties, along with about 1,000 more by air force fighter-bombers and some planes from the Seventh Fleet.

Although the bombing did cause vast destruction, it also demonstrated the ineffectiveness of what remained of U.S. military might in Vietnam. The Pentagon admitted losing twenty-one B-52s (fifteen shot down over Vietnam and six permanently disabled) and thirteen fighter-bombers, though Hanoi's claims of thirty-four B-52s and forty-seven fighter-bombers were probably closer to the truth. At this late date, at least 121 airmen were lost, including forty-four captured, increasing, ironically enough, by 8 percent the number of U.S. military POWs held in North Vietnam.[62] The Christmas bombing also intensified the antiwar movement within the air force, with potentially ominous consequences.

Individual pilots — one with more than two hundred previous combat missions — refused on moral grounds to participate in the bombing.[63] After the first nights of heavy losses, many of the B-52 crews voiced their opposition to the kinds of risks they were being asked to take in a conflict that had obviously been decided. The most serious actions took place among air crews of the supersecret 6990th Air Force Security Service based on Okinawa, whose mission was eavesdropping on North Vietnamese air defense communications in order to give timely warnings to the B-52 crews. Because they had firsthand knowledge of the DRV's preparations for peace and were outraged by the nature of the bombing, they staged a work stoppage verging on open mutiny. According to Seymour Hersh, who interviewed at least ten members of the unit in early 1973, during the work stoppage there were cheers whenever a B-52 was shot down. Some of the men were later court-martialed under stringent security.[64]

The Christmas bombing was designed, among other things, to create the postwar myth that the United States had forced the DRV "back to the bargaining table." But the peace agreement signed by Richard Nixon in January 1973 was in fact an almost total capitulation to terms Washington had been offered throughout the war, with the addition of a secret pledge of several billion dollars to help repair all the devastation the United States had inflicted. In this agreement the United States finally recognized precisely what it had been attempting to deny by every possible means since 1954, that Viet Nam was and is one country, not two: "The United States and all other countries respect the independence, sovereignty, unity, and territorial integrity

THE ANTIWAR MOVEMENT

of Viet-Nam as recognized by the 1954 Geneva Agreements on Viet-Nam." Indeed, the agreement incorporated *word for word* most of the "Ten-Point Program" put forward by the National Liberation Front as its initial negotiating position in May 1969.[65]

The antiwar movement initiated back in 1945 by those hundreds of merchant seamen protesting U.S. participation in the French attempt to reconquer Vietnam was thus consummated in a movement of tens of millions of ordinary American citizens spearheaded by soldiers, sailors, fliers, and veterans which finally ended the war with a recognition that Vietnam could be neither divided nor conquered by the United States.

No, it was not Vietnam but the United States that ended up divided by America's war. And the division cut even deeper than the armed forces, biting down into the core of the secret government itself. When members of the intelligence establishment joined the antiwar movement, they had the potential to inflict even greater damage than mutinous soldiers and sailors. The perfidy of the Central Intelligence Agency in Vietnam was revealed by one of its highest-level agents in South Vietnam, Ralph McGehee, author of *Deadly Deceits: My Twenty-Five Years in the C.I.A.*[66] Philip Agee decided in 1971 to publish what eventually became *Inside the Company: CIA Diary* because of "the continuation of the Vietnam war and the Vietnamization programme," writing, "Now more than ever exposure of CIA methods could help American people understand how we got into Vietnam and how our other Vietnams are germinating wherever the CIA is at work."[67] Nineteen seventy-one was also the year when one of the authors of the Pentagon's own supersecret history of the war, Daniel Ellsberg, exposed it to the American people and the world. As manifested in the eloquent declarations of W. D. Ehrhart and Senator Mike Gravel, quoted in the previous chapter, these *Pentagon Papers* were an earthquake that demolished all the official narratives, revealing the shameful swamp of lies on which they had been constructed.

Interviewed three years after the release of the *Pentagon Papers*, Ellsberg outlined the history of the Vietnam War by tracing the "lies" told by Presidents Truman, Eisenhower, Kennedy, Johnson, and Nixon. "The American public was lied to month by month by each of these five administrations," he declared. And then he added, "It's a tribute to the American public that their leaders perceived they had to be lied to."[68]

The end of the war did not end the lies. Since then, both the war and the antiwar movement have been falsified so grossly that we risk forfeiting the most valuable knowledge we gained at such great cost to the peoples of Southeast Asia and to ourselves. Nor can we understand what America is becoming if we fail to comprehend how the same nation and its culture could have produced an abomination as shameful as the Vietnam War and a campaign as admirable as the thirty-year movement that helped defeat it.

The present model of the fire bomb, the M116A1, was designed specifically for delivery by high-performance jet airplanes. When released at low altitudes, the tank and the igniters burst upon contact. . . . The blazing contents are scattered over an area approximately the size of a football field. The resulting flash fire ignites readily combustible material and burns or suffocates exposed personnel. It is particularly useful in jungle operations.

"Chemical and Biological Warfare," *Fundamentals of Aerospace Weapons Systems,* U.S. Government Printing Office, 1961

The lie works only as long as it takes to speak
And the girl runs only as far
As the napalm allows
Until her burning tendons and crackling
Muscles draw her up
Into that final position
Burning bodies so perfectly assume. Nothing
Can change that; she is burned behind my eyes . . .
Bruce Weigl, "Song of Napalm"

CHAPTER FOUR

Burning Illusions

THE NAPALM CAMPAIGN

It was early 1966. A woman in the suburban town of Redwood City, California, answered her doorbell. Asked to sign a petition against the local production of napalm, she responded: "Napalm? No thank you. I'm not interested. I always use Tide."

She represented the majority, for in early 1966 most Americans had never heard of napalm. By the end of that year, a national and global campaign against its use had changed the consciousness of tens of millions. That campaign had been initiated by a handful of people in and around Stanford University in January 1966. It was a turning point in the lives of many people, including me.

Looking backward, I realize that I cannot understand how I became the person I am today without mentally recapitulating the stages of my metamorphosis during that napalm campaign, a campaign that destroyed the cocoon of illusions within which much of our consciousness had been formed. Revisiting the early days of that campaign may allow readers of today to penetrate some of their own illusions in order to comprehend how the movement against the Vietnam War changed the lives of ordinary individuals and a nation.

How could a campaign directed against a single weapon profoundly transform minds and lives? The answer lies mostly in the process of activism and the discoveries about self and society made in this process. That will be the main story I tell in this chapter. But just probing the history of this particular weapon also has transformative powers, as I learned. Because I had flown in the Strategic Air Command, I was assigned the job of doing this research. What I found clashed with my perception of America and its history, a perception mainly shaped between the ages of seven and eleven during World War II.

Napalm is a highly flammable sticky gel originally made by adding to aviation gas a chemical compound of aluminum naphthenates and palmitates. The Chemical Warfare Service developed napalm during World War II for two purposes. First, because it sticks to clothing and flesh and continues to burn into the bone, it was an effective weapon on the battlefield. Its second use in World War II was for what was called "strategic bombing," that is, attempts to destroy cities — and their populations — from the air.

"Strategic bombing" was explicitly part of the ideology of Fascism, raised to the level of theory by Mussolini's commissioner of aviation, General Giulio Douhet, who argued that incendiary bombs are even more useful than high explosives in creating the desired "terror from the air."[1] Before the United States entered World War II, Secretary of State Cordell Hull claimed to be "speaking for the whole American people" when he denounced this fascist theory and practice, declaring, "No theory of war can justify such conduct."[2] On September 1, 1939, the day World War II started in Europe, President Franklin D. Roosevelt communicated an "urgent appeal to every Government which may be engaged in hostilities publicly to affirm its determination that its armed forces shall in no event, and under no circumstances, undertake the bombardment from the air of civilian populations." Alluding to Axis air assaults on Ethiopia, China, and Spain, he declared that "the ruthless bombing from the air of civilians . . . has sickened the hearts of every civilized man and woman, and has profoundly shocked the conscience of humanity." He warned that "hundreds of thousands of innocent human beings" would be victimized if the warring nations were to sink to "this form of inhuman barbarism."[3]

But this is precisely what napalm was originally designed for. Shortly after the United States entered World War II, university professors and

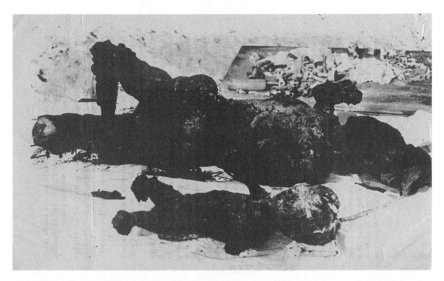

"Mother and Child." Between January and February 1966, 250,000 copies of this leaflet were dropped from airplanes over Los Angeles, Disneyland, troopships in San Diego harbor, San Francisco, and Oakland. The Stanford law student who organized the operation, along with three of the six pilots involved, was arrested; he was charged with a felony: conspiracy to litter.

other American scientists under contract to the Chemical Warfare Service supervised the construction of replicas of the working-class districts of Japanese industrial cities, including the houses made of paper and wood. Their goal was to develop an incendiary weapon that would leave a fiercely flaming substance sticking to structures long enough to generate an urban firestorm so intense that its winds would make it self-sustaining and inextinguishable.

Other incendiary bombs were used, primarily by the British Royal Air Force, against a number of German cities, the most notorious example being the firebomb raid that incinerated Dresden. Napalm itself as a "strategic" weapon was reserved for people of color. Designed to be used against Japanese cities, it was tried out first on the occupied Chinese city of Hankow, which was cremated in December 1944, with fires raging for three days after the raid. The attack, I learned, was led by my former commanding officer, General Curtis LeMay, who soon launched a napalm offensive on Japan that caused many more casualties among Japanese civilians than their armed forces suffered throughout the war. For example, the March 9, 1945, raid on Tokyo was as devastating as the Hiroshima atomic bomb.

The target was a twelve-square-mile rectangle housing one and a quarter million people. For three hours, hundreds of B-29 super-fortresses unloaded their firebombs. The results were indeed spectacular. Instead of mere firestorms, the blazes produced a new, even deadlier phenomenon—the sweep conflagration, a tidal wave of fire igniting every combustible object in its path by radiant heat, melting asphalt streets and metal, leaping over canals, and searing the lungs of anyone near its superheated vapors. The heat was so intense that it generated towering thunderheads shooting bolts of lightning. The last waves of bombers had difficulty finding anything left to bomb, and were tossed around like leaves by the thermal blasts from the fires below. Sixteen square miles of the city were burned out. More than 267,000 buildings were destroyed, and well over a million people were rendered homeless. At least 84,000, and probably more than 100,000, died that night in the Tokyo inferno.[4]

Years later, while exploring more deeply the history of napalm and its role in American weapons culture, I learned that back in Hollywood, First Lieutenant Ronald Reagan was taking part in what he would later call one of the major "secrets of the war, ranking up with the atom bomb project": creating a complete miniature of Tokyo, so authentic in detail that even top air corps generals could not distinguish films of it from films of the real city. In his autobiography, Reagan described his voice-over narrative of fake bomb runs on the toy city and told how his Hollywood team would "burn out" their counterparts in "our target scene," evidently obliterating, along with the city, the boundaries between illusion and reality.[5]

By early August 1945, every Japanese city with a population over fifty thousand had been burned out—except for four reserved for an experimental secret weapon. Two of these were Hiroshima and Nagasaki.

Napalm was used again in the Korean War, so effectively that vast areas were turned into scorched wastelands. Almost every city, town, and village in North Korea and many in South Korea were incinerated. Whole forests were burned to the ground. Decades after the war, Koreans in the northern half of the country would show visitors a lone tree that had survived the holocausts, referring to it as a "prewar tree." Much of the population was forced to live underground.[6]

But U.S. weapons technology never stands still. In early January 1966, when I was teaching at Stanford University, a worker from a local corporation, United Technology Center, secretly communicated to a few of us antiwar activists the news that his company had just received a subcontract from Dow Chemical to develop a new, improved kind of napalm. The contract, we discovered, was for the development of Napalm-B, a thicker gel that would ignite more reliably, burn more intensely, and stick more tenaciously.

Napalm-B consisted of 25 percent gasoline, 25 percent benzene, and 50 percent polystyrene, the marvelous new thickener, which was to be manufactured in quantity for the napalm by Dow Chemical at Torrance, California. If UTC (United Technology Center) could successfully complete the research and development, production was scheduled to reach mammoth proportions. The information we gathered was later verified in the March 1966 issue of *Chemical and Engineering News,* which reported that the forthcoming use of polystyrene in Napalm-B would be 25 million pounds a month, so much that the normal industrial supplies would be severely overstrained. According to this figure, the production of Napalm-B was to reach 500 million pounds each year, three times the total dropped on Japan during World War II.

The antiwar movement at Stanford was then embodied by the Stanford Committee for Peace in Vietnam, accurately described by its vague, innocuous name. SCPV consisted of about two dozen students, faculty members, and residents of the surrounding suburbs, each more or less fitfully active against the war. It included a few people who called themselves pacifists, two who called themselves Marxists, and most who no longer knew what to call themselves.

My wife, Jane, and I fitted into the last category. Sometime after I had gotten out of the Strategic Air Command in 1959, in which I had flown as a navigator and squadron intelligence officer, we had inclined toward pacifism. We still didn't allow our two-and-a-half-year-old son to play with toy guns, and we were in favor of something then known as "militant, nonviolent protest." But we no longer considered ourselves pacifists, and our opposition to "violent" protest was not philosophical but tactical (it might "alienate" people). We were opposed to aggressive anticommunism, but we avoided political ideology, particularly Marxism, about which we knew virtually nothing except that it was a musty old nineteenth-century dogma of little relevance to the modern world, especially to an advanced industrial society such as the United States. We were in favor of anything that would work to stop the war.

SCPV as a whole expressed a similar outlook. This was about a year after opposition to the Vietnam War had taken shape as an organized national movement, dedicated principally to convincing the government and the American people that U.S. involvement in the war was a "mistake." Each weekly SCPV meeting was spent mainly debating proposals for actions to take the following week. We were looking for the one spectacular action that would quickly educate the American people, make the government recognize its folly, and end the "senseless killing" in Vietnam. We felt an urgency about this because we believed that the Vietnamese would soon be destroyed as a people. SCPV had no interest in any long-term programs to change American society.

When SCPV got word about the local contract to develop Napalm-B, we thought we could at last do something concrete: stop local production. And practically all of us saw a great potential for some kind of mass campaign that would swiftly educate people about the "immoral" nature of the war and the illusions of our government. Only two members disagreed.

One of the two, a self-declared Marxist, argued something like this: "A campaign against napalm would only build false consciousness. It would suggest that the Vietnam War would be fine if it were fought with conventional weapons. Who would this kind of campaign appeal to? Only middle-class liberals. In fact, it will alienate working-class people, because they want to use whatever weapons are necessary to support our troops. We must focus all our efforts on demanding immediate withdrawal of all our troops. That's the only demand that working-class people can support." The other naysayer took a position that seemed almost the precise opposite: "There's only one way to deal with a napalm plant, and that's to deal with it. Anybody who is interested, see me after this bullshit meeting is over."

These two seemingly opposite positions in fact had much in common, for both were based on the assumption that we could not build effective mass opposition to napalm. I do not believe that either of these other proposed courses of action was wrong. It was necessary to build a mass movement calling for withdrawal of the troops, and that movement certainly did get built. At some point the napalm plant should have been sabotaged. But a mass movement against napalm, as it turned out, was hardly a diversion from either of these goals.

One person, possibly the only one in our little group, understood all this back then. He was Keith Lowe, a doctoral candidate in Stanford's English department. Evidently Keith saw both the potential and the limitations of the situation. He also had the patience to lead some of the rest of us step by step through a process of political and personal development that produced not only a mass anti-napalm campaign spreading from the San Francisco Peninsula across the country and around the world, but also a number of people, including Jane and me, who came to see the problem finally not as napalm or the war but the entire political-economic-cultural order responsible for the Vietnam War.

Keith was a short, slim, soft-spoken, and self-effacing Jamaican, whose features reflected the mixture of European, Asian, and African peoples who had mingled on that island. He responded to other human beings as though he were a stranger to none of them. He was later rewarded by the government of the United States and the administration of Stanford University, which worked together closely on his case, when, in 1969, Keith, then a highly regarded assistant professor of English at the University of California, San Diego, was denied a visa to reenter the United States after a visit to Jamaica. The main evidence against him in his immigration file consisted of statements from the Stanford administration identifying him as a "subversive."

Keith's response to the news of the napalm contract was something unheard of—at least to most of us at the time. He proposed that we carry the issue right to the people in the napalm company. Most of the members of SCPV were excited by this proposal, but there were two contradictory views of how to apply it. Some thought this meant we should go directly to the workers and try to persuade them not to help develop and produce the new form of napalm. Others thought that only the management had the power to pull the company out of the napalm business, so we should go to them. Most groups of activists I have known since would have plunged into endless debate. One side would have argued that it was hopelessly impractical to go to the workers. The other side would have attacked this argument, and those who put it forth, as anti–working class. They in turn would have been attacked as dogmatists. If any action had come out of the debate, it would have been crippled by the divisive struggle that had brought it forth. What Keith apparently understood was that the proponents of neither position had ever verified their arguments in experience, and that most of us would use the debate, if we could, as an excuse to avoid the arena of practical struggle. Keith did not discount the importance of theory, but he pointed out that many theories seem persuasive until they are tested and modified in practice. So we soon found ourselves testing both ideas. Because we ourselves were so naive, we applied each in a fairly ridiculous manner. We leafleted the workers, as if a leaflet could persuade them to quit their "immoral" jobs, and we sat down with the top management to convince them that they should cease being war profiteers.

The main office of United Technology was in Sunnyvale, about ten miles south of Stanford, in the heart of what was later to be called Silicon Valley. In 1950 Sunnyvale had been a sleepy little burg with a population of 9,800. The aerospace and electronics complex developed by Stanford had changed all that, transforming Sunnyvale into a boomtown. By 1960 its population was almost 53,000; in 1966 it had reached 100,000.

Four delegates were selected to visit the shimmering modernistic office complex of UTC, strung out amid similarly well landscaped offices of other corporate, manufacturing, and banking centers in Sunnyvale. Our mission: to meet with the president of UTC and convince him, through rational dialogue, that the development and manufacture of napalm were immoral and so his company should refuse the contract. Off we went on January 25, 1966, all neatly and conservatively attired, the three men in jackets and ties, the one woman in an unobtrusive dress.

After some last-minute dickering, we were admitted into the office of Barnet Adelman, the president. He was flanked by three other officers of UTC. Two were retired generals, one a retired admiral. We then held our rational dialogue about the Vietnam War and Napalm-B.

Barnet Adelman seemed a pleasant, mild-mannered scientist. We knew that he was Jewish, had got his master's degree in chemical engineering from Columbia in 1948, and then worked in rocketry for the Jet Propulsion Lab, Cal Tech, the rocket-fuels division of Phillips Petroleum, and RamoWooldridge. He belonged to the American Ordnance Association and the American Rocket Society. He assured us that he was just as interested as we were in seeing the Vietnam War end quickly. "After all," he said, "our business has suffered a great deal from the war. Our main work is in long-range liquid-fueled space rockets. These have no immediate military application. The Defense Department has taken away all our funds for these rockets because of Vietnam. So we have no choice. Even if we didn't want to work on napalm, we would have to just to stay in business."

"So you would do anything just for money?" asked an Asian American Stanford student who was part of our delegation.

"Napalm will help shorten the war," responded Adelman. "Isn't that what we all want? Besides, whatever our government asks us to do is right."

Elena Greene, who had visited China and Vietnam with her husband, Felix Greene, brought up Nuremberg, and pointed out that one of the main defenses of the war criminals for what they had done was that their government had ordered them to do it.

"But that was not a legally elected government," said Adelman.

Someone appealed to him directly as a person whose own people had been the victim of war crimes. He responded, "That was Germany. This is America."

As I mentioned earlier, I had been assigned to do much of the research for our materials. So now I went into some of the history of Dow Chemical itself and its connections with Nazi war crimes, professorially reading from my research notes: "In the 1930s, Dow Chemical and the giant German chemical corporation I. G. Farben formed an international cartel. They agreed to restrain U.S. production of magnesium and allow Germany to take world leadership in this element. So, when World War II began, Germany was producing five times as much magnesium as we were. During the war, it was the Farben subsidiary, Badische Anilin and Soda-Fabrik, that developed and manufactured Zyklon-B, the poison gas used at Auschwitz and Dachau. Actually Dow maintained secret ties with Badische throughout the war. As soon as the war was over, they formally renewed their prewar connection with Farben by going directly through Badische. Right now, Dow Chemical and Badische are in partnership in a giant chemical plant in Freeport, Texas, called the Dow-Badische Company."

My little speech had no visible effect on Adelman, not to mention his three colleagues. Finally, one of the other delegates asked if we could have an opportunity to discuss the issue with the employees.

"I *am* the employees of UTC," said Adelman. He then informed us that he had to "take care of other business," and our discussion was "terminated."

Next we went to the workers, taking with us a leaflet asking, "*Is Barnet Adelman the employees of UTC?*"

UTC's napalm test site was located on a rambling old ranch off a dirt road several miles from the rural crossroads community of Coyote, south of San Jose. A few hundred yards back from the narrow dirt road stood several mysterious-looking low buildings, a small tower, and some large chemical storage tanks. Along the road ran a barbed wire fence, and the property stretched as far back as the eye could see into the hills.

We were nervous the first day, especially since all the workers in America, according to the media, staunchly supported the war. We stood at the gate and tried to hand leaflets to the workers as they drove through. That first day, most of them stopped to take the leaflet. Some went out of their way to be friendly. A few, though, tried to run us down. On the second day, the company posted plainclothes security guards and a photographer at the gate. Almost every worker driving through now pretended that we didn't exist, except for a few who again tried to run us down. It looked as though the workers were as reactionary as the media said. Then some of us tried leafleting back down the road, where it met U.S. Highway 101, three miles away from the company guards and photographer. Here the response was even more friendly than on the first day. Some workers got out of their cars to talk. They told us that the management was very nervous, and had posted plainclothes security guards inside the plant to keep an eye on the workers. Most employees, they told us, were very fearful of losing their jobs if they showed any sympathy for our position.

One of our leaflets asked the workers, of all things, to quit their jobs in protest. Two or three actually did, and were quickly blacklisted from all employment in the area.

In the first week of February, we held an open meeting at Stanford to organize a caravan to Coyote, where we would hold a rally as the day-shift workers were leaving. At the Stanford meeting, one of the speakers was a young black man from the Student Nonviolent Coordinating Committee (SNCC). Tall, thin, unsmiling, he seemed wound up tight enough to explode. Speaking in a soft voice filled with barely restrained anger, he told us about a new political party he had helped organize in Alabama. It had split off from the regular Democratic Party of Alabama in order to conduct voter registration and run candidates in predominantly black Lowndes County. Since the symbol of the Alabama Democratic Party was a snowy white rooster, they had chosen the black panther as their symbol. The speaker, Stokely Carmichael, then said that he had just received his draft induction notice. He spoke of draft resistance. "I intend to walk right into that draft office and tell them," he said so quietly you had to cock your head to hear, "I don't belong to you, so you have no power over me." I heard this then as an existentialist affirmation, as well as an act in the civil disobedience tradition of Thoreau. I realize now that I missed altogether the significance of what Carmichael was saying because I knew nothing then about revolutionary black nationalism. I heard Carmichael projecting himself as a representative of every individual human being. In reality he was defying the draft as a representative of the African American people. He was disputing the power of the draft board to claim ownership not so much of his own human essence but of the lives of a people kidnapped from Africa.

At the Coyote rally Carmichael spoke again. Standing at a microphone directly facing the gate in the barbed wire fence across the dirt road, covered with the red dust churned up by the workers' cars, he spoke about the Vietnam War itself, his voice now loud, his words ringing out toward the napalm test site and the rolling hills beyond. Afterward, I walked up in my tweed sport jacket, white button-down shirt, and striped tie, and was introduced. I enthusiastically put out my hand and said, "That was a wonderful speech." Carmichael limply put his hand in mine for a second, glanced at me, stared past my head toward the chemical storage tanks, and mumbled something like "Yeah?"

Several weeks later, SNCC held a national conference, at which Stokely Carmichael was elected chairman. It was this conference that issued the historic paper titled "The Basis of Black Power," a modest statement demanding self-determination for blacks and asking "progressive whites" to organize in white communities. The mass media suddenly bombarded the country with the name of Stokely Carmichael, depicting him as a "black racist," a "disciple of hatred and race war," "a fiery inciter of passions." This obviously did not describe the man who had come to help in our campaign against napalm. It never occurred to me then that Carmichael had stuck his neck out to try to ally the black movement with the antiwar movement and that we ought to be thinking about what we could do to further that alliance. I was too busy working to stop the production of napalm.

At about this time, both Jane and I began to notice cars following us and mysterious sounds on our telephone line. Jane was then often on the phone, turning the San Francisco call-in shows into discussions of the war. Once, after dialing but before the phone was picked up at the other end, she heard a man's voice say, "Oh, she's just calling one of those damned shows again." One afternoon one of the workers who had quit UTC telephoned and asked me to come to his home in Santa Clara, another aerospace and electronics boomtown. After supper I drove to his moderately prosperous suburban community and, wary enough already to try to conceal our meeting, parked a few blocks away. He was still in contact with some of the other UTC workers, who told him that many employees were privately opposed to making napalm, but the plant had been turned into a virtual police state. Their casual conversations were being spied on, and even their personal reading matter was being inspected surreptitiously.

On my way home, I thought I was being followed on the freeway. When I got to Palo Alto, I drove to a gas station and went to a telephone to call Jane to find out where SCPV was meeting that night. Suddenly a car pulled in and rolled right up to the phone booth, blocking the door and fixing me in its headlights. I could barely make out the silhouettes of two men, wearing what seemed to be felt hats and business suits, in the front seat. I quickly told Jane what was happening. I could see the front license plate, so I made it obvious to the men in the car that I was reading its numbers into the phone. I continued facing the car and kept talking to Jane. After what seemed a very long time, probably only a few minutes, the car backed up and sped off, ostentatiously burning rubber. Somebody seemed to be sending me a message.

By the middle of March, UTC had completed its contract for the development of Napalm-B. They received their reward: a large contract for the production of actual napalm bombs. The company selected as the site for this production an unused Standard Oil storage facility in the port of Redwood City, at the end of a causeway sticking two miles out into the San Francisco Bay. This site was on publicly owned tidal land. Therefore, all leases and uses of it were under the jurisdiction of the Redwood City Port Commission, whose rulings were legally subject to override by the citizens of Redwood City.

On March 21, the Port Commission convened in an old frame building amid the unused petroleum storage tanks Standard Oil was asking to sublease to UTC. About fifty protesters showed up. Some were members of Concerned Citizens, a Palo Alto peace organization in which Jane participated. Others were from a Unitarian congregation in Redwood City. Most of the men wore jackets and ties, the women dresses. The most casually dressed were a few Stanford students. The room where the commissioners met could hold only about a dozen of us, so we presented them with our formal written protest and asked them to move to a larger facility. After much arguing, they agreed to adjourn to an auditorium in the county office building in downtown Redwood City.

By the time the meeting reconvened, almost two hundred people had gathered. The middle-aged white gentlemen on the commission set up ground rules for public participation, specifically ruling out of order "the moral question" and "the federal policy of war in Vietnam." Speaker after speaker rose to reason with the commissioners: a local minister, several Redwood City housewives, workers, students. Olive Mayer, an engineer from Redwood City who had inspected the gas ovens of Belsen, calmly stated: "As a professional engineer I knew that other members of my profession planned and engineered these ovens as execution chambers. The manufacturer's name was proudly displayed over the door of the ovens. Engineers had to calculate the number of victims to be accommodated, means of ingress and egress, how many to be executed at one time, and so on. Local government and professional people had to be involved in providing locations for the manufacture of these ovens, just as you commissioners are now called upon to make a decision concerning a napalm factory."

I rose, intending to speak about the specific qualities of napalm, based on my air force experience and recent research. I got as far as my name. The chairman turned tomato red and burst out angrily, "We know who you are and what you have to say, and we don't want to hear it. Sit down!" I couldn't believe my ears. I tried to ask why I shouldn't be allowed my opportunity to speak. The chairman yelled to the policemen at the back of the room, "Get that man out of here! Right now!" Two cops rushed up, twisted one arm behind my back, and started dragging me backward down the aisle. Our seven-year-old daughter burst into tears. The people in the audience were all staring in shocked disbelief at the scene in the aisle. By the time the police got me to the rear door, I noticed that the commissioners were packing their briefcases and starting to leave. I broke loose, ran back down the aisle, and demanded, "What are you doing?" People began calling out: "What's going on?" "Why are you leaving?" "Aren't you going to discuss it?" "Aren't you even going to bother to vote?" The chairman looked over his shoulder, laughed, bent down to a microphone, and said: "We just did vote to grant the sublease. We also voted to adjourn. You probably couldn't hear because of all the commotion you were making."

During the next few days, we investigated the legal options open to us. We discovered that the vote of the commission could be overturned in a referendum called by an initiative petition signed by 10 percent of the registered voters of Redwood City. When our lawyer went for help in preparing the papers, the city attorney gave him false information that cheated us out of thirteen days of the thirty we were entitled to have. So we had only seventeen days to find volunteers, build an organization, and collect the signatures of 10 percent of the voters. And this at a time when, according to the media and their polls, all but a handful of "dissidents" supported the war.

Signatures could be solicited only by registered voters of Redwood City. Redwood City was a suburban bedroom community of about fifty thousand, almost 100 percent white, mostly middle-income working-class, small business, and professional people. The city boundaries had been drawn to exclude the sizable population of Chicano, black, and poorer white working-class people, mostly concentrated in the unincorporated area known informally as East Redwood City. Redwood City had no history of radical politics. There wasn't even a liberal political organization to be found in town. On top of all these obstacles, the local press launched a campaign to block the petition. On April 16, the influential *Palo Alto Times* tacitly encouraged violence against us, and then, in two most revealing editorials, pointed out that if the people were allowed to vote on such matters, the country would be unable to wage war and the national government would be shattered:

> There is no question that considerable pressure is being brought by a small but vocal minority that objects to our use of napalm in the Viet Nam war. It is the same minority that objects to our involvement in the war at all. . . . The voters of Redwood City do not have the right to preempt these decisions for themselves, to make the decisions for the rest of the country. . . . [T]o place on a municipal ballot decisions on military and foreign policy is to invite chaos. If all cities in the United States were to decide for themselves whether to permit the manufacture of military aircraft, bombs, rifles, grenades, rockets, torpedoes and other war material, they would wreck our armed forces. If all of them were to arrogate to themselves decisions on foreign policy, they would wreck the national government.

Four days later a second editorial appeared:

> While there may be some question about the use of napalm in warfare, it is not a question to be decided by the voters of Redwood City or any other municipality. . . . It is easy to see what would happen if every city were to be allowed to make its own decision as to what war material is acceptable to its citizens.
>
> The people of Sunnyvale could vote on whether Polaris missiles should be manufactured by Lockheed. The people of Palo Alto could vote on whether electronics equipment for guided missiles should be built in the city. The citizens of San Francisco or Oakland could vote on whether their municipal port facilities should be permitted to load materials of war, such as napalm and atomic weapons, onto ships headed for the war.
>
> The result would be chaos.

But in a few days we had our volunteers and an organization. One hundred ten citizens of Redwood City, most of them working people, were out actively soliciting signatures. The regional local of the International Longshoremen and Warehousemen's Union sent a telegram of support, a small donation, and three volunteers. Thirty-four local clergymen signed a statement of support. Although the *Redwood City Tribune* had at first called us "treasonous," it began editorializing about the people's right to vote. On April 17 the *New York Times* ran a story on the campaign, and in the next three days NBC and CBS television news broadcast on-the-scene reports, both concluding that the reaction of the citizens of Redwood City to our campaign ranged from indifferent to hostile. ABC television did interviews but never aired them. On the seventeenth day we stayed up all night verifying and counting the signatures on the petitions. Fifteen percent of the registered voters of Redwood City had signed.

Anyone who has circulated a petition knows that this figure represents overwhelming support. In a petition campaign, it's good work just to *see* 15 percent of the registered voters in *thirty* days. On April 20, as we officially filed the petitions, we were confident that we were going to win the election, and we knew that this would have national and even international significance.

Meanwhile, UTC had started production of napalm bombs. If you drove out along the causeway to the napalm facility, you now passed acres of stacked crates of 500-pound and 750-pound bombs. You could even stand at the high chain-link fence and watch as the empty bomb casings were swung over to a raised platform and pumped full of napalm. On May 1 a barge partly loaded with napalm bombs mysteriously developed two holes in its hull and began to sink. A vigil began across the road from the plant. On May 16 and 17 a Palo Alto psychiatrist, two students from Stanford, and a Chicano jazz musician named Aaron Manganiello were arrested for lying down in front of trucks bringing empty bomb shells to be filled.

Meanwhile, the petitions still lay, uncounted, in the city clerk's office. The city attorney had been using one legal maneuver after another to block the election. On May 20, Superior Court judge Melvin Cohn ruled that the petition was invalid because it opposed the original sublease from Standard Oil to UTC. He disclosed that on April 26, six days after we had filed the petition, Standard Oil, UTC, and the Port Commission had secretly scrapped the old sublease and arranged a new one. Judge Cohn informed us that, in order to be valid, a petition would have to oppose this new lease. Since this new lease had gone into effect on April 26, we would have until May 26, only six days, to draw up a new petition, collect signatures, and have it filed. It was now obvious that, even if we could have performed that miracle, Standard Oil, UTC, and the Port Commission would merely draw up still another lease. A few weeks later we discovered that Judge Cohn was a personal friend of Barnet Adelman, president of UTC; their children attended the same Sunday school class. Nevertheless, we understood that their friendship had little to do with the judge's Alice-in-Wonderland decision. We had been forced to recognize that judges—like port authority commissions, city attorneys, policemen, FBI agents, newspapers, and armies—were there to do whatever corporations required of them.

The following day, Aaron Manganiello began a one-man fast and vigil across the road from the napalm plant. Aaron had just been suspended from the College of San Mateo, the local community college where he had been studying music, for distributing literature against the Vietnam War. Each night of his vigil and fast, men from UTC would hose him down every hour. After six days Aaron developed pneumonia and had to give up the vigil. He also soon gave up his pacifism, later becoming minister of information of the Brown Berets, a militant Chicano organization, and then head of the revolutionary California organization Venceremos.

On May 28 we officially launched the national campaign against napalm with a rally at a stadium in downtown Redwood City and a march to a concluding assembly at the gates of the napalm plant out on San Francisco Bay. The speakers at the rally included three antiwar congressional candidates, the publisher of *Ramparts* magazine, African American publisher and California gubernatorial candidate Carleton Goodlett, Felix Greene, retired admiral Arnold True, and a truck driver running as a peace candidate for the state assembly. Despite a virtual news blackout before the event, 3,500 people, including many families with small children, showed up. The demonstrators were "mostly well-dressed and clean-shaven," noted the *Redwood City Tribune*.

Our son, who had just celebrated his third birthday, rode his trike on the four-mile march through downtown Redwood City and out along the causeway to the napalm plant. Our older daughter, looking back decades later on this and many experiences that were to follow, remembered that "family outings were marches, demonstrations, sit-ins against the war." The march ended with more speeches, delivered from a flatbed truck outside the front gates of the napalm plant. The princi-

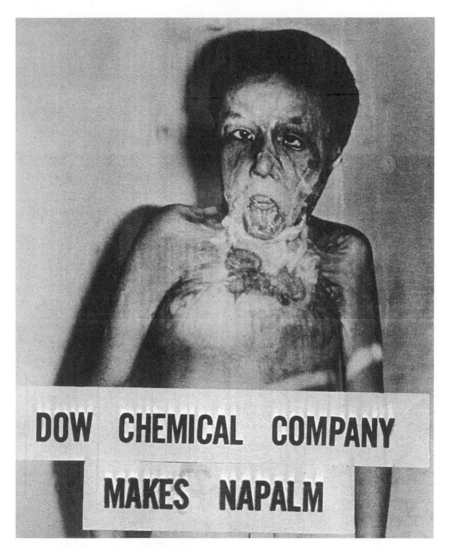

DOW CHEMICAL COMPANY MAKES NAPALM

pal speaker was Senator Wayne Morse of Oregon, who rambled on for half an hour, telling a couple of anecdotes to show that he was still a good friend of Lyndon Johnson's, never mentioning napalm. The rally concluded, and people began strolling to the buses we had chartered to take them back to their cars. Suddenly dozens of squad cars appeared, as if from nowhere. They had been carefully concealed behind buildings surrounding the rally. We counted hundreds of police from five different agencies. Many of the squad cars displayed shotguns and contained six police officers in full riot gear, something most people there had seen only on television. The Redwood City police depart-

BURNING ILLUSIONS

ment and the San Mateo County sheriff's office had prepared an elaborate ambush, and they were obviously disappointed that they had not
found a chance to "teach you some patriotism," as one cop yelled at the
protesters from a car window.

Only local newspapers reported that the march and rally had taken
place, and they underestimated the size of the crowd, reporting that
most citizens of Redwood City were hostile to such activities. Bruce
Brugmann, the *Redwood City Tribune* reporter who had been covering
the napalm campaign, became so disgusted by the blatant censorship
and rewriting of his stories that he left to found the radical weekly
newspaper the *Bay Guardian.* Even a mere twenty miles away, the press
and radio in San Francisco imposed a total news blackout. This did
keep many people in ignorance. But it also educated tens of thousands
about the role of the media. Almost everyone in the area knew that an
important event had taken place and could not help but wonder why it
was not reported and how many events from other areas were not being
reported to us.

In fact, we had succeeded in breaking through the wall of media
isolation and misrepresentation. The national boycott of Dow Chemical Corporation products, announced at the rally, had already begun.
That very day, fifty pickets demonstrated outside the New York offices
of Dow Chemical, and over two hundred picketed Dow's big polystyrene production plant in Torrance, outside Los Angeles. But none
of us would have predicted that over the next few years there would be
hundreds of demonstrations, involving hundreds of thousands of people, against Dow Chemical, its campus recruiters, and its subcontrac-
tors. Through the campaign against napalm, tens of millions of people
in the United States and around the world were to learn deep lessons
about the real nature of America's war against Vietnam.

"They are, it appears, trying to make 1968 the year of
decision in South Vietnam—the year that brings, if not
final victory or defeat, at least a turning point in the
struggle."
    President Lyndon Baines Johnson,
    address to the nation, March 31, 1968

CHAPTER FIVE

1968; or, Bringing the War Home

THE MOVEMENT, ITS PRESS, AND ALTERNATIVE PERCEPTIONS OF REALITY

In 1968 the armed forces of the United States suffered a stag-
gering setback in Vietnam; the incumbent president was so
discredited and crippled by the war that he had to abandon his
bid for reelection; the economy entered a prolonged plunge
into runaway debt and inflation; two preeminent political leaders were assassinated; and waves of rebellion swept the nation's
cities and campuses. In this cauldron, the movement against
the Vietnam War began to merge into something different,
something that called itself "the Movement," divorced from
the two parties that controlled American politics, profoundly
alienated from the dominant culture, increasingly militant in
practice and revolutionary in aim — and armed with its own
press.

"The Movement" — that turbulent confluence of political,
cultural, racial, and sexual rebellions — had to create its own

communications media, without, needless to say, the benefit of corporate sponsors or advertising. Of course it owned no television networks or even stations, for these were almost all under the control of an interlocking conglomerate of corporations that either owned outright or controlled through advertising the national radio networks, almost all national magazines, and the metropolitan, suburban, and regional newspapers. Hollywood was practically ignoring the war when it wasn't supporting it with jingoistic harangues such as *The Green Berets,* directed by and starring John Wayne, released in 1968. There was no Internet to offer any bypass around the corporate media. The only significant opening to the airwaves was the small but expanding Pacifica radio network, especially its founding station, listener-supported KPFA, which had been broadcasting alternative voices from Berkeley since 1949. Necessity being the mother of invention, the movement created a new kind of theater as well as a new form of movie production, and the leading innovators of each — the San Francisco Mime Troupe and NewsReel — have both survived into the twenty-first century. But mainly the movement would have to rely on its own print journalism. So what it built with astonishing speed and influence was the "underground" or "alternative" press.

Near the beginning of 1968, the *Wall Street Journal* estimated that the underground press had a third of a million readers; ten months later *Newsweek* estimated that readership had climbed to 2 million. The movement now had its own news services — Liberation News Service and the Underground Press Syndicate — which were claiming between 4.6 and 30 million readers.[1] By 1969, there were at least five hundred underground newspapers, with another five hundred to a thousand dissident high school papers.[2] There were already several dozen GI newspapers, which would soon number close to three hundred, many put out by active-duty soldiers and sailors on military bases and warships around the globe.[3] By 1969, veterans found it necessary to create the GI Press Service to serve these journals as "the Associated Press of the GI movement."[4] In addition, hundreds of prison newspapers were beginning to voice radical views, and dozens of leftist theoretical journals were adding readers at geometrical rates.

Yet the role of the underground press during the Vietnam War soon disappeared into the black hole of national amnesia that has swallowed much of our consciousness. Although there has been serious debate about the absurd proposition that the establishment press helped lose the war by not loyally supporting it, everybody seems to have forgotten that the establishment press eventually lost its monopoly on reporting the war, as millions of Americans began to rely primarily on the un-abashedly disloyal movement press for accurate and truthful reporting. Peter Braestrup's *Big Story: How the American Press and Television Reported and Interpreted the Crisis of Tet 1968 in Vietnam and Washington* never finds room in its 740 pages even to mention the existence of any press other than the corporate media.[5] By the 1990s, this erasure was virtually total. *Reporting Vietnam,* the purportedly definitive two-volume 1998 collection published as part of the Library of America, includes in its 1,715 pages a grand total of nine from the underground press.[6] Two major 1990s studies that attempt to give conclusive accounts of the media's role in the war — Clarence Wyatt's *Paper Soldiers: The American Press and the Vietnam War* and William Hammond's *Reporting Vietnam: Media and Military at War* — both demonstrate how government manipulation of the media led first to unreliable reportage and later to media distrust of the government, but both unaccountably fail even to mention the movement press.[7] Yet it was this alternative press that exposed the con-ventional media's initial complicity with the government and exposed their corollary unreliability — partly by doing the job that the establish-ment media were supposed to be doing.

The phenomenal growth of the alternative press in the late 1960s was generated by specific historical events as well as the inability or unwillingness of the establishment press to predict these events or ex-plain them adequately. The most spectacular expansion and radicaliza-tion of the movement and its press came in the decisive year of the war — 1968. What allowed the movement's press to challenge the hege-mony maintained by the traditional organs of corporate America over the public interpretation of events was the one that shaped many other major events of 1968: the month-long Tet offensive launched in late January by the National Liberation Front and Hanoi.

The Tet offensive offered an acid test for the comparative reliability of the underground versus the mainstream media. To people who got their news only from television and the establishment press, the offen-sive seemed to come out of nowhere. By contrast, it authenticated the reportage of the movement press, which had accurately assessed the military situation and predicted just such an eventuality.

In the waning days of 1967, the *New York Times* featured a series of front-page analyses of the Vietnam War by Hanson Baldwin, ace mili-tary correspondent of the establishment press. Baldwin began by an-nouncing in the December 26 issue that "nearly all United States officials" in Saigon, "from Ambassador Ellsworth Bunker and Gen. William C. Westmoreland down, believe that the main battleground in 1968 will be in the United States."

U.S. officials had good cause to think that the war was coming home. During the summer of 1967, dozens of American cities had been swept by rebellions. It had taken the 101st Airborne to quell the uprising in Detroit; machine guns, tanks, and helicopters were becoming commonplace features of urban life. In October, Stop-the-Draft Week had climaxed with a massive confrontation at the Pentagon, while ten thousand demonstrators in Oakland ended five days of street demonstrations by seizing much of the downtown area and thus successfully blockading northern California's main induction center for hours. The Justice Department was indicting thousands of Americans for draft resistance, while the antiwar movement was organizing to prevent the incumbent president from even being nominated.

What kind of warfare did those U.S. leaders foresee in the United States, their "main battleground" for 1968? With their old goal of "winning the hearts and minds" of the Vietnamese becoming ever more illusory, they would have to shift to the more realistic target of winning the hearts and minds of the Americans. The reality of the Vietnam War now seemed to them far less crucial than its public image. To secure the battleground, they needed mastery of the media.

Following this logic, President Johnson had summoned General Westmoreland home in November 1967 for a public relations offensive, featuring a major address to the National Press Club. As faithfully reported in the *New York Times* of November 22, Westmoreland told the nation's leading opinion makers that "the enemy's hopes are bankrupt," his forces "declining at a steady rate," and "he can fight his large forces only at the edges of his sanctuaries" in other countries; the war had entered the phase "when the end begins to come into view," a time when the South Vietnamese army would "take charge of the final mopping up of the Vietcong."[8] In the same issue of the *Times,* James Reston echoed the official assertions that "the Vietcong now control only 2,500,000 people," little more than half the number they had controlled in 1965, and "it is now merely a matter of time until this trend forces the enemy not to negotiate but to fade away into the jungle."[9]

Westmoreland's speech set the main line of the corporate press for the ensuing two months, and Hanson Baldwin's late December series, based on high-level, top secret briefings, spelled out the details. But the American public, having watched Lyndon Baines Johnson renege on his campaign promise "never to send American boys to Asia to do the job Asian boys should do," and then having learned some of the lies about the Tonkin Gulf incidents and subsequent deceptions about the conduct of the war, was becoming daily more skeptical and disenchanted, if not yet overtly opposed to the war.

Imagine — or remember — yourself as an American at this time. You are trying to sort truth from falsehood about the war. What is happening in Vietnam? Why? When will it ever end? How?

If you turned to Hanson Baldwin, you would read that "the enemy is weaker than he appears to be" and is gripped by "desperation," that his recent offensive is just a public relations ploy keyed "to strengthening opposition to the war in the United States and influencing American and world public opinion during a Presidential election year," that the morale of U.S. troops is "excellent," whereas there is "irrefutable evidence of a decline in enemy morale," that "the enemy can no longer find security in his South Vietnamese sanctuaries," that "the allies are winning" and "there seems little reason to doubt that Hanoi has abandoned the hope of conquest of South Vietnam by military force."[10]

If you turned to the underground press, you would find a totally contradictory reality. Just as the establishment press relied for military analysis on Hanson Baldwin, the alternative press relied on Wilfred Burchett. Unlike any of the reporters anthologized in the 1,700 pages of *Reporting Vietnam,* most of whose sources were limited to the briefings conducted by U.S. military authorities in downtown Saigon's Rex Hotel (dubbed the "Five-O'Clock Follies" by the press corps) and visits to U.S. combat units, Burchett knew from personal experience how things looked from the other side's combat units, a view entirely discounted by the U.S. mainstream press. As early as 1964, Burchett had actually accompanied insurgent fighters all the way to the outskirts of Saigon.[11] Writing in the *National Guardian* on December 23, 1967, Burchett claimed that the National Liberation Front had taken the initiative in the war, had begun a major offensive, and was "now able to mount simultaneous attacks on widely separated objectives in divisional strength." On January 6, 1968, Burchett argued in the *National Guardian* that "the true facts about the war have been denied the U.S. public by the extraordinary antics of Gen. William Westmoreland and his public relations team in Saigon": "Unable to present any successes in terms of terrain reoccupied or population won back from areas controlled by the NLF, the U.S.-Saigon command has resorted to an old trick the French used until the fall of Dien Bien Phu — the claim to be wiping out tens of thousands of enemy troops for the loss of a handful of their own." Burchett boldly declared:

> As the new year begins, the National Liberation Front of South Vietnam (NLF) is on the offensive at all points.
>
> This indigenous peasant army is clearly winning the war in Vietnam against all the might short of nuclear arms that the world's most developed, technologically advanced power can deploy.

Rarely have two conflicting versions of reality been so sharply defined by a disagreement about objective facts, and even more rarely has the outcome of the dispute been determined more clearly by those facts. Americans — and people around the world — would dramatically discover within weeks who was telling the truth: the government of the United States and its semiofficial corporate media or the antiwar movement and its hand-to-mouth press. And if the underground press was a more reliable guide to the reality of the Vietnam War, what implications did that have for information concerning other aspects of reality, including American democracy?

Although the official line still dominated editorials and analyses in the establishment media through the first thirty days of January, battlefield reports did not seem to corroborate the notion that the "Viet Cong" and "North Vietnamese" were desperately trying to pull themselves together in remote jungles and foreign sanctuaries. Between January 2 and 10, for example, the *New York Times* reported: "Enemy attacks U.S. air base at Danang"; "smashes at two American artillery bases in Queson Valley"; "almost wipes out allied platoon defending hamlet near Hoian"; "strikes district headquarters town of Phuloc 25 miles SE of Hue" while attacking five U.S. Marine Corps positions in the area; attacks government forces 24 miles northeast of Saigon; "fights way to center of Khiemcuong 21 miles west of Saigon"; "overruns U.S. airfield at Kontum, blowing up several planes." Then came the Tet offensive.

On January 30, during the Vietnamese New Year's Tet holiday, the National Liberation Front and the People's Army of Viet Nam exposed the official U.S. version of reality as a flimflam of illusions and lies. Simultaneously they attacked in every part of South Vietnam, hitting U.S. and puppet forces in five of the six major cities, thirty-six provincial capitals, sixty-four district capitals, and at almost every military base. Many U.S. airfields, ammunition dumps, and supply centers were devastated, and some were overrun, providing the insurgent forces with vast quantities of modern arms. Possibly as many as 200,000 prisoners were freed, more than making up in numbers for battlefield losses. Vietnam's old capital city of Hue was overwhelmed in hours, and held for weeks against all-out U.S. air, sea, and ground attacks. Sections of Saigon itself were seized, forcing the United States to bomb and strafe the capital with fighter-bombers and helicopter gunships.[12] U.S. authorities now claimed that they had won a great victory in Saigon by recapturing the American embassy compound, repulsing an assault on the Presidential Palace, and driving NLF forces back to the perimeter of Tan Son Nhut, the city's main military air base. Standing amid dead bodies and ravaged buildings on the grounds of the American embassy, with munitions exploding in the background, General Westmoreland declared on national television that the whole offensive was merely a "diversionary" tactic for an imminent invasion "across the Demilitarized Zone."[13] Perhaps he could hardly do otherwise without acknowledging that he had just committed one of the most colossal blunders in military history, moving his most effective combat units to counter the feint at the remote and insignificant outpost at Khe Sanh, thus stripping the defenses from the cities and densely populated regions that were the real targets of the offensive.[14]

Actually, sporadic fighting was to go on in Saigon for months, while sections of the capital and its surrounding suburbs would remain covert rebel strongholds throughout the rest of the war. Despite the absence of any open uprisings in the cities, it was obvious that the offensive could not have been possible without wide support from the populace. If either side was gripped by "desperation," it was the United States, which now launched frenzied massive counterattacks on the Vietnamese people. As a result, both the establishment and alternative media found the U.S. war aims expressed most trenchantly in the infamous words of an officer who explained why our warplanes and artillery had devastated the Mekong Delta city of Ben Tre, capital of Ben Tre Province: "It became necessary to destroy the town to save it."[15]

In fact, the military picture painted by the establishment media had now become almost indistinguishable from that found in the alternative press. The *Wall Street Journal* editorialized on February 23: "We think the American people should be getting ready to accept, if they haven't already, the prospect that the whole Vietnam effort may be doomed; it may be falling apart beneath our feet. The actual military situation may be making academic the philosophical arguments for the intervention in the first place." A *Washington Post* column by Art Buchwald datelined "Little Big Horn, Dakota, June 27, 1876," revealed how many in the media now viewed General Westmoreland's public statements:

> Gen. George Armstrong Custer said today in an exclusive interview with this correspondent that the Battle of the Big Horn had just turned the corner and he could now see the light at the end of the tunnel.
>
> "We have the Sioux on the run," Gen. Custer told me. "Of course, we still have some cleaning up to do, but the Redskins are hurting badly and it will only be a matter of time before they give in."[16]

The judgment of most Americans who had been trying to comprehend the war was succinctly summed up in the front-page headline for Wilfred Burchett's article in the February 10 *National Guardian:* "Vietnam: The Lies Crumble."

There is now general agreement that the Tet offensive and its immediate aftermath constituted the turning point of the war, ending any prospect that Washington had of "winning." From then on, it was almost inevitable that the NLF and Hanoi would eventually achieve their goal: a unified and independent sovereign nation of Vietnam.

Nevertheless, debate still rages about whether the Tet offensive was actually a "military defeat" for the Vietnamese revolutionaries, which was turned into a decisive "psychological victory" by a craven American administration and a complicit American press. Indeed, the history of the war most widely promulgated in the 1980s and 1990s adopts this view, retailing General Westmoreland's argument that the Tet offensive was a desperation move that exhausted the strategic potential of the "VC," producing a "colossal military defeat" for them and a decisive military victory for the United States, which had "never been in a better position in South Vietnam."[17] There are several fatal flaws in this argument.

Most fundamentally, it is based on a fallacious distinction between "military" and "psychological." A guiding principle for the other side, spelled out in detail by Vo Nguyen Giap in his 1961 *People's War; People's Army* and elsewhere, is that the main purpose of military action is to demoralize the enemy and inspire the people (and even Washington avowed the primacy of "winning hearts and minds").

If Westmoreland had achieved a decisive military victory with the forces on hand, why did he submit an emergency request for an additional 206,000 soldiers, an increase of 40 percent? And if the White

March? And if the insurgents were crippled by their losses in the Tet offensive, how were they able to mount subsequent attacks on bases and cities throughout South Vietnam? The NLF and Hanoi would launch an equally devastating offensive in May, another coordinated attack in August, a repeat of Tet on its 1969 anniversary, and an even larger offensive in May 1969, when U.S. troop strength (which had steadily increased while the United States was supposedly deescalating) was at its maximum of over 542,000.[18]

The Pentagon's public claims of "victory" are belied by its own top secret history and analysis in the *Pentagon Papers,* containing these assessments:

> The Johnson Administration began 1968 in a mood of cautious hope about the course of the war. Within a month those hopes had been completely dashed. In late January and early February, the Viet Cong and their North Vietnamese supporters launched the massive Tet assault on the cities and towns of South Vietnam and put the Johnson Administration and the American public through a profound political catharsis on the wisdom and purpose of the U.S. involvement in Vietnam. . . . One of the inescapable conclusions of the Tet experience . . . [was that] the bombing had been a near total failure.[19]

> The enemy's TET offensive . . . although it had been predicted, took the U.S. command and the U.S. public by surprise, and its strength, length, and intensity prolonged the shock.[20]

> The primary focus of the U.S. reaction to the TET offensive was . . . avoiding defeat or disaster in the South.[21]

> The enemy is operating with relative freedom in the countryside, probably recruiting heavily and no doubt infiltrating NVA units and personnel. . . . To a large extent the VC now control the countryside.[22]

The *Pentagon Papers* display in detail how the administration and Pentagon were forced to recognize that the Tet offensive proved that all their previous beliefs in U.S. military "progress in many ways had been illusory" and that a U.S. "military victory was probably not possible."[23] Furthermore, as Robert Buzzanco has discovered in previously classified archives, both Westmoreland and General Earle Wheeler, chairman of the Joint Chiefs of Staff, privately acknowledged that the Tet offensive was anything but a U.S. victory and held a very pessimistic view of its military outcome.[24]

The claims of military victory made by the Pentagon and White House were so preposterous that even the establishment media would not or could not peddle them to the public. Indeed, if the media had based their reporting on the secret papers of the president, his head of the Joint Chiefs of Staff, the commander of his forces in Vietnam, and his other top generals, their reports of the Tet offensive would have differed little from the version they did report.

But then came the outlandish sequel: the generals, politicians, and, later, other apologists for the war blamed the media for losing the war by reporting the Tet offensive as a communist victory. Today, even some of the establishment media, now far more firmly under control, blame the establishment media of the 1960s for losing the war.

As the disagreeable facts about the Tet offensive forced their way more and more into the television and radio networks, the newsweeklies, and the daily press, reporting and analyzing the military situation in Vietnam became less and less a priority of the movement press. Its analysis confirmed beyond all expectation by the Tet offensive, the movement itself would be profoundly transformed in the national and international sequels.

One of the first casualties of Tet was the stability of the entire system of international capitalist finance. Parts of the movement press were already predicting that financing the Vietnam War and bearing the other burdens of empire would lead to ever-increasing deficits in the U.S. budget and balance of payments, endemic inflation, and the demise of the gold standard.[25] Unable to raise taxes to finance an unpopular war, the government had been forced to budget for 1968 the largest deficit since World War II, greater than the deficits of the previous five years combined. As the Tet offensive punctured the myth of U.S. invincibility, U.S. dollars were dumped by investors on a grand scale, thus shattering by early March the $35 per ounce fixed price of gold, which had held steady since 1934, through World War II and the Korean War. Before the end of that month, Eugene McCarthy, running as an antiwar presidential candidate, received only 524 votes fewer than the incumbent president from his own Democratic Party in the New Hampshire primary; Robert Kennedy entered the race for the Democratic presidential nomination as another antiwar candidate; the commander of

U.S. forces in Vietnam had been replaced; and President Johnson startled the nation on March 31 by withdrawing from the presidential campaign. The movement press had already predicted that neither the Republican nor the Democratic Party would allow any choice on the issue of the war, and therefore "millions of people are going to feel doors closing on their high school conception of American democracy."[26]

Within a week of Johnson's announcement, Martin Luther King, Jr., was assassinated. The reaction to his murder in some ways resembled the Tet offensive, as rebellions broke out in 125 U.S. cities and towns. Before 55,000 troops and tens of thousands of police were able to quell this uprising, television viewers around the world had seen federal combat soldiers defending Washington itself, as columns of smoke from torched buildings towered above the Capitol. The alternative press charged that the establishment media were understating the scale and nature of these rebellions, and proved it by providing detailed coverage available no place else.[27] And it demonstrated the purpose of the corporate media's coverage by reprinting purloined copies of official policy statements, such as "Civil Disorder Coverage Guidelines," which stated explicitly that "the primary goal" of the media is to provide "maximum assistance in the reestablishment of control," and therefore "broadcast newsmen should be dispatched to law enforcement command posts, rather than directly to the scene," since "an authoritatively staffed command post will undoubtedly be in communication with the scenes of disorder and be capable of providing newsmen with any desired information."[28]

While antiwar liberals threw themselves into the McCarthy and Kennedy campaigns, the more radical journals explained the co-optative purposes of these maneuvers and predicted their futility.[29] One even suggested that Robert Kennedy might be the next target for assassination. An April 19 article in the widely read *Los Angeles Free Press* presented evidence that Robert Kennedy had maintained silence about his brother's assassination because of possible CIA involvement and consequent political pressure, that he planned to reopen the investigation if he became president, and that his life might therefore be in danger from the killers.[30]

McCarthy and Kennedy swept the primaries, winning between them 83 percent in Pennsylvania, 63 percent in Wisconsin, 78 percent in Massachusetts, 63 percent in the District of Columbia, 69 percent in Indiana, 83 percent in Nebraska, 82 percent in Oregon, 67 percent in

New Jersey, 70 percent in South Dakota, 72 percent in Illinois, and 88 percent in California. Altogether the two antiwar candidates polled 69 percent of the total popular vote in the Democratic primaries, while slates of electors representing Vice President Hubert Humphrey, who stood for a continuation of the administration's Vietnam policy, garnered a mere 2.2 percent.

But on June 4, less than two months after the *Los Angeles Free Press* had warned of the possibility, Robert Kennedy was assassinated. Somehow, by the time the Democratic convention opened in Chicago at the end of August, a majority of the delegates were pledged to Humphrey. Outside, thousands of antiwar demonstrators and supporters of Eugene McCarthy, confronted by 6,000 federal troops, 6,000 National Guardsmen, 1,000 Secret Service agents, and 12,000 Chicago police, were teargassed and beaten before the television cameras of the world. No establishment organ could afford to label this confrontation as effectively as a typical headline in the alternative press: "System Unmasks Itself in Streets of Chicago."[31] Nor would it report this reaction among the soldiers ordered to suppress the demonstrators: "Sunrise, Friday, August 23: 43 GI's were arrested at Fort Hood, Texas. As of this writing, the base is still in a state of near rebellion. These guys were shafted for one beautiful reason: they refused to go to Chicago to bust our heads. Maybe they got squeezed into Uncle Sam's Salvation Army, but they don't dig it, and they sure as shit ain't going to come to Chicago to play cops for the 'democratic process.' "[32]

Although much has been written about the demoralizing effects of the Tet offensive on that mythical creature "the American public," precious little attention has been given to its effects on those millions of Americans already passionately opposed to the war. Ever since the beginning of the organized movement against the Vietnam War, a steadily increasing number of Americans found themselves identifying with the aspirations of "the enemy." By mid-1967, some demonstrators were even marching with the NLF flag, chanting, "Ho, Ho, Ho Chi Minh, the NLF is going to win" — a slogan that turned out to be truer than any words coming out of the White House. The Tet offensive, which Wilfred Burchett had called a "feat unprecedented in military history,"[33] induced a qualitative transformation in this quantitative process. No one has described more trenchantly than David Hunt in *Radical America* how Tet proved to the movement that the Pentagon's Harvard-trained experts "had been wrong, and we had been right, more right even than we had dared to imagine":

As the insurgents burst into view, "shouting their slogans and fighting with nerve-shattering fury," we realized that they were not just noble victims, but that they were going to win the war. Trying to make sense of the details of the Offensive, we were bowled over by the sheer ingenuity of it, the thrilling spectacle of people performing miraculous feats. Tet brought into focus with blinding clarity just how much human beings are capable of accomplishing. Carried along by the momentum of their endeavor, we wanted to be associated with the Vietnamese revolutionaries . . . and to figure out how our newly discovered vision of "power to the people" might be realized here in the United States.[34]

An indelible record of this metamorphosis is preserved in the alternative press. From February 1968 on, the dominant image of the Vietnamese would no longer be decapitated or napalm-mutilated bodies but triumphant fighters, not victims but heroes, as in the soon-to-be-famous picture of a woman guerrilla wearing a rifle with fixed bayonet slung over her shoulder, which appeared alongside Burchett's first article on Tet in the February 10 *Guardian*.

Take, for example, the *Peninsula Observer,* referred to by Liberation News Service as one of "North America's most respected underground papers" (November 7, 1968). In 1967 it portrayed the Vietnamese as victims, emphasized the need for humanitarian aid, and consistently referred to "the peace movement." Its first issue after the Tet offensive openly identifies with the NLF for the first time, and in a most revealing way. The front page, devoted to an article about women's contrasting roles in American society, in the movement, and in Vietnam, consists mainly of three recent pictures from other periodicals: a model in scanty lace lingerie, captioned "Women Power, Playboy Style"; a headless torso bearing a political button worn next to deep cleavage, captioned "Women Power, Ramparts Style"; and that heroic guerrilla, captioned "Women Power, Guardian Style." The vocabulary of the opening sentence suggests how thoroughly the military victories of the NLF were influencing the movement's conceptualizations, even of domestic concerns: "Somewhere between playmate-of-the-month and liberation soldier, today's U.S. radical woman is fighting on several fronts."[35] Before the end of 1968, the *Observer* would bring the war even closer to the American home, with a jolly Santa Claus on the cover, about to slide down the chimney, his finger on the trigger of his grenade launcher, chanting, "Ho! Ho! Ho Chi Minh!"[36]

The same month, *New Left Notes,* the official weekly newspaper of Students for a Democratic Society (SDS), made the message more explicit. A cover picture of NLF guerrillas brandishing assault rifles bore this caption: "December 20 marks the 8th anniversary of the founding of the NLF. The NO [National Office] is planning on issuing this picture as a poster. Revolutionaries are invited to show solidarity through appropriate actions."[37] Liberation News Service itself, the AP and UPI of the movement, spelled out its role as a revolutionary alternative to the media of the "corporate rich" in a midyear article equating in its punning title the underground press with the deadly sorceress of Greek myth: "1968: Year of the Heroic Guerilla MEDEA." All subsequent 1968 issues of *LNS* would bear on the masthead page the Cuban version of that slogan honoring Che Guevara, executed in Bolivia in 1967 while attempting to lead a guerrilla insurgency: "Año de guerrilla heroica."[38] Liberation News Service thus proclaimed the movement press's own guerrilla task in a global revolution.

The movement's images of itself were changing even more rapidly than its images of the war. Until the fall of 1967, the people beaten in police attacks on demonstrations were, like the Vietnamese, portrayed by the movement press mainly as victims. These images began to shift with the emergence in 1967 of the anti-draft organization pointedly named "the Resistance," and the increasingly militant demonstrations of that fall. For example, *The Movement,* which was evolving from an organ of SNCC and SDS into an influential independent monthly about revolutionary community organizing, bannered its front-page story about Stop-the-Draft Week with the headline "The Days We Seized the Streets of Oakland."[39] After Tet, alternative press reports of antiwar demonstrations no longer registered great shock at police brutality; they read, more and more accurately, like battlefield reports.

The movement's images were not mere metaphor and hyperbole. The prophecy shared in late 1967 by "nearly all United States officials in Saigon," as Hanson Baldwin had reported, "that the main battleground in 1968 will be in the United States" was coming true far more literally than perhaps had been foreseen. A second front was being added to the combat that had been raging in the nation's ghettos since 1964 as real blood began to flow in struggles on college campuses. For instance, on February 8 hundreds of National Guardsmen and police invaded the campus of South Carolina State College at Orangeburg, an African American institution, and opened fire on unarmed students, killing three and wounding dozens.

No matter what the ostensible issue in these struggles — at Orange-burg it was desegregation of the town's bowling alley — Vietnam was always present. The main target of the police at Orangeburg was actually Cleveland Sellers, a SNCC organizer who had recently been sentenced to five years in prison for draft resistance.[40] Although the Columbia University sit-in of April was touched off by the university's attempt to demolish community housing to make room for a gymnasium, the influence of the Tet offensive was unmistakable and pervasive. *CAW!,* a new SDS national magazine, wrapped around its front and back covers a photograph of demonstrators waving an NLF flag from a tower atop Columbia's mathematics building; *New Left Notes* ran the same picture over the front-page headline "Two, Three, Many Columbias . . . ," echoing Che Guevara's 1967 call to create "two, three, many Vietnams."[41] The five-month San Francisco State College strike, begun in November 1968 and finally put down only after repeated teargassings and savage police sweeps of the campus in which hundreds of students were beaten and jailed, was called to demand open admissions for nonwhite students and a degree program in Black Studies, issues having no explicit connection with the Vietnam War. But it was led by the Black Student Union and the Third World Liberation Front, whose name revealed the growing perception of local struggles as part of a global anti-imperialist revolution with Vietnam in the vanguard. In the words of one of the strike's leaders: "The central demand of the BSU and TWLF is not for equality but for self-determination. . . . Since the ruling class is not at all interested in giving self-determination to the black and third world people, here or in Vietnam, this struggle will by necessity be a prolonged one."[42]

The Tet offensive signaled the transformation of the antiwar movement into an anti-imperialist movement. In what might seem a paradox, reportage about Vietnam appeared with far less frequency in the alternative press after Tet than before. For example, even *Viet-Report,* which had been one of the antiwar movement's principal sources of in-depth information and analysis about the war ever since it began publication in July 1965, printed practically nothing about Vietnam itself in its first two post-Tet issues. Yet these two issues were signs not that the war was being ignored but that it was being perceived as part of that worldwide anti-imperialist conflict extending much further into the past and future. The editors of the first post-Tet issue explained why they were devoting it to what they called "prewar Latin America": "Opposition to the war in Vietnam finally led us to reassess official histories

of American foreign policy interests in Asia. How many American boys
will have to die before analysts decide to reappraise Latin American
history? To ignore the parallels to Vietnam which prewar Latin America presents is to run the risk of standing by helplessly while America
steps into another quagmire." In a postscript, they added that the next
issue "will focus on still another front: Urban America."[43]

While the issue was being prepared, Martin Luther King, Jr., was
assassinated, and for eleven days in April the resulting casualties on the
urban front approached in numbers those in Vietnam. When it appeared, *Viet-Report*'s special report on "Urban America in Revolt,"
titled "Colonialism and Liberation in America," focused on the inter-
relations between the wars at home and abroad:

> The question is not can America police the Third World. The
> question is can *America* be policed?
>
> With this Summer 1968 Issue, *Viet-Report* turns to the nation's
> number one foreign policy problem: domestic racial and economic
> insecurity. It is an open question . . . whether the American people
> will tolerate the economic inequities and social injustices which the
> aggressive pursuit of empire abroad has produced.
>
> In the ghetto, the people have decided: submission is intolerable.[44]

Even before the Tet offensive, much of the African American movement and parts of the antiwar movement had understood that the
domestic conflagrations were fueled by the war and that they con-
sumed the foundations of the government's ability to wage the war. As
early as 1965 and 1966, key organizations in the African American
movement were equating the war against the Vietnamese with the oppression of African Americans, and King's April 1967 speech at a huge
antiwar rally in New York explained the inseparable fates of the two
struggles.[45] The Tet offensive then served as an inspiration to the most
militant sectors of the African American movement, showing that revolutionary people of color could defeat the common enemy. For example, the March 16, 1968, issue of *The Black Panther* sandwiched a long
article on the Tet offensive, titled "Ocean of People's War Engulfs
South Viet Nam Cities and Villages Alike," between calls for armed
black self-defense and this quotation from Huey Newton: "20,000,000
unarmed black people is one thing; but 20,000,000 black people
armed to the gills cannot be denied."[46] The next month brought those
huge rebellions that followed King's assassination.

In late 1967 and early 1968, while the predominantly white or
nized antiwar movement saw itself moving from protest to resistance
press was already seeking paths that would unite it in practical actio..
with the African American rebellions. Liberation News Service gave
national circulation to an article from the *East Village Other* that lam-
basted the "middle class peace movement" for failing to recognize "its
obligation to link up" with "the black revolution." Ridiculing the common complaint among organizers of mass marches that "the blacks
refuse to come into the peace movement," the article argued that the
rioters had been doing "more all along to stop the war than the whole
white middle class antiwar movement put together," that, in fact, "they
are the antiwar movement."[47]

The Tet offensive convinced the movement that its main task was to
develop tactics and strategy to merge the wars at home and abroad.
Secretly the Pentagon made a similar assessment. In an agonizing reap-
praisal of its ability to control "public opinion" sufficiently to maintain
the economic and military "resources for the ghetto fight," the Department of Defense despaired of its ability "to convince critics that we are
not simply destroying South Viet Nam in order to 'save' it," and concluded that U.S. strategy had failed because the Tet offensive had done
so much damage on both the Vietnamese and domestic fronts. The
Pentagon strategists foresaw "increased defiance of the draft and growing unrest in the cities" combining to provoke "a domestic crisis of
unprecedented proportions."[48]

As the crisis of 1968 kept intensifying, both the movement and the
government understood with increasing clarity that the most crucial
nexus between Vietnam and America lay within the armed forces themselves. And it was here that the decisive links between the antiwar movement and the African American rebellions were forged.

According to the rewritten history of the Vietnam War, U.S. soldiers
and veterans were cursed at, spat on, reviled as "baby killers," and
generally perceived as the enemy by antiwar activists. This postwar concoction, as discussed in chapter 3, has obfuscated the history of the
movement, its press, and the subsequent course of the Vietnam War.

The movement's own press preserves the evidence in black and
white. Throughout 1967 it was reporting with sympathy and enthusiasm on the powerful antiwar upsurge among active-duty GIs, including
many examples of coherent resistance and the surfacing of an organized deserters' movement. By the fall of that year, the first antiwar GI

newspapers had joined the ranks of the underground press, and an antiwar veterans' newspaper was able to list twenty-two organizations of veterans against the war.[49]

The current myth about GIs being abused by the antiwar movement was certainly not accepted by the military authorities, who were alarmed by the rise of that movement within the ranks. *The Bond,* published by veterans and circulated among GIs, reported official warnings posted on military ships: "Criticism of our government, of military leaders or command . . . may be considered disloyal . . . and place an individual in a position of possible violation of U.C.M.J. article 134 . . . for which the maximum punishment is . . . three years confinement at hard labor."[50]

The Tet offensive intensified the process that was uniting antiwar GIs, veterans, and other activists. In February the movement press covered activities such as joint appearances by an ex–Green Beret and a SNCC leader at a statewide antiwar conference in Kentucky; a public declaration of resistance by soldiers at Fort Gordon in Georgia; a press conference in Paris at which a group of deserters displayed "copies of their underground newspaper, which encourages other soldiers to desert"; and a militant antiwar demonstration by "twenty-five soldiers in uniform" at Fort Jackson, South Carolina, who leafleted the other soldiers and received support from "students at the nearby University of South Carolina."[51]

Liberation News Service reported that by April "already 12,000 servicemen" had joined the American Servicemen's Union.[52] Leafleting soldiers was now a routine activity for antiwar groups, and "Support Our GIs" was a typical caption on pictures of antiwar soldiers.[53] SDS created a special workshop on GI organizing which resolved to "support in our Draft work those individuals who wish to continue the struggle against imperialism by entering the Military for the purpose of politicizing and organizing our brothers in the Military."[54] *Vietnam GI,* a newspaper published by Vietnam veterans, jumped its printing from ten thousand copies in January to thirty thousand in October, including thousands read by soldiers in Vietnam; it headlined its April issue "War in the States?"[55]

Feeling the futility of demonstrating and of working within a rigged electoral system, the movement and its press turned increasingly toward the one group capable of ending the war with direct action: the people forced to fight it. Liberation News Service's "Special Issue on Soldiers" gave prominence to stories from *Vietnam GI* and *The Bond.*[56]

antiwar movement.

The main focus was on coffeehouses, which were already centers for active-duty and other resisters near major bases in Missouri, Texas, South Carolina, and Washington state, while new ones were being opened in California and New Jersey. When the manager of the Oleo Strut, the coffeehouse near Fort Hood in Killeen, Texas, "stood up before the G.I.s and announced that the Oleo Strut was part of the Summer of Support," *LNS* reported, the soldiers "responded with a standing ovation" because "this was their coffee-house, and, should trouble come, many of them will defy the army."[57] Indeed, within weeks the Oleo Strut proved to be a center of the insurrection that led to dozens of soldiers refusing to go to Chicago to suppress the antiwar demonstrations taking place outside the Democratic convention.[58] Simultaneously there emerged at Fort Hood itself *The Fatigue Press,* an underground paper published by the GIs, whose editor was arrested by base authorities two weeks after the Chicago confrontation.[59]

As the underground press threw itself into the Summer of Support, there was a noticeable shift away from civilians leading soldiers toward soldiers providing leadership for the entire antiwar movement. Before long, this trend would dramatically change the form and content not just of opposition to the Vietnam War but of the war itself.

The reversal of roles was aptly symbolized by a teach-in held in Berkeley's Provo Park on August 10, 1968, chaired by ex–Green Beret Donald Duncan. Students now came not to teach soldiers about the war, but to learn from them. *The Ally,* a GI newspaper whose first issue in February had explained the profound significance of the Tet offensive, now reported the lessons brought to the teach-in by vets and active-duty GIs from the army, navy, coast guard, and marines.[60] The underground press, especially the rapidly proliferating papers published by military personnel, were filled with stories of the insurrections, mutinies, and fraggings that were crippling U.S. combat potential in Vietnam. SDS criticized itself for not having taken previous work within the military seriously enough and emphasized that "showing that the Left supports the soldiers" is no less important than showing "that the soldiers support the Left."[61]

In October, GIs and Vets for Peace became the main organizer of a mass march to be held in San Francisco. Many of the bases in the area responded by scheduling special inspections or drills for the Saturday of the march.[62] Nevertheless, on October 12, over 500 active-duty men and women, many risking court-martial by participating in uniform, led 14,000 antiwar marchers through the streets of San Francisco to the Presidio.[63] The following day, 120 active-duty soldiers from Texas bases participated at an antiwar rally organized by University of Texas students.[64]

The National Mobilization Committee to End the War in Vietnam, whose main previous activity had been organizing large demonstrations, declared the first week of November — the week of the national elections — to be National GI Week. Vietnam veterans arranged to conduct teach-ins on twenty to thirty major college campuses. "They will show army training films and talk about military life," the *Guardian* reported — without commenting on how radically this showed things had shifted since January — "in an attempt to get students to resist the draft."[65]

By January 1969, some activist Vietnam veterans and soldiers were making revolutionary demands on the movement. For example, a wounded white Vietnam combat veteran now organizing at the Oleo Strut had this to say to Bernardine Dohrn, interorganizational secretary of SDS: "We're not trying to build a GI union. We're not trying to reform the army or form no union inside the army. We're trying to overthrow the system. We're not interested in getting up front in a demonstration and giving reformist organizations legitimacy. Those ones that say we're going to help you GIs . . . [t]hey see themselves in supportive roles, and we don't need no supporters, we need fellow combatants."[66] Ultimately, the insurrectionary upsurge within the armed forces, inspired and led by African American rebellions, was to guarantee the victory of the Vietnamese revolutionaries, as many U.S. military authorities acknowledged.[67] In this sense, the war at home was brought to Vietnam. But despite the profound national crises of 1968, the movement proved to be far less successful in launching from the war back home a sustainable movement to transform the political and economic structure of American society, much less a revolution.

Indeed, by the 1980s, powerful reactionary forces were firmly in control of politics at all levels, owing in part to the unrestrained influence of wealth, which attained hegemonic dominion over all media. Newspapers, magazines, TV and radio stations were gobbled up by multimedia corporate conglomerates, including right-wing ideologue Rupert Murdoch's vast global media empire.[68] Television and radio talk shows, which had opened to a fairly wide political spectrum during the Vietnam War, were now given over to hosts who tirelessly raced one another to the right. The alternative news media were swept away like fallen leaves in a hurricane. GI newspapers disappeared, high school newspapers were subjected to severe censorship, and the hundreds of prison newspapers that had carried some of the movement's politics on into the late 1970s were soon virtually wiped out, turning the two-century-old tradition of prison journalism into a historical artifact.[69] By 1999, the last broadcast stronghold of alternative politics — the Pacifica network — was besieged on one side by a Clinton ally chairing its own governing board and on another by corporations eager to devour its flagship stations: KPFA in Berkeley, WBAI in New York, and KPFK in Los Angeles. Founding station KPFA found itself fighting for its own life and, as the many thousands of supporters who rallied to its aid understood, the survival into the twenty-first century of any truly alternative broadcast voices.[70]

With the alternative media marginalized where not silenced, the corporate media have with impunity been able to rewrite and reimage the history of the Tet offensive, 1968, the war, the antiwar movement, and even the reporting of the war. As shown in chapter 1, post–Vietnam War administrations have masterfully used the obedient national media to inspire support for the invasions of Grenada and Panama, intermittent warfare against Iraq from 1991 into the twenty-first century, and a militarized political economy and culture.

The impeccably trained performances of the media were effectively displayed in 1999, when the United States, Britain, France, Germany, Turkey, Italy, and thirteen other NATO nations decided to complete the dismemberment of Yugoslavia. Warplanes and missiles were once again the stars of the show, but added was the major component missing from the Gulf War circus: pictures of human suffering caused by the villain. After aerial technowar was unleashed on Serbia in 1999, non-stop TV footage of Kosovo refugees fleeing Serbian repression and NATO bombing was used to equate Serbian president Slobodan Milosevic with Adolf Hitler. "As far as keeping the American people behind this," Secretary of Defense William Cohen revealingly commented, "I think they only have to turn on their television sets every day and to see the kind of horrendous suffering that is now portrayed on the evening news."[71]

With war-sponsoring institutions having a near-monopoly over TV, radio, and print news, even many people who had been active against the Vietnam War and Washington's subsequent invasion and bombing of other countries found themselves at first supporting the "humanitarian" bombardment of the villages, cities, and countryside of Kosovo and Serbia. Yet opposition soon started to build, and one of its main sources of news, background, and analysis was a medium that by its very nature is congenial to alternative views: the Internet.

The Internet also contributed much of the information and organization that led to the astonishingly large, sophisticated, and successful demonstrations against the World Trade Organization in Seattle in December 1999. Whether the Internet has the potential to play a role comparable to that of the alternative media of the Vietnam War epoch, or whether it will, like the other media, function mainly as an instrument of establishment control remains to be seen. But two clear lessons of 1968 are that the medium is not the movement, and a dedicated movement can create its own media.

The Vietnam War and the Culture Wars; or, the Perils of Western Civilization

Talking about the Vietnam War and the culture wars in the same breath is risky. After all, one was a real war in which more than 58,000 Americans and perhaps 3 million Vietnamese, Laotians, and Cambodians were killed, whereas the victims of the culture wars are not zipped into body bags or bulldozed into mass graves—although there are real casualties. But these very different forms of conflict share some common origins and content, because both involve revolts against the rule of "Western civilization" over nations and cultures. And one cannot understand the culture wars of contemporary America without recognizing how they were shaped by the Vietnam War.

In the decades since the end of the Vietnam War, many Americans have come to believe that the culture wars are just as divisive and crucial for the fate of the nation. As Pat Buchanan declared in 1992 to the Republican national convention, "There is a cultural war going on in our country for the soul of America."[1] Many also believe that in this war the United States is being defeated even more catastropically than in Vietnam. "I wonder if after this culture war is over," declared Representative Henry Hyde in 1999 as he helped lead the drive to impeach President Clinton, "an America will survive that's worth fighting to defend."[2] And Americans have been led to believe that those responsible for this current menace to the nation are the same internal enemies blamed for the Vietnam debacle: self-indulgent students, the allegedly liberal press, African Americans and other people of color, feminists, and those left-wing professors and unionized public school teachers misleading all these un-American malcontents. As Senator Robert Dole said while campaigning for the presidency in 1996, the blame lies with "the liberal education establishment."[3]

These alarms are all part of a nonstop campaign waged for decades and designed to portray the culture wars as a new phenomenon, a desperate struggle for the nation's future, a contest that is being won by "tenured radicals" who exert a tyranny of rabid multiculturalism, radical feminism, and "political correctness" over American universities, which have thus been transformed into bastions of subversion and barbarism, pouring forth fanatical legions who have already largely succeeded in nullifying "Western" culture, thereby threatening the very survival of civilization.

The cultural tides that have caused all this consternation come from the confluence of two historical streams. One flows from America, the other from Vietnam.

Our contemporary American culture wars are neither new nor peculiar to the United States. The entire social history of the United States (not to mention its prehistory as North American British colonies) can be charted through its culture wars fought over contradictions among race, gender, and class. In education, these issues have always centered on what is to be studied, who should be allowed to study it, who should be selected to teach it, and how it should be taught.

In the first three decades of the nineteenth century, throughout New England and the Middle Atlantic states, there were (as Dorothy Canfield Fisher wrote in 1927) "horrified outcries over the revolutionary, poisonous idea of teaching all children to read and write, even the children of parents who had no money to pay tuition fees."[4] In the ensuing decades, religious opponents of public schools kept making dire predictions that would not seem out of place in today's debates.

For example, in 1845 the Presbyterian Synod of New Jersey warned that "irreligious and infidel youth, such as may be expected to issue from public schools, *deteriorating more and more* with revolving years will not be fit to sustain our free institutions."[5] In an 1830 article titled "Argument against Public Schools," a Philadelphia newspaper explained why education should be reserved for the wealthy:

> Literature cannot be acquired without leisure, and wealth gives leisure. . . . The "peasant" must labor during those hours of the day which his wealthy neighbor can give to the abstract culture of his mind; otherwise, the earth would not yield enough for the subsistence of all: the mechanic cannot abandon the operations of his trade for general studies; if he could, most of the conveniences of life and objects of exchange would be wanting; languor, decay, poverty, discontent would soon be visible among all classes. No government . . . can furnish what is incompatible with the very organization and being of civil society.[6]

In the 1830s, as the industrial revolution was transforming plantation agriculture, most of the slave states outlawed literacy for Afro-Americans. A Virginia law of 1831, for instance, decreed "that all meetings of free negroes or mulattoes, at any school-house, church, meeting-house or other place for teaching them reading or writing, either in the day or night, under whatsoever pretext, shall be deemed and considered an unlawful assembly."[7]

The Morrill Act which established the land-grant colleges to provide higher education for working-class young men — and, later, women — could come about in 1862 only because of the wartime absence of congressmen from the slaveholding states. In 1857 President James Buchanan had vetoed the bill, declaring that it violated states' rights and set a dangerous precedent of federal aid to education.

At the beginning of the twentieth century, those who were struggling to open more doors of higher education to women were branded dangerous radicals and subversives. After all, according to one university president in 1904, "It is now well established that higher education in this country reduces the rate of both marriage and offspring. . . . I think it established that mental strain in early womanhood is a cause of imperfect mammary function which is the first stage of the slow evolution of sterility."[8] A 1905 magazine article titled "Higher Education of Women" explained further:

Not only does wifehood and motherhood not require an extraordinary development of the brain, but the latter is a decided barrier against the proper performance of these duties. . . . [I]n this rivalry between the offspring and the intellect how often has not the family physician seen the brain lose in the struggle. The mother's reason totters and falls, in some cases to such an extent as to require her removal to an insane asylum. . . . [M]ost of the generally admitted poor health of women is due to over education, which first deprives them of sunlight and fresh air for the greater part of their time; second, takes every drop of blood away to the brain from the growing organs of generation; third, develops their nervous system at the expense of all their other systems, muscular, digestive, generative, etc.; fourth, leads them to live an abnormal single life until the age of twenty-six or twenty-seven instead of being married at eighteen, which is the latest that nature meant them to remain single.[9]

U.S. public schools long operated under an apartheid system, which was legally mandated in the South (where the races lived mostly intermingled in agricultural settings) but which was almost as rigidly determined in the North (where African Americans were forced by economics and "gentlemen's agreements" to live in segregated districts). It took a 1954 Supreme Court decision to delegitimize de jure apartheid while its de facto form still prevails throughout most of the nation's cities and suburbs. Well into the mid-1960s — that is, before the Vietnam War began to have a major impact on American society — the faculty at most eminent American universities was still just as white (and almost as male) as major league baseball had been a decade before. When I arrived at Stanford University to begin graduate study in 1959 after three years in the air force, the English department was all white and all male. When I received my Ph.D. in 1961, I had not been required — or even advised — to read a single author of color. By the time I was fired from Stanford as a tenured associate professor in 1972 because of 1971 speeches against the university's active participation in the Vietnam War, the English department was no longer all male, but it was still as white as it always had been.

As for the proper study of literature in America, we need to keep reminding ourselves that the holy canon of great literature presented to us by today's conservative cultural warriors as a timeless gift of God, somewhat akin to the Ten Commandments given to Moses on Mount Sinai, is in fact quite recent and has been continually changing throughout our history. Until the Civil War, the only literature considered worthy of serious study was the Greek and Roman classics. Defenders of the canon then were as alarmist as those today. For example, a Cincinnati magazine issued this jeremiad: "Should the time ever come when Latin and Greek should be banished from our Universities, and the study of Cicero and Demosthenes, of Homer and Virgil, should be considered unnecessary for the formation of a scholar, we should regard mankind as fast sinking into absolute barbarism, and the gloom of mental darkness as likely to increase until it should become universal."[10] The Modern Language Association — the organization of college and university teachers of postclassical literature and languages — was formed in 1883 as part of the struggle against the monopoly of Greek and Roman literature. English literature, American literature, modern literature — each new transformation of the canon was greeted with howls of outrage and alarm. As Gerald Graff has written:

> After English literature had replaced the ancient languages and civilization did not crumble, Anglophiles issued the same dire warnings against new upstarts who wanted to teach the barbaric trash that was presumptuously starting to call itself "American literature." This phrase, said the Anglophiles, was clearly a contradiction in terms, for anyone with taste knew that the few works of any merit written in the United States constituted at best a minor rivulet of the great stream of English letters.[11]

In the first two decades after World War I, the worst fears of the cultural conservatives seemed to be materializing. Not only were aesthetic standards being challenged and inferior modern writers displacing the classics, but also the very definition of literature was being brazenly widened to include the most vulgar forms, some not even written at all.

By the early 1930s, anthologies of American literature often included generous selections of Native American poetry, African American spirituals and blues, ballads and work songs, folk tales, and other forms of popular and oral literature. The most widely used anthology of poetry, for example, was Louis Untermeyer's two-volume opus, *American Poetry from the Beginning to Whitman* and *Modern American Poetry*. The first volume included examples and analyses of the earliest African American poetry, plus sections titled "American Indian Poetry"; "Spanish-Colonial Verse"; "Early American Ballads"; "Negro Spirituals"; "Negro Social, 'Blues' and Work-Songs"; " 'Negroid' Melodies"; "Cowboy Songs and Hobo Harmonies"; "Backwoods Ballads"; and "City Gutturals."[12] The various editions of *Modern American Poetry* track the rise of African American literature. The first editions, of 1919 and 1921, contained poems by Paul Laurence Dunbar. By the fifth edition, in 1936, there was major representation of other black poets, including James Weldon Johnson, Claude McKay, Jean Toomer, Langston Hughes, and Countee Cullen.[13] These same black poets were also well represented in such other widely used anthologies as Alfred Kreymborg's *Lyric America: An Anthology of American Poetry, 1630–1930* (Coward-McCann, 1930) and *The New Poetry: An Anthology of Twentieth-Century Verse in English*, edited by Harriet Monroe and Alice Corbin Henderson (Macmillan, 1932). To meet the growing demand, anthologies of African American literature poured from major publishers.[14] Yet from at least the mid-1950s until the late 1960s, African American literature was entirely eliminated from the standard American literature anthologies, bibliographies, histories, criticism, and college and university courses (except for some in the "Negro" colleges).[15]

How did all that multicultural and popular literature manage to escape from its ghettos and get accepted into the prestigious neighborhood of literary studies? And how did it get forced back into its ghettos in the 1940s and 1950s—and even wiped from the pages of literary history? And what does all of this have to do with the Vietnam War and the postwar culture wars? To answer these questions in a way that will offer the deepest insights into the subject matter of this book, it is necessary to place them in the context of the most important historical event of the past five hundred years: the rise and fall of a global imperialist system dependent on racial domination and colonialism. In this light it is also possible to see the fullest significance of the Vietnam War, which plays a unique and crucial role in this history.

Europe began its colonization of the planet toward the end of the fifteenth century. Guided by the magnetic compass and the newly emerging ideology of racism, driven by the needs of burgeoning mercantile capitalism, conducted in vessels of the most modern technological design, and armed with the world's most advanced weapons, the so-called voyages of "discovery" soon provided Spain with the world's first global empire. As early as 1494, Pope Alexander VI, in the Treaty of Tordesillas, divided the entire non-European planet between Spain and Portugal along a line drawn from pole to pole. For the next three centuries, the nations of Europe kept redrawing the lines that defined their empires, often in blood. At the same time, the mineral, forest, and agricultural wealth skimmed from the colonies vastly enlarged the power of their colonizers, whose imperial status continually influenced their own internal politics, economy, class relations, technology, and culture.

By 1800, as the industrial revolution was beginning to transmute the political economy of the planet, Europeans and their descendants — that is, "white" people — owned or controlled 35 percent of the earth's land surface. By 1875 this figure had approximately doubled, with white people ruling 67 percent of the earth's surface. Imperialism's rapid expansion had entered a period of ferocious struggle over the last remaining lands available for colonization. As part of this process, continental powers such as the United States and Russia wiped out most of the indigenous populations blocking their expansion, whether westward across North America or eastward across Siberia. As another part of the process, the United States invaded and annexed the northern half of Mexico in 1848–49 and became a self-proclaimed global imperialist power in the 1890s with the seizure of Hawaii, the Philippines, Guam, Puerto Rico, and Cuba. As still another part of the same process, France between 1858 and 1883 completed its conquest of the nation of Vietnam. By 1914 white people owned or controlled 85 percent of the earth's land.

To make all this seem rational, moral, and just, European culture had to be fundamentally racist, deeply imperial, and, at the same time, intensely nationalistic. Axiomatic within the dominant culture of each nation-state was a belief in the superiority not simply of the white race but of that nation's particular culture.

Such was the background of "the Great War," later aptly renamed the First World War. It was not caused by the assassination of some Austrian archduke by a Serbian nationalist. This was a war about redividing the planet. On one side the main combatants were the three largest colonial empires of the world — England, France, and Russia — while on the other side were the would-be great colonial empires landlocked in Europe (the Central Powers), allied with the Ottoman Empire, which was being dismembered by the European empires. When the United States plunged in on the side of the global empires, it began its role as the preeminent power of the twentieth century.

World War I produced two unforeseen events with profound implications for the rest of the twentieth century, including the cultural wars of our historical epoch. The first was the Russian Revolution, which sparked communist revolutions and revolutionary movements from Mongolia to Germany and then around the world. The second was the national liberation movements of the colored peoples in the colonies and neo-colonies of the great empires.

The embattled French and British empires had taken two very dangerous steps during the war: they had brought troops from their colonies in Africa and Asia into the European battlefield, and they had ordered many of their African and Asian subjects to violate the most fundamental taboo underlying white colonial rule, the prohibition against people of color ever committing violence against white people. What happened to the consciousness of the African troops from the French and British colonies, for example, when they were ordered to kill white Germans? Even more dangerous was the light shed on the fundamental rationale of white colonialism—what the British called "the white man's burden" and what the French called "la mission civilisatrice"—that the "West" was bringing "civilization" to the backward, benighted colored peoples of the world. The colonized peoples were of course already aware of the misery and oppression brought to their homelands by these civilizers, and so were some people from the colonizing nations. For example, back in the middle of the nineteenth century, a young American author and ex-sailor named Herman Melville, whose global voyages had allowed him to witness some of the ravages of European colonialism, became convinced that "the white civilized man," as he put it in 1845, is "the most ferocious animal on the face of the earth."[16] During World War I, what Africans and Asians, as well as American "Negroes," saw in the great cradle of "Western civilization" was an insane orgy of mass murder and devastation on an unprecedented scale, as the hallmark of this civilization, its miraculous technology and vast production, was used to turn portions of Europe into poisonous wastelands.

One of the colonial subjects on the scene during World War I was a young Vietnamese then known as Nguyen Ai Quoc, who, believing in the Enlightenment ideals of the American and French revolutions, beseeched President Woodrow Wilson in 1919 to support basic rights for his people. At the conclusion of World War II, this Vietnamese patriot, now named Ho Chi Minh and the leader of a guerrilla army allied with the United States, would make a similar request of President Harry Truman. His 1919 and 1945 letters still lie, unanswered, in U.S. State Department files.[17]

In the global cultural and political wars emerging from World War I, the hegemony of European culture, as well as its alleged aesthetic and moral superiority, was directly challenged by people of color everywhere. This was the period, for example, of the May Fourth Movement in China, the Harlem Renaissance with its roots in the British Caribbean colonies, and the *négritude* movement among francophone peoples in Africa and the Caribbean. Among the political and intellectual leaders who were to emerge from this awakening were Jomo Kenyatta, first president of Kenya; Sukarno, first president of Indonesia; Kwame Nkrumah, first president of Ghana; Mao Tse-tung of China; Carlos Bulosan of the Philippines; Agostinho Neto, first president of Angola; Léopold Senghor, first president of Senegal; and Ho Chi Minh. Many of these leaders were also distinguished literary figures, including such fine poets as Neto, Mao, Ho, and Senghor, who, together with Aimé Césaire, co-founded the *négritude* movement and translated many works from the Harlem Renaissance into French. Culture, especially literary culture, in the lives of these anti-imperial revolutionaries was never divorced from political issues and action.

The explosion and recognition of multicultural and popular literature in America during the 1920s and 1930s must be seen in this global context of the anticolonial movement among people of color, the revulsion against the carnage of war, and the Russian Revolution, which was soon offering a theoretical basis for proletarian and ethnic literatures. It is no mere coincidence that the 1920s was the decade of both the Harlem Renaissance and the Jazz Age, a term borrowed from African American popular culture. Then, when the Great Depression struck the United States in 1929, it also blasted holes in dams that had long separated "high" and "low" culture, releasing a flood of multiethnic, working-class, and sometimes even revolutionary literature that threatened to overwhelm the dominant British tradition.

The conservative reaction against the radicalization of 1930s culture was swift and increasingly powerful. In literary studies it took three interrelated forms. First was the cult of the "great books," originally codified by overtly racist propagandists and soon institutionalized at Columbia and the University of Chicago, two universities in urban centers most threatened by the rising flood of radicalism.[18] Second was a rigidly tightened definition of the canon of "major" or "great" literature to be included in anthologies and courses, one that eliminated all writers of color.[19] But most important in shaping the study of literature in the 1940s, 1950s, and 1960s before the impact of the Vietnam War was New Criticism.

Although New Criticism came to be regarded as an apolitical methodology designed to study literature for "its own sake," without any corrupting influence from ideology or social context, that was neither its founding purpose nor its enduring effect. The original New Critics, first coalescing at Vanderbilt University, explicitly presented themselves as "reactionary" saviors of the culture of Western civilization from the encroachments of the subcultural influences of colored and other working-class people. Their announced purpose, spelled out in *I'll Take My Stand* (1930; a title taken from the song celebrating the slave South) and *Reactionary Essays on Poetry and Prose* (1936), was to combat "vulgar" culture, promulgating in its place the "finest" values of "the Old South" and literature congenial to their ideology. For example, the leading New Critic Allen Tate declared that "the Negro" has "had much the same thinning influence upon the class above him as the anonymous city proletariat has had upon the culture of industrial capitalism," and then went on to explain that "the Negro" "got everything from the white man," but "we could graft no new life upon the Negro; he was too different, too alien."[20] The hallmark of New Critical methodology — intricately detailed and nuanced readings of texts — was actually a corollary of those texts deemed worthy of study, texts filled with elaborate ambiguities and ironies, texts therefore not easily accessible to common readers.[21] In the two decades after World War II, New Criticism triumphed not only in American higher education but in the teaching of literature throughout elementary and high schools as well.

Graduating in 1955 from Amherst College, a bastion of the most extreme forms of New Criticism, I had no notion of the political agenda of this professedly nonpolitical way of studying literature. I saw no connection between the texts we studied and the absence of a single person of color or a single woman on the faculty. Nor was I aware that the rising dominance of New Criticism was an aspect of the blanket repression stifling American society in this first decade of the Cold War. I certainly had not the slightest inkling that any of this could possibly relate to a nation called Vietnam. And there was no way I could possibly know that Vietnam would trigger the culture wars of the past few decades and, in the course of these wars, eventually make me conscious of everything that I am writing about in this chapter.

The purification of the canon of American literature was a relatively minor incident in the global culture wars of the 1930s, where the major new force was fascism, especially as manifest in Nazism, with its far more comprehensive drive for racial purification. But as Aimé Césaire ar-

gued in 1955 — just when the United States was replacing France as the
nemesis of Vietnam — Nazism had only committed upon Europeans
what Europeans long had been and still were routinely committing
upon their colonized peoples.[22]

Except for Russia, the three largest colonial empires had survived
World War I intact. But in the midst of the worldwide depression of the
1930s, they confronted a new, more menacing challenge as the Axis
alliance launched a global offensive that evolved into the Second World
War. In this war, the French and British empires were far more seriously
endangered than in World War I. Half of France itself was occupied by
the Nazis, while the other half was placed under the Nazi puppet Vichy
government, which claimed legitimate rule over all of France's colonies
in Africa and Asia, including what was then called French Indochina —
Cambodia, Laos, and Vietnam. England was subjected to a new form of
warfare first tested against colonized people and soon to be developed
as the most original and influential attainment of Western civilization:
"strategic" bombing, that is, massive aerial attacks on civilian populations.[23] Meanwhile, Japan was attacking and in many cases successfully
occupying Dutch, British, French, and U.S. colonies in the Pacific and
Southeast Asia, where the French colonial infrastructure, operating as
an agency of the Vichy regime installed by the Nazis, compliantly ad-
ministered Vietnam for the Japanese invaders. Whereas World War I
and its aftermath had merely generated the nascent culture of national
liberation, World War II and its aftermath produced organized struggles for national liberation that were to prove the doom of colonialism.

Between 1945 and 1949, one fourth of the world's people attained
national independence from colonialism. In 1949 anticolonialism
gained a powerful ally when the communist revolution triumphed in
China, freeing another fourth of the world's population from domination by the great empires. In the thirty-year period from 1945 to 1975,
outright colonialism, which had ruled 85 percent of the earth's surface, was utterly destroyed as a global system. The end was marked in
1974–75 by the simultaneous victories of Vietnam, Laos, and Cambodia and of the Portuguese colonies in Africa (Angola, Mozambique,
Guinea-Bissau, and the Cape Verde Islands).

The significance of Vietnam in the destruction of the colonial system — truly one of the most significant events in all human history —
can hardly be overstated. Vietnam's wars against France and the United
States span precisely that crucial 1945–1975 period. Vietnam was the
first nation after World War II to launch an armed struggle for inde-

THE VIETNAM WAR AND THE CULTURE WARS

pendence from colonialism. Its military defeat of France in mid-1954 sent shock waves around the world. One of these waves carried Algerian veterans of the conflict home to help spark the Algerian revolution in late 1954, which was to be the decisive battle against French colonialism throughout Africa.

Vietnam's even more astonishing defeat of the United States may have inaugurated a new epoch in world history, though hardly the revolutionary ascendancy that many thought imminent at the time. Dominoes did not fall all over the world, and the definitive end of overt colonialism led rapidly to the consolidation of "the New World Order" — a marvelously engineered form of neocolonialism — as the system that was to rule the planet into the next century.

What befell the United States in Vietnam induced a protracted culture shock that transformed many aspects of American society, even the writing and study of literature. Like most thinking Americans during this period, numerous historians and humanists found themselves being forced by the war to reexamine both their received ideological assumptions and their overall vision of America's history and culture. Many who began with the naive belief that the Vietnam War was an aberration, some kind of wayward "mistake" by a nation long leading the world's march to progress, discovered instead that the war actually typified the nation's history from colonial settler regime to global empire. In the process of reassessing that history, they also discovered how much their own vision of that history had been shaped by ideological demands evolving from the nation's origin through the Cold War. Most obviously, both the conduct of the Vietnam War and the justification for it bore inescapable resemblances to the genesis of "America" in the genocidal wars against the "Indians." GIs even called Vietnam "Injun country." A student of American literature watching "Zippo squads" torching Vietnamese villages might feel like the protagonist of Hawthorne's "Young Goodman Brown" when Satan tells him, "It was I that brought your father a pitch-pine knot, kindled at my own hearth, to set fire to an Indian village." But the truly seismic culture shock came from the recognition that this war was being won by the Indians.

To understand the impact of Vietnam on America's culture wars since the late 1960s, literally fabulous help comes from an American author writing just as European imperialism was rocketing to global hegemony. Way back in 1809, Washington Irving published an attack on imperialism in the form of an imagined colonization of the earth by the men from the moon. These "Lunatics," in Irving's words, "pos-

sessed of vastly superior knowledge to ourselves; that is to say, posses
of superior knowledge in the art of extermination," are therefore
terly convinced of the superiority of their culture, which of cou
sanctions their imperial actions. Irving offers this thinly veiled c
parison with the Europeans' colonization of the lands they had supposedly "discovered":

> Finding that we not only persist in absolute contempt of their rea-
> soning and disbelief in their philosophy, but even go so far as dar-
> ingly to defend our property, their patience shall be exhausted, and
> they shall resort to their superior powers of argument: hunt us with
> hippogriffs, transfix us with concentrated sunbeams, demolish our
> cities with moon-stones; until having, by main force, converted us to
> the true faith, they shall graciously permit us to exist in the torrid
> deserts of Arabia, or the frozen regions of Lapland, there to enjoy
> the blessings of civilization and the charms of lunar philosophy, in
> much the same manner as the reformed and enlightened savages of
> this country are kindly suffered to inhabit the inhospitable forests of
> the north, or the impenetrable wildernesses of South America.[24]

Parallels with the American war against Vietnam are obvious. Even
the Lunatics' logic of using their technological superiority and wonder
weapons to save us by destroying our cities is echoed in that infamous
explanation offered by a U.S. officer for the destruction of the capital
city of Ben Tre Province: "It became necessary to destroy the town to
save it." But what would have happened to Irving's imagined Lunatics
if we earthlings had defeated their supposedly omnipotent machinery
of war?

Would they have plunged into self-doubt and radically questioned
their Lunatic imperial culture? Would their defeat at the hands of
primitive, inferior aliens have led to psychological agonies, domestic
turmoil, and internal conflict? Or would they have militarized their
culture even more and committed their political economy to producing more and better superweapons so that they could become truly
invincible world conquerors? Or all of the above?

These questions offer an illuminating perspective on American culture since 1968, the year when the American people and their government realized that the United States was losing the Vietnam War. Inter-
cutting some of the major events of that year explored in chapter 5 with
some educational events gives a sense of their cultural impact.

Nineteen sixty-eight had begun with assurances from the government and the media that the United States was on the verge of total victory in Vietnam. But on January 30 came the month-long Tet offensive, in which the allegedly vanquished enemy launched simultaneous attacks on all U.S. military bases in Vietnam and 110 cities and towns in South Vietnam. On March 31, President Johnson announced that because of the conflict over the Vietnam War, he was withdrawing from the presidential race. Four days later came the assassination of Martin Luther King, Jr., who a year earlier had called the Vietnam War evidence that the United States was on "the wrong side of a world revolution" and denounced the U.S. government as "the greatest purveyor of violence in the world today." In response to King's murder, a week of rebellions broke out in 125 U.S. cities. The same month, students at Columbia University, protesting the university's role in the war and domestic oppression, joined with community activists in a two-month siege of the campus. On June 4, Robert Kennedy, campaigning against the war, won the California Democratic presidential primary, with 88 percent of the votes going to him and to rival antiwar candidate Eugene McCarthy. That night Kennedy was assassinated in Los Angeles. In May the government of France was almost overthrown by a movement arising in part from protests against the Vietnam War and led at first by students. In early August the Republican presidential convention in Miami Beach nominated Richard Nixon, who had campaigned on a pledge to end the war as soon as he took office. A line of tanks sealed off Miami Beach from a black rebellion in Miami; gunfights, described by a police official as "firefights like in Vietnam," came within a mile of convention headquarters.[25] Later that month the Democratic Convention in Chicago nominated Vice President Hubert Humphrey, although he had won only 2.2 percent of the delegates in the state primaries, which had been swept by McCarthy and Kennedy. Outside, thousands of antiwar demonstrators were attacked by the Chicago police, the National Guard, and regular army units; dozens of soldiers were court-martialed for refusing to participate. On November 5, Richard Nixon was elected president. The next day a strike began at San Francisco State College, with demands for ethnic studies programs and open admissions for blacks, Latinos, Asians, and other people of color. The strike, later joined by the college's chapter of the American Federation of Teachers, lasted until the following March. The strikers were repeatedly gassed by the police; many were savagely beaten; some of the leaders were brutally tortured while in police custody.[26]

It was in the midst of these events that the profession of the teaching

THE VIETNAM WAR AND THE CULTURE WARS

of literature itself turned into an open battleground over issues such as the literary canon, multiculturalism, and critical methodologies, as well as the overt racism and sexism that determined not only which works should be taught and how, but also who should be allowed to teach literature in the highest academies of the land.

In December 1968, the Modern Language Association convention in New York had on its schedule a major panel titled "The American Scholar and the Crisis of Our Culture" and a seminar arranged by a small group of activists titled "Student Rebellions and the Teaching of Literature." After Louis Kampf, chair of the Department of Literature at M.I.T., was arrested in the Americana Hotel for preventing the removal of a poster advertising the seminar, the convention was plunged into a maelstrom from which the profession of literature has yet to emerge. Hundreds of those at this normally staid old boys' meeting marched from a teach-in on the Vietnam War to stage a sit-in in the lobby of the Americana, while busloads of New York City Tactical Squad police in riot gear awaited the signal to attack. By the time four days of tumult at the convention were over, the Modern Language Association had adopted resolutions condemning the Vietnam War and the repression of African American activists, moved the following year's meeting from Chicago as a protest against the police attacks on antiwar protesters in August, elected Kampf to succeed to the presidency of the organization, and established a Commission on the Status of Women. Out of that convention also came an outpouring of critical essays, many published in a seminal collection, *The Politics of Literature: Dissenting Essays on the Teaching of Literature* (1972). Unifying the activism of the late 1960s with the ideological transformation induced by this activism, this volume explored the role of class, race, and gender in determining aesthetic criteria, defining literary canons, anointing cultural authorities, and structuring cultural hierarchies. It thus drew the battle lines of American culture wars on the literary front for the rest of the twentieth century.[27]

But the main front in the educational culture wars was not literary. In April 1969 students sat in at City College of the City University of New York (CUNY), denouncing what they saw as the university's discrimination against people of color and the poor in its admissions policy. In response, the Board of Higher Education initiated a program of open admissions whereby every graduate of a New York City high school could enroll in the city's famous university.

At the time, CUNY was the nation's third-largest system of public higher education, behind the University of California and the State University of New York. Never, since its first college was founded in 1847, had CUNY charged tuition. For well over a century, it had thus been a boulevard to success for many tens of thousands of poor and working-class New Yorkers. Now combining open admissions with free tuition, CUNY appeared as the vanguard in the democratization of American higher education.

At this point, a fierce counteroffensive against the progressive movements on campus was launched and coordinated by the White House, occupied since January by Richard Nixon. In June, President Nixon delivered a speech at General Beadle State College in South Dakota in which he equated "drugs, crime, campus revolts, racial discord, [and] draft resistance," expressed horror at the "patterns of deception" in American life stemming from contempt for moral, legal, and intellectual standards, and denounced the campus movement as central to this national crisis: "We have long considered our colleges and universities citadels of freedom, where the rule of reason prevails. Now both the process of freedom and the rule of reason are under attack. At the same time, our colleges are under pressure to collapse their educational standards, in the misguided belief that this would promote 'opportunity.' "[28] Vice President Spiro Agnew (not yet indicted for his own criminal activities) was even more explicit. Speaking at an Iowa Republican fund-raising dinner in April 1970, Agnew argued that there was too high a percentage of black students in college and condemned "the violence emanating from Black student militancy." Declaring that "college, at one time considered a privilege, is considered to be a right today," he singled out open admissions as one of the main ways "by which unqualified students are being swept into college on the wave of the new socialism."[29]

Later in 1970, Roger Freeman — a key educational adviser to Nixon then working for the reelection of California governor Ronald Reagan — spelled out quite precisely what the conservative counterattack was aimed at preventing: "We are in danger of producing an educated proletariat. That's dynamite! We have to be selective on who we allow to go through higher education. If not, we will have a large number of highly trained and unemployed people."[30] The two most menacing institutional sources of the danger described by Freeman were obviously those two great public university systems charging no tuition: the University of California and the City University of New York. Governor Reagan was able to wipe out free tuition at the University of California

of crippling CUNY was to go on for six more years, outlasting the Nixon
administration and falling to his appointed successor, Gerald Ford.[31]

Speaking to the National Press Club in late 1975, President Ford
explicitly declared that he would withhold federal aid from New York
City, which was then in a severe financial crisis, until it eliminated the
self-indulgent luxury of open admissions and free tuition at City University. To be financially responsible, the president declared, New York
must no longer be a city that "operates one of the largest universities in
the world, free of tuition for any high school graduate, rich or poor,
who wants to attend."[32] Ford's press secretary, Ron Nessen, speaking in
highly charged code language, explained the president's determination to block federal aid for New York City, which he compared to "a
wayward daughter hooked on heroin": "You don't give her $100 a day
to support her habit. You make her go cold turkey to break her habit."[33]

Finally, in 1976, the assault on public education succeeded in termi-
nating City University's 129-year policy of not charging for tuition, thus
wiping out the last stronghold of free public higher education in the
United States. Simultaneously, the university fired hundreds of young
faculty members who had been hired to implement the open admissions program.[34]

In the decades since then, with free tuition looking like a relic of
some ancient past or a dream of some utopian future, tuition and other
charges have kept rising at public colleges and universities across the
nation. Compounded by reduced budgets for scholarships, these escalating costs have made it ever more difficult for poor and working-class
students to obtain a college education, a trend accelerated in the late
1990s by open attacks on affirmative action. In 1998 and 1999, CUNY
and the poor of New York City again became targets as the administrations of Mayor Rudolph Giuliani and Governor George Pataki moved
to forbid remedial education at any of the city's four-year colleges.[35]

Meanwhile, just as the state and federal governments were taking
away the funds to open up the universities, they were beginning to
spend enormous sums on alternative institutions for the poor — institutions with exceptionally easy entrance requirements and lengthy en-
rollments for people of color. From 1976, the year when free higher
education was eradicated, until the end of the century, on average a
new prison was constructed in America every week. The prison population ballooned from under 200,000 in 1971 to more than 2 million in
2000 as the United States became the prison capital of the world. The

state of California alone now ran the world's second-largest prison system. By the late 1990s, many states had followed California's lead in spending more money for prisons than for higher education, and across the country far more young black men were in prison than in college.[36] Felony convictions had permanently stripped the vote from 4.1 million American citizens.[37] This has been culture war with a vengeance — and with a very effective strategy.

At the same time, within colleges and universities, business and accounting programs have continually expanded at the expense of the humanities, which in some schools have been reduced to service programs. One generation of young scholars in the humanities was decimated by political repression in the late 1960s and early 1970s, and a new generation, deprived of opportunities for full-time employment as teachers, has been reduced to a kind of peonage as adjuncts. Corporate domination of higher education has gone virtually unchallenged except briefly by the anti-apartheid movement when it focused on university endowments' investments in South Africa. Administrations, answerable only to political and corporate governing boards, have continually inflated in size and power, eliminating most vestiges of faculty and student participation in making significant decisions. It might seem that the conservative restoration is close to victory in the culture wars.

But if so, why have countless politicians, talk-show hosts, and editorialists continued to bemoan the loss of the culture wars to the "liberal educational establishment" — tenured radicals, feminists, multiculturalists, homosexuals, and a ruthless dictatorship of "political correctness" that has allegedly turned American universities into virtually the last citadels of leftism, subversion, and insurrection remaining after the Cold War? Why does the *Wall Street Journal* keep wailing about how Western civilization is menaced by the choice of books that students are asked to study?[38] Strangely enough, just when the conservative offensive was attaining victory after victory, an endless stream of heavily promoted and therefore often best-selling books, many financed by right-wing think tanks and foundations, proclaimed catastrophic conservative defeat in the culture wars.[39] To name just a few marching to the same rousing drumbeat since the closing years of Reagan's second term as president: Allan Bloom's *The Closing of the American Mind: How Higher Education Has Failed Democracy and Impoverished the Souls of Today's Students* (1987); E. D. Hirsch's *Cultural Literacy: What Every American*

Needs to Know (1987); Roger Kimball's *Tenured Radicals: How Politics Has Corrupted Our Higher Education* (1990); Dinesh D'Souza's *Illiberal Education: The Politics of Race and Sex on Campus* (1991); Arthur Schlesinger, Jr.'s, *The Disuniting of America: Reflections on a Multicultural Society* (1992); *The Devaluing of America: The Fight for Our Culture and Our Children* (1992) by William Bennett, former chair of the National Endowment for the Humanities and secretary of education; *Dictatorship of Virtue: Multiculturalism and the Battle for America's Future* (1994) by leading *New York Times* cultural critic Richard Bernstein; *Telling the Truth: Why Our Culture and Our Country Have Stopped Making Sense and What We Can Do About It* (1995) by Lynne V. Cheney, chair of the National Endowment for the Humanities in the Reagan and Bush administrations; *The Shadow University: The Betrayal of Liberty on America's Campuses* (1998) by Alan Charles Kors and Harvey A. Silverglate; and Gertrude Himmelfarb's *One Nation, Two Cultures* (1999).

Well, maybe there is some reason for this conservative anxiety. The literary canon cannot be restored to its white male purity of the pre–Vietnam War era. Nor can literature departments become, as most then were at the more prestigious institutions, 100 percent white and almost all male. And no intelligent thinker about culture can any longer believe that the choice of cultural materials to study or of the critical methodologies used to study them can possibly be apolitical. The consciousness formed in the crucible of the movement against the Vietnam War has not entirely disappeared. The imperial hegemony over culture has been shattered. After all, millions of Americans did become aware that there are other ways of looking at the emperor's new clothes.

While teaching a course on the Vietnam War and American culture, I have been struck by two responses expressed by students who came to consciousness after the combat was over. One is nostalgia for what they call "the sixties." A typical comment is, "I wish I could have been the same age I am now in the sixties." The other is to treat me as if I were some naive kid when I explain how our consciousness about American society changed during the movement against the war. Some of the most radical views of the antiwar movement—especially about corporate control of the government—now seem to be taken for granted. "What did you expect?" is a typical response. "We've known this stuff all our lives." These are, admittedly, working-class, multiethnic students at the state university campus in Newark, New Jersey. Maybe Roger Freeman, who gave such telling advice to President Nixon and Governor Reagan, foresaw just such a lurking menace when he said, "We are in danger of producing an educated proletariat. That's dynamite!"

Although the economic and political attack on public education at all levels has certainly diminished the danger of our producing an educated proletariat, Freeman's explosive metaphor is appropriate to the culture wars, which are indeed real combat, with real victims and, possibly, victors. The outcome of these wars has by no means been decided. There are probably two safe predictions that can be made: The culture wars will continue into the foreseeable future. And in that near future, the course of the culture wars within the United States will determine and be determined by struggles between transnational capital and peoples exploited by it, peoples whose revolutionary aspirations were once inspired by the example of Vietnam.

Much may depend on how well people remember and comprehend Vietnam's defeat of the mightiest war machine the world had yet known. Looking backward, historians of the future may recognize that this war machine was, up to that date at least, the most stupendous achievement of American culture. By defeating this war machine, the people of Vietnam not only exposed the myth of its invincibility but also ignited a series of wars within the culture that had created it.

> "With regard to space dominance, we have it, we like it, and we're
> going to keep it."
>> Keith Hall, Assistant Secretary of the Air Force for Space, 1997
>> (quoted in Karl Grossman, "Master of Space," *The Progressive* 64
>> [January 2000], 28)

CHAPTER SEVEN

Star Trek and Kicking
the Vietnam Syndrome

Operation Desert Storm, America's technowar blitzkrieg against Iraq, was launched in January 1991. To prepare for the big show, Washington initiated Operation Desert Shield, a massive buildup of troops and wonder weapons in Saudi Arabia and the Persian Gulf, along with a corollary media barrage, in August 1990.

Meanwhile, the same month but tens of millions of miles away, another miracle of American technology was beginning to beam home some startling images, very different from the war icons already streaming into American households. The robot spacecraft *Magellan,* peering with its radar imaging devices through the boiling acid clouds that shroud Venus, was transmitting, in a live-action display, the first coherent human view of the surface of Earth's sister planet. The handful of geologists, astronomers, and physicists privileged to attend the debut of *Magellan*'s imaging wizardry were astonished to see nonstop detailed pictures of great swaths of landscape, as sharp and clear as photographs.[1]

For more than a year and over three thousand orbits, *Magellan* poured back a complete topographic map of the alien planet. "We now have a better global map of Venus than of Earth," exclaimed one Jet Propulsion Laboratory scientist a year later, explaining that no map of our own planet had so completely traced the topography beneath the oceans.[2] One of the most exciting achievements of space exploration, this topographic picture of Venus was extraordinarily relevant to our own destiny because it displayed what could happen to a geologically similar planet when global warming leads to a catastrophic greenhouse effect. With the aid of computers, scientists were able to create a color video that unified *Magellan*'s images into a thrilling three-dimensional flying tour of the planet.

In late 1991 I was working at the Smithsonian Institution's National Air and Space Museum as the advisory curator for "*Star Trek* and the Sixties," the exhibition due to open in February 1992. Each day, as I passed through the main lobby on my way to meet with Mary Henderson, art curator of the museum and organizer of the exhibition, I saw two large video monitors in prominent, equivalently spaced positions in the lobby. The one on the left was playing that spectacular video of *Magellan*'s grand tour of Venus. The one on the right was playing "Weapons of the Gulf War," familiar footage of missiles and warplanes that had aired endlessly on TV. Sometimes nobody was watching the Venus video; the largest group I ever saw at that monitor was three people. But every day a huge crowd jostled for viewing space in front of "Weapons of the Gulf War," with blissful smiles plastered on the faces of many, especially boys and young men.

When "*Star Trek* and the Sixties" opened, it turned out to be the most popular exhibition in the history of the Air and Space Museum, which had to issue tickets to control the huge influx. After more than a million people attended in Washington, the exhibition traveled to the Hayden Planetarium of New York's American Museum of Natural History to be seen by another huge audience.

What was the appeal, not just of the exhibition, of course, but of *Star Trek*, which by then had already become a major component of American culture? Where did *Star Trek*'s allure fit in the continuum between the video of the Venus flyby and the video of "Weapons of the Gulf War"? And how many of the million viewers were interested in our contextualization of the original *Star Trek* in the crises of the 1960s, especially the Vietnam War?

Although the original 1960s series flopped in the ratings and r
aged to survive three seasons only because of ardent advocacy fr
limited audience, by 1992 *Star Trek* had become its own cultural
try. Episodes from the original series were being rebroadcast on U.S.
television two hundred times a day; *Star Trek: The Next Generation* was in
its fifth season and was being seen by 17 million Americans each week.[3]
Hundreds of *Star Trek* novels had been published, giving steady employment to many prominent science-fiction authors; Hollywood had produced the first six feature films starring the original cast; *Star Trek*
conventions attracted up to tens of thousands of "Trekkies," or, as they
preferred to be called, "Trekkers," who also produced innumerable
fanzines and thousands of *Star Trek* stories; warehouses could have
been filled with all the *Star Trek* encyclopedias, paintings, clocks, jew-
elry, beach towels, biographies, coffee mugs, tricorders, dictionaries,
posters, Klingon battle cruisers, magazines, handheld phasers, comic
books, retrospectives, lunch boxes, calendars, dissertations, costumes,
chess sets, scholarly and critical books and articles, videos, T-shirts,
action figures, games, puzzles, toys, Christmas ornaments, and, yes,
translations of classic books into the language of the Klingons. There
was even an entire subgenre of fan fiction, known as K/S and mostly
written by women, that featured homoerotic relations between Kirk
and Spock.[4] Interwoven through this gargantuan hodgepodge, this
"mega-text" of *Star Trek* culture, there have always been some serious
and important topical themes.[5]

The actual exploration of space had of course been part of the
historical context of the original series. In 1961, after Soviet cosmonaut
Yuri Gagarin had become the first human in space, President John F.
Kennedy committed the United States to landing humans on the moon
during the 1960s. The first episode of *Star Trek* was broadcast in 1966
and the last episode was aired in June 1969, the month before *Apollo 11*
landed on the moon. But this context is as problematic as *Star Trek*
itself. Was the enormous U.S. space program and its attendant hoopla
designed primarily to advance human knowledge or to win a Cold War
contest with the Soviet Union? Where did it fit in the psychological
space between those two competing videos and among all those other
artifacts of flight, exploration, and warfare housed in the National Air
and Space Museum? During those three years of *Star Trek*, American
attitudes toward the space race, like opinions about many other matters, were transformed and splintered by the Vietnam War. Indeed, by

the time of the moon landing, many Americans saw it as a Nixon administration attempt to glorify the military and deflect attention from the war.

If the U.S. race to send people beyond Earth was really about the exploration of space, why did the program abort in 1972, so soon after that first lunar landing and the four that followed? For the rest of the twentieth century, no human was to venture to the moon or any other extraterrestrial body, despite all those predictions about lunar and Martian colonies by the late 1980s or 1990s. Indeed, the last time a human being traveled beyond the earth's orbit was on December 18, 1972, the day President Nixon began Linebacker II, the twelve-day aerial blitzkrieg of North Vietnam, a few weeks before the United States officially ended its war in Vietnam by accepting peace terms originally proposed by Hanoi and the National Liberation Front in 1969.

And if *Star Trek* was really about the exploration of space, why was its audience so meager during the days of space travel and so immense after that era ended? *Star Trek*'s meteoric popularity came after the simultaneous conclusion of manned space flight beyond Earth and the U.S. war in Vietnam. The show with the slogan "to boldly go where no man has gone before" thus became a central feature of American culture just as America was abandoning human extraterrestrial travel, at least for the rest of the century. A perfect symbol of this cultural juncture occurred in 1974, when an eleven-foot model of the *Enterprise* used for special effects on the TV show went on permanent exhibit at the National Air and Space Museum, taking its place with such actual spacecraft as the *Apollo 11* command module.[6]

The manned space program of the 1960s was not, of course, the dominant feature of that decade in America, a distinction that clearly belongs to the Vietnam War. Our exhibit's contextualization of *Star Trek* in the 1960s spotlighted the war and related crises. We attempted to have the endless queue of visitors experience this context as they waited to enter the exhibition by having them file slowly past an eye-level series of large black and white photographs with captions such as:

1961 Soviet cosmonaut Yuri Gagarin became the first person to
   orbit the Earth in a spacecraft.
1962 The U.S. Navy blockades Cuba during the Cuban missile
   crisis.
1963 During a gigantic civil rights rally in Washington, D.C., Dr.
   Martin Luther King, Jr., delivered his "I have a dream" speech.

1963 President and Mrs. John F. Kennedy ride through Dallas, Texas. Moments later, President Kennedy and Texas Governor John Connally were shot.

1964 Many of the dreams of the civil rights movement died with the murder of Andrew Goodman, James Earl Chaney, and Michael Henry Schwerner during the voter registration campaign known as Mississippi Freedom Summer.

1964 The "sit-in" came to the campuses in the Free Speech movement at the University of California, Berkeley.

1965 Discontent in the cities burst out in the form of rebellions, such as this one in the Watts section of Los Angeles.

1967 Military police confronted anti-war demonstrators on the steps of the Pentagon.

1967 Members of the Black Panther Party displayed weapons in protest against anti-gun legislation, at the State Capitol in Sacramento, California.

1968 A Viet Cong prisoner was executed by the chief of the Saigon secret police.

1968 Dr. Martin Luther King, Jr., was assassinated in Memphis, Tennessee.

1968 Washington, D.C., was one of the 125 cities that erupted in rebellion in the week after the assassination of Dr. Martin Luther King, Jr.

1968 Senator Robert F. Kennedy is assassinated during a victory celebration after winning the California presidential primary.

1968 Demonstrators and police clashed at the Democratic National Convention in Chicago, Illinois.

1968 American atrocities in Vietnam were revealed through photos of a massacre at the village of My Lai.

1968 President Lyndon Johnson offers to negotiate with North Vietnam and announces that he will not run for reelection.

1969 American astronauts Edwin E. Aldrin and Neil Armstrong become the first humans to land on the Moon.

1969 At the Woodstock festival, 300 to 400 thousand people came to listen to music and celebrate the counter culture.

The exhibition was designed to show that the original *Star Trek* series was conceived, produced, and broadcast during one of the most profound crises in American history.[7] At the center of the maelstrom was the Vietnam War, which was remolding American consciousness dur-

the thirty-three months—from September 1966 to June 1969—
n the series was first broadcast. In the midst of a disastrous war,
1al warfare in the nation's own cities, increasing crime, inflation
and debt, campus rebellions, and deep challenges to hallowed cultural
values and gender roles, *Star Trek* assumed a future when Earth had
become a wonderfully prosperous, harmonious world without war and
social conflict, a future in which the aptly named starship USS *Enterprise*
embodied an undivided, self-contained, disciplined society capable of
making traditional American values and roles triumphant throughout
the galaxy.

Looming in the mind of every thinking American, the Vietnam War
was threatening to tear the nation asunder. As a matrix for *Star Trek*,
the war was in one sense a subtext for the entire series. Earth's utopian twenty-third-century future assumed in *Star Trek*—though never
shown—was presented as a sequel to the Vietnam era, just as the starship *Enterprise* was presented as an alternative to the actual world of
viewers in the America of the 1960s.

As one of television's first dramatic series to confront the Vietnam
War, *Star Trek* was actually quite daring.[8] TV networks rarely allowed
disturbing or controversial issues into shows designed for entertainment. So following its usual gambit for dealing with contemporary
issues, *Star Trek* parabolically displaced the Vietnam War in time and
space. Conceived just as the war was becoming an openly American
affair, the serial shows dramatically how America was being transformed
by the war.

In early November 1963, Ngo Dinh Diem, who had been installed by
Washington in 1954 as the puppet dictator of South Vietnam, was
overthrown and assassinated by a cabal of his generals, whose efforts
were coordinated by U.S. ambassador Henry Cabot Lodge. Although
President John F. Kennedy had authorized the coup, he reportedly was
shocked by the assassination of Diem, for Kennedy's own family had
been instrumental in selecting Diem to serve as the U.S. proxy. At this
time there were between 16,000 and 21,000 U.S. troops in Vietnam,
officially designated as "advisers." Deprived of its figurehead Diem, the
United States now had two possible courses of action: withdrawal or a
large-scale U.S. war. There is no evidence that Kennedy was leaning
toward the latter course. But three weeks later, President Kennedy himself was assassinated. Within four days of being sworn in, President
Lyndon Baines Johnson approved the top secret plan for covertly at-

tacking North Vietnam in order to provoke retaliation and thus legitimize an overt U.S. war.[9]

Four months later, in March 1964, Gene Roddenberry submitted
the first printed outline for *Star Trek*, which he described as an "action-
adventure science fiction" designed "to keep even the most imaginative stories within the general audience's frame of reference."[10] In August, the Johnson administration, falsely claiming that U.S. ships had
been repeatedly attacked by North Vietnam in the Gulf of Tonkin,
ordered "retaliatory" bombing of North Vietnam and received from
Congress the Gulf of Tonkin Resolution, the blank-check authorization
for full-scale U.S. war in Southeast Asia. Meanwhile, Johnson was in the
process of winning a landslide victory over Barry Goldwater on the
basis of his promise that he would "never send American boys to Asia to
do the job that Asian boys should do." In February 1965, Roddenberry
delivered the intended pilot episode of *Star Trek*, "The Cage," which
was rejected. The same month, Lyndon Johnson, a few weeks after
being inaugurated as the elected President, began nonstop bombing of
North Vietnam, followed swiftly by dispatch of the first openly acknowledged U.S. combat divisions to Vietnam.

By the time the first *Star Trek* episode was broadcast in September
1966, the United States was fully engaged in a war that was devastating
Indochina and beginning to tear America apart. By the time the final
Star Trek episode was aired in June 1969, the war seemed hopeless and
endless. Four episodes broadcast between the spring of 1967 and January 1969, the most crucial period in the war and for America, relate
directly to the war. Taken as a sequence, these four episodes dramatize
a traumatic metamorphosis in the war's impact on both the series and
the nation.

The first of the four was "The City on the Edge of Forever," aired on
April 6, 1967, one week before the end of *Star Trek*'s first season. Prior
to this date, the most astonishing domestic manifestation of the war was
the spectacular growth of the antiwar movement, whose size and fervor
were without precedent in the history of America's wars. In April 1965,
just a few weeks after the first overt dispatch of U.S. combat troops to
Vietnam, the first large antiwar demonstration took place in Washington. In the same period, an intense campaign began to educate the
American people about the history of the war, a campaign featuring
the teach-in movement on college campuses and the publication of an
avalanche of historical books, journals, and pamphlets. Millions of

Americans were beginning to learn that the government had been deceiving them about how and when the United States had intervened in Vietnam, as well as about the conduct and current status of the war. They discovered that the war had begun not as the defense of a nation called "South Vietnam" from invasion by the communist nation of "North Vietnam," but as a war of independence by Vietnam first against France and then against a dictatorship installed in the south in 1954 by the United States in violation of the Geneva Accords. They read and heard about how the Eisenhower, Kennedy, and Johnson administrations had gradually escalated a covert war into what could already be considered America's longest overseas military conflict. Two days before "The City on the Edge of Forever" aired, Martin Luther King, Jr., threw himself into the burgeoning antiwar movement with his "Declaration of Independence from the War in Vietnam," a sermon which summarized much of this history and which he gave as a speech two weeks later to a throng of hundreds of thousands of antiwar demonstrators in Central Park.

"The City on the Edge of Forever" opens with the *Enterprise* being buffeted by strange ripples in time. Doctor McCoy accidentally injects himself with a potent drug, and, in a paranoid delirium, hurtles through a time portal into New York City of 1930. Evidently something he does there will annihilate the future in which the *Enterprise* exists, so Captain James Kirk and First Officer Spock follow him through the portal to prevent his action and thus reestablish the proper course of history. While searching for McCoy, Kirk falls in love with social worker and "slum angel" Edith Keeler. But he and Spock discover that for their future to come into being, Edith Keeler must soon die in a traffic accident. If she is not killed then, she will become the founder of a peace movement that would change the outcome of World War II. At the crucial moment, Kirk prevents McCoy from saving Edith from an oncoming truck, thus restoring the history familiar to the audience and the crew of the *Enterprise*.

The subtext of this episode and its significance are highlighted by the evolution of the script and key pieces of dialogue inserted into the version that was broadcast in April 1967. The original script of May 13, 1966, written by Harlan Ellison, was a poignant tragedy of doomed love. Though using the science-fiction convention that any change in the past, no matter how slight, might radically alter the future, this script made no reference to Edith as a peace activist, much less to a peace movement that could misguide history. In Ellison's revised script

of June 3, 1966, Spock imagines possible futures that might com
pass if Edith were to live, such as, "She might give birth to a child
would become a dictator." "What if her philosophy spread," he
speculates, thus delaying America's entry into World War II so that "the
outcome of the war would be reversed?"[11]

In the episode as it aired in 1967, Spock's speculation has been
turned into a major plot element that viewers could hardly fail to relate
to the growing movement against the Vietnam War. Asked by me in
1992 whether the makers of this episode consciously intended it to
employ the contemporaneous anti–Vietnam War movement as subtext, producer Robert Justman replied, "Of course we did."[12]

In the televised episode, Spock works feverishly with the materials
available in this primitive period to build a rudimentary computer so
that his tricorder can actually display the possible futures unreeling
from the temporal focal point of 1930 New York. He discovers an
obituary for Edith Keeler, indicating that she was killed in a 1930 traffic
accident. But he also discovers newspapers with later dates indicating
that Edith has become the founder of a gigantic "peace movement":
that will keep the United States out of World War II long enough for
Nazi Germany to develop the atomic bomb, win the war, and rule the
world, thus annihilating the future in which the USS *Enterprise* exists. So
in order for the wondrous twenty-third century of *Star Trek* to come
into being, as Spock ruefully tells Kirk, "Jim, Edith Keeler must die."
And of course it is Kirk who must take the action to ensure her death.

As an embodiment of a dangerously misguided peace movement,
Edith is not portrayed as contemptible or ridiculous. She has only the
most admirable and worthy motives. Indeed, she is a true visionary,
who, in the midst of the miseries of the Depression, offers a prophecy of
a magnificent future as inspiration to the homeless and unemployed.
The future she describes is, in fact, the very one dramatized by the *Star
Trek* series: "One day, soon, man is going to be able to harness incred-
ible energies. Maybe even the atom, energies that could ultimately hurl
us to other worlds, maybe in some sort of space ship. And the men who
reach out into space will be able to find ways to feed the hungry millions of the world and to cure their diseases. . . . And those are the days
worth living for." But this apostle of peace, technological progress,
prosperity, and space exploration has the misfortune to be living in the
wrong time and place.

As broadcast in the spring of 1967, "The City on the Edge of Forever" was clearly a parable suggesting that the peace movement di-

rected against the U.S. war in Vietnam, no matter how noble, alluring, and idealistic in its motivation, might pose a danger to the progressive course of history. The episode projected the view that sometimes it is necessary to engage in ugly, distasteful action, such as waging remorseless warfare against evil expansionist forces like Nazi Germany or the communist empire attempting to take over Indochina — and perhaps even doing away with well-intentioned, attractive people who stand in the way of such historical necessity.

At this point in the Vietnam War, the peace movement, though growing rapidly, still represented only a minority of the American people, for it seemed to most that victory in Southeast Asia was not only necessary but also feasible, and perhaps even imminent. This view would soon change.

In the months that followed, the American people, despite the media's general support of the war, began to receive ever more appalling glimpses of its reality. Napalmed children, villages being torched by American GIs, the corpses of young Americans being zipped into body bags — all these became familiar images within the typical American home.

As public opposition to the war kept growing, a major public relations campaign was launched in November 1967, designed to convince the American people that victory was almost in view and before long, as General Westmoreland promised, the Saigon army would "take charge of the final mopping up of the Vietcong."[13] As I discussed in chapter 5, the pundits of the establishment media dutifully echoed these claims, assuring the public that "the enemy" is gripped by "desperation," the morale of U.S. troops is "excellent," whereas there is "irrefutable evidence of a decline in enemy morale," "the allies are winning," "Hanoi has abandoned the hope of conquest of South Vietnam by military force," and "it is now merely a matter of time" before the enemy is forced "to fade away into the jungle."[14] So, according to the White House, the Pentagon, and the media, the Johnson administration's strategy of gradual escalation was on the verge of success; the American people only needed to be patient, rejecting both those who called for withdrawal and those who demanded a speedy end to the war through massive escalation, including the possible use of nuclear weapons.

It was during this period that *Star Trek* was producing "A Private Little War," the episode designed explicitly as a policy statement about the Vietnam War. In a series of internal letters written from May through September 1967, *Star Trek*'s three main producers — Gene Roddenberry, Gene L. Coon, and Robert Justman — defined the message about Vietnam they wanted this episode to bring to the TV audience.

The first script, written by Don Ingalls, was criticized by Roddenberry for opposing U.S. intervention in Vietnam. Disregarding *Star Trek*'s "Prime Directive" — banning interference in the natural development of alien societies — Roddenberry wrote to Coon in May: "The things at stake in Vietnam are much more important and powerful than a charitable attitude toward simpler people in the world."[15] Coon, a major *Star Trek* writer as well as producer, spelled out in August the politics of the episode:

> We have always played [the Klingons] very much like the Russians. . . . In the current situation in Vietnam, we are in an intolerable situation. We are doing what we are forced to do, and we can find no other way to do it. . . . If we are to honor our commitments, we must counter-balance the Klingons. If we do not play it this way, the Klingons will take over and threaten the Federation, even as the situation is in Vietnam, which is as I remember, if Vietnam falls all southeast Asia falls. . . . At this point, it should be evident to everyone that we have essentially been talking about Vietnam. . . . What we are trying to sell is the hopelessness of the situation. The fact that we are absolutely forced into taking steps we know are morally wrong, but for our own enlightened self-interest, there is nothing we can do about it."[16]

These were the politics of the broadcast episode, with a final script written by Roddenberry himself.

The *Enterprise* visits Neural, a planet Kirk remembers from an earlier visit as so primitive and peaceful that it seemed like "Eden." However, an unequal war has begun on Neural, with one side — known as "the villagers" — mysteriously armed with firearms, devices far beyond the technological level of any society on the planet. The villagers, who represent the official U.S. view of the North Vietnamese, have been attacking and attempting to conquer the peaceful "hill people," who represent the official U.S. view of the South Vietnamese. Like the National Liberation Front (the "Viet Cong"), the villagers at first seem to be armed with primitive hand-forged weapons, in this case flintlocks. But these weapons in fact have been mass-produced by some outside imperialist power, which has been smuggling them in and making them appear to be indigenous. Who could this evil empire be? The Klingons, of course, *Star Trek*'s analogue to the Soviet Union. Their aim, needless to say, is to subvert and take over this primitive planet, itself an analogue to Vietnam, Indochina, and the rest of the Third World, menaced, according to the domino theory, by communist expansion.

Thus "A Private Little War" promoted the official administration version of the history of the Vietnam War: that it had begun as an intervention by an outside evil empire — the Soviet Union. In fact, as millions of Americans were then discovering, the war had begun as a defense of an existing empire, France, against an indigenous movement for national independence, and was transformed into a war of conquest by another nation attempting to advance its own imperial interests in Southeast Asia — the United States of America.

This is not to say that the episode implicitly endorsed major enlargement of the Vietnam War. Indeed, it seems to suggest that the main danger to be avoided is any form of military intervention that could lead to direct warfare between the United States, represented by the Federation, and the evil communist empire, represented by the Klingons.

The *Enterprise*'s options are presented in a debate between Kirk and McCoy. It is revealing that in the "teaser," Spock, after issuing a stern warning against interfering in the planet's affairs, is gravely wounded and spends the rest of the episode recovering on the ship, thus conveniently removing him from all further discussion and decision making. Perhaps, as Rick Worland has suggested, Spock's usual role as an objective outside commentator on human affairs "might have made him too dangerous here," for, being a superrational Vulcan, he might "have perceived instantly the illogic of the whole situation and denounced the Neural/Vietnam War."[17] Before McCoy challenges him, Kirk has decided to provide military training to the hill people and to arm them with the same weapons as the villagers. McCoy, appalled by this course of action, points out its hideous potential consequences for the people whom the Federation would supposedly be aiding in a speech loudly evoking Vietnam in the minds of viewers: "You're condemning this whole planet to a war that may never end. It could go on for year after year, massacre after massacre." Kirk argues that he is merely establishing a balance of power, and makes the parallel with the Vietnam War explicit:

McCoy: I don't have a solution. But furnishing them with firearms is certainly *not* the answer!

Kirk: Bones, do you remember the twentieth-century brush wars on the Asian continent? Two giant powers involved, much like

the Klingons and ourselves. Neither side felt that they could
pull out?

McCoy: Yes, I remember — it went on bloody year after bloody
year!

Kirk: But what would you have suggested? That one side arm its
friends with an overpowering weapon? Mankind would never
have lived to travel space if they had. No — the only solution is
what happened, back then, balance of power.

McCoy: And if the Klingons give their side even more?

Kirk: Then we arm our side with *exactly* that much more. A balance
of power — the trickiest, most difficult, dirtiest game of them
all — but the only one that preserves both sides!

Kirk here aligns himself closely with the avowed policies of the
Johnson administration and suggests that, although the road may be
long and ugly, a patient application of *Realpolitik* will eventually lead out
of the Vietnam morass and into humanity's glorious future. At the
time, the growing impatience of the American people with a seemingly
endless war was producing an increasingly bitter conflict between advo-
cates of total war, such as retired Strategic Air Command chief Curtis
Le May ("bomb North Vietnam back into the Stone Age") and Ronald
Reagan ("pave the country over and put parking stripes on it"), and
the already huge peace movement, which was demanding more and
more that the United States withdraw from Vietnam and let the Vietnamese settle their own affairs. With the logical Spock absent, McCoy is
unable to articulate any coherent alternative to the captain's analysis
and is reduced to mere moral outrage. Kirk's own moral anguish in
making his choice precisely mirrors that being projected by Lyndon
Johnson, who presented himself as a realistic moderate torn by his
rejection of seductive but illusory extremes.

Just like "The City on the Edge of Forever," "A Private Little War"
warns the audience that it must support unpleasant policies in the
primitive epoch of the 1960s or else the world of the USS *Enterprise*
might never come into being. But now, just months later, that warning
is mainly directed not against the doves but against the hawks, who
could bring about a catastrophe in which "mankind would never have
lived to travel space."

The episode ends with a sense of foreboding and disillusion un-
characteristic of *Star Trek*. When he orders Scotty to manufacture a
hundred flintlock weapons for the hill people, Kirk refers to these

instruments as "a hundred serpents . . . for the garden of Eden." Then, as McCoy tries to comfort him, the captain says somberly, "We're very tired, Mr. Spock. Beam us up home."

Even as it was being produced, "A Private Little War" was anachronistic in its view of the Vietnam War, referring more clearly to the period of covert U.S. involvement prior to the assassination of Ngo Dinh Diem in 1963 than to the open U.S. war of 1968. Kirk even points out early in the episode that "keeping our presence here secret is an enormous tactical advantage" over the Klingons. The leader of the hill people has a wife obviously modeled on President Diem's wife, Madame Nhu, the infamous "dragon lady"; and the fictional wicked woman, like her model in Saigon, helps precipitate the event that triggers escalation by the good outside power. In late 1967 and the first month of 1968, despite all official and media reassurances, Kirk's policy of measured escalation had certainly not led to any resolution, and McCoy's warnings about "a war that may never end" could not be easily dismissed.

Nevertheless, "A Private Little War," like "The City on the Edge of Forever," suggests that the Vietnam War is an ugly necessity that forms part of the pathway to the glorious twenty-third century in which the adventures of *Star Trek* take place. But two days before the episode aired, an event began that was to challenge even such guarded optimism.

Although "A Private Little War" was produced while the government and media were proclaiming that the United States was nearing victory, it was originally telecast on February 2, 1968, while the nation was in shock at the news of the devastating Tet offensive, when the insurgent forces simultaneously attacked most U.S. bases and over a hundred cities and towns in South Vietnam. When the next episode directly relevant to Vietnam was broadcast one month later, it dramatically expressed the effect of the Tet offensive on America's consciousness. Completed in December 1967, while antiwar newspapers were debunking official optimism with accounts of the rapidly deteriorating U.S. military situation, this episode suggests that the makers of *Star Trek* themselves had moved much closer to the antiwar movement.[18] Sardonically titled "The Omega Glory," it displayed a profound darkening of *Star Trek*'s vision of the Vietnam War and its possible consequences.

By the time "The Omega Glory" aired on March 1, 1968, the Tet offensive had shattered any expectations of victory in Vietnam. The episode, written by Gene Roddenberry, examined the consequences of a possibly endless war in Vietnam from a perspective much closer to the grim view McCoy had expressed in "A Private Little War." Indeed, the main victims of such a war are no longer seen as alien peoples confined to some remote location like the planet Neural or Southeast Asia, for America itself is imagined as a devastated former civilization reduced to barbarism.

Kirk, Spock, and McCoy visit the planet Omega IV, whose dreadful history is gradually revealed to them. The planet is now dominated by a race of Asian villagers known as "the Kohms," who are engaged in unending warfare against a fair-haired, fair-skinned race of savages known as "the Yangs." The Yangs, who are so primitive they seem scarcely human, are beginning to overwhelm the Kohms with the sheer ferocity of their hordes. Meanwhile, starship captain Tracey, a mad renegade, has violated the "Prime Directive," directly intervening in the planet's war on the side of the Kohms and personally using his phasers to slaughter many hundreds of Yangs.

McCoy's medical research reveals that once there had been very advanced civilizations here, but they had destroyed themselves in this constant warfare. The survivors show signs that they had even waged "bacteriological warfare," similar to Earth's "experiments in the 1990s." "Hard to believe," he says, "we were once foolish enough to play around with that." Spock's logic ultimately concludes that this planet presents a case of parallel evolution: "They fought the war your Earth avoided, and in this case the Asiatics won and took over the planet." He comes to this conclusion as soon as he and Kirk realize the significance of the names of the two warring races:

> KIRK: Yangs? Yanks. Yankees!
> SPOCK: Kohms. Communists!

At this point, the Yangs, who have conquered the Kohm village, are being incited by Captain Tracey to execute Kirk, Spock, and McCoy. The scene is dramatically punctuated by the entrance of the sacred banner of the Yangs, a tattered American flag, evidently the "Omega Glory" of the episode's title. Forgetting all the principles for which they were fighting in their endless war against the communists, these Yankees have become savage barbarians teetering on the very edge of bestiality. All they have left of their great American ideals are their worship words—garbled versions of the Pledge of Allegiance and the Preamble to the Constitution of the United States—which they recite as sacred gibberish.

In a melodramatic ending, Kirk grabs their holiest of holies, a printed version of the Preamble, and recites it, with emphasis on "We the People." He explains to the Yangs, who now worship Kirk as a god because of the seemingly miraculous appearance of a rescue team from the *Enterprise,* that "these words . . . were not written only for the Yangs, but for the Kohms as well." Such thoughts constitute a shocking heresy for the Yangs, but Kirk insists, "They must apply to everyone, or they mean nothing." The eyes of the Yangs gradually seem more human as Kirk thus awakens them from their eons of mindless anticommunist warfare, and the thrilling sight of Old Glory and strains of "The Star-Spangled Banner" suggest that this planet too may return to the true path of American ideals.

"The Omega Glory" implies that the war in Southeast Asia, which no longer held any promise of victory or even any suggestion of an end, could evolve into an interminable, mutually destructive conflict between the "Yankees" and the "Communists" capable of destroying civilization and humanity. True Americanism is shown as antithetical to mindless militarism and anticommunism, and the episode rather paradoxically uses ultrapatriotic images of a tattered Old Glory and the strains of the U.S. national anthem to preach a message of globalism. Kirk's emphasis on "We the People" might even be a suggestion to the American people that they must reassert their own role in the nation's affairs.

If there were any doubts where the makers of *Star Trek* now stood on the Vietnam War itself, they were resolved in the pages of the nation's leading science-fiction magazines. Like other Americans, science-fiction writers were profoundly and bitterly divided about the Vietnam War, and in early 1968 more than a hundred and fifty of them took out rival advertisements supporting and opposing continuation of the conflict.[19] These ads, signed before the Tet offensive, appeared first in the March issue of the *Magazine of Fantasy and Science Fiction,* which came out just before "The Omega Glory" was broadcast. Not one person associated with *Star Trek* joined the seventy-two signers of the ad that stated "We the undersigned believe the United States must remain in Vietnam to fulfill its responsibilities to the people of that country." Among the eighty-two who signed the ad that stated "We oppose the participation of the United States in the war in Vietnam" were *Star Trek* scriptwriters Jerome Bixby, Jerry Sohl, Harlan Ellison, and Norman Spinrad, as well as Gene Roddenberry himself.

Nineteen sixty-eight was not only the decisive moment in the Vietnam War but also the period of the most intense domestic crisis of recent American history, as discussed in chapter 5. Most of the countryside of South Vietnam was lost to the insurgents, and U.S. forces were busy defending their bases and the cities and towns of the south. General Westmoreland was dismissed from his command. The president of the United States was forced to withdraw from the election campaign, and antiwar candidates swept every Democratic primary. Tens of thousands of troops and almost all urban police forces had to be mobilized to put down the uprisings in 125 cities the week after the assassination of Martin Luther King, Jr. Police and sometimes soldiers battled demonstrators on college campuses across the country. The international finance system reeled from blows to the U.S. economy and its credibility, and the Johnson administration was forced into negotiations with the Democratic Republic of Vietnam and the National Liberation Front of South Vietnam. Robert Kennedy, running as an antiwar candidate for president, was assassinated on the evening when he had seemingly clinched the Democratic nomination. Twenty-five thousand soldiers, police, and Secret Service agents battled antiwar demonstrators outside the Democratic convention in August. As discussed in chapter 6, the Republican convention earlier that month had taken place on the edge of an armed combat zone. In his acceptance speech, Richard Nixon, after noting that "as we look at America, we see cities enveloped in smoke and flame," vowed that "if the war is not ended when the people choose in November," "I pledge to you tonight that the first priority foreign policy objective of our next Administration will be to bring an honorable end to the war in Vietnam."[20] Nixon won that 1968 election as a peace candidate.

On January 10, 1969, ten days before Nixon's inauguration and four years before the end of official U.S. participation in the Vietnam War, *Star Trek* broadcast an aptly titled episode, "Let That Be Your Last Battlefield." This episode views the racial conflict of the 1960s in a parable about two races on an alien planet, each half black and half white, who annihilate each other in an increasingly violent struggle between oppression and revolution. The master race, white on the left half and black on the right, has enslaved and continues to exploit the other race, black on the left half and white on the right. Enraged by millennia of persecution, the oppressed are led by a fanatic militant. In a clear allusion to the disproportionate fatalities being suffered by African Americans in Vietnam, he asks crew members of the *Enterprise*, "Do you know what it would be like to be dragged out of your hovel into a war on another planet, a battle that will serve your oppressor and bring death to your brothers?"

The ultimate end of the mutual hatred between these races is spelled out when the *Enterprise* reaches their home planet. Spock reports that there are now "no sapient life forms"; "they have annihilated each other totally." As the last representatives of the two races continue their fight to mutual doom, behind them flash scenes of actual footage of America's burning cities. The vision of global disaster projected as a possible outcome of the Vietnam War in "The Omega Glory" has now, less than a year later, literally come home.

The first of two of these episodes, "The City on the Edge of Forever" and "A Private Little War," suggested that the Vietnam War was merely an unpleasant necessity on the way to the future dramatized by *Star Trek*. But the last two, "The Omega Glory" and "Let That Be Your Last Battlefield," broadcast in the period between March 1968 and January 1969, are so thoroughly infused with the desperation of the period that they openly call for a radical change of historic course, including an end to the Vietnam War and to the war at home. Only this new course presumably would take us to the universe of the USS *Enterprise*.

But the universe of the *Enterprise* was also one inhabited by evil empires, the Klingons and the Romulans. Without evil empires, there would be no space combat. And what would *Star Trek*—and its audience—be without Klingon battle cruisers, phasers, shields, and photon torpedoes?

In the original series, space warfare was not nearly as important as it became in the *Star Trek* mythos. The first actual image of a Klingon battle cruiser did not appear until December 1968, and then only as a secondary plot device (in "Elaan of Troyius"). But unending battles against Klingon ships became central to *Star Trek* culture in the 1970s, in the wake of the Vietnam War.

January 1973 saw two historic milestones in American culture: the United States formally agreed to end its war in Vietnam, and the first *Star Trek* convention was held in New York City. Meanwhile, an obscure phenomenon was gathering momentum, helping to expand *Star Trek*'s role in the transition from the Vietnam War to the Gulf War.

In October 1972 a new *Star Trek* computer game was invented and soon placed in the Hewlett Packard program library. By mid-1973, this game was spawning a whole breed that would soon inhabit every university's mainframe computer and then spread to personal computers in homes and offices throughout America.[21] Known as "Star Trek" or just plain "Trek," the game allowed millions of Americans, mostly young, to command the *Enterprise* and wage thrilling electronic warfare against an unending host of battle cruisers from the evil Klingon empire.

The blastoff of *Star Trek* culture coincided with the end of the Vietnam War and the simultaneous end of manned extraterrestrial travel. *Star Trek* culture went into orbit in the 1970s and early 1980s just as the exploration of space was being replaced by the militarization of space. By 1976, trekkers had enough clout to persuade President Gerald Ford to change the name of the U.S. space shuttle *Constitution* to the *Enterprise*.

By 1981, multibillion-dollar military space programs had gobbled up the space budget. Most future plans for the peaceful exploration of space had been dumped; as a NASA astronomer lamented, "The space science program has been almost destroyed." That fall, the civilian director of NASA's shuttle project was replaced by air force general James Abrahamson, a leading proponent of space war. In 1982, air force chief of staff General Lew Allen announced the creation of the Space Command, making air force space operations coequal with tactical and strategic air operations. A few weeks later, General Allen was named head of the Jet Propulsion Laboratory, the nation's principal center for the exploration of deep space.[22] In 1983, General Abrahamson was made program manager of a vast new project announced by President Ronald Reagan, the Strategic Defense Initiative, known more accurately as "Star Wars."

By the end of the twentieth century, the Space Command — whose motto "Master of Space" is emblazoned on its uniform patch — was moving toward the center of the U.S. government's vision of future war. "We're going to fight from space, and we're going to fight into space. . . . We will engage terrestrial targets someday — ships, airplanes, land targets — from space," proclaimed General Joseph W. Ashby, former commander-in-chief of the U.S. Space Command, in 1996.[23] So on November 1, 1999, the United States was one of two nations (the other was Israel) that refused to join the otherwise unanimous vote of the General Assembly of the United Nations reaffirming the Outer Space Treaty and pledging to use "outer space for peaceful purposes."[24]

Those visitors to the National Air and Space Museum in 1991 gawking at "Weapons of the Gulf War" while ignoring the spectacular panorama of Venus were living embodiments of the cultural triumph of militarization in the 1980s. The weapons of the Gulf War were truly miraculous: freeing us from the memories of Vietnam while linking the shields that protected the USS *Enterprise* from Klingon phasers with the Star Wars shield that promised to make America invulnerable to missiles. The *Wall Street Journal* hailed the advent of true technowar, bragging about how these "advanced weapons spare civilians."[25] In "Robowar: The Day the Weapons Worked," the *New Republic* proclaimed that the "pinpoint" accuracy of these "wonder weapons" guaranteed a clean victory, free of the civilian blood and misery and "general destruction" caused by outdated "cruel" weapons.[26] But in March 1991, a United Nations investigation revealed that the bombing of Iraq had caused "near-apocalyptic" devastation, hurling a modern nation into a "pre-industrial age" where "most means of modern life support have been destroyed or rendered tenuous" because of the deliberate targeting of the urban superstructure. And later it was revealed that even the miraculous Patriot anti-missile missiles had probably destroyed only one Iraqi Scud missile, while causing more damage to Israel than the incoming Scuds.[27]

American bombing of Iraq was to continue throughout the rest of the twentieth century and into the twenty-first century. Combined with draconian economic sanctions, it proved responsible for the deaths of many hundreds of thousands of Iraqi children.[28] But the fantasies on TV screens continued to screen out this reality. Those smart bombs that had helped us kick the Vietnam syndrome proved even more wondrous than the deadliest weapons of the USS *Enterprise,* because not even photon torpedoes could beam into our television sets their own photographic vision of their perfectly antiseptic annihilation of the alien enemy.[29]

Meanwhile, the Air and Space Museum itself was being purged of any ambivalence about militarism. When it attempted in 1994 to display the fuselage of the *Enola Gay* (the B-29 that dropped the atomic bomb on Hiroshima) as the centerpiece of a multifaceted history of the event, a jingoistic campaign waged by military officials, veterans' organizations, and most of Congress purged the planned exhibit of any content except for glorification of the bomber and the bomb. Many historians came to understand the profound and shocking significance of this triumph of militarist culture.[30] Then, in late 1999, the museum got a new director, retired marine general John R. Dailey, who had flown 450 missions bombing Vietnam.[31]

CHAPTER EIGHT

The Vietnam War as American Science Fiction and Fantasy

America's war in Indochina cannot be separated from American science fiction, which shaped and was reshaped by the nation's encounter with Vietnam. Out of American pulp, comic book, and movie science fiction of the 1930s, 1940s, and 1950s poured two streams of images that profoundly influenced how the war was conceived and conducted: fantasies of techno-wonders and of superheroes. Of course these streams inter-mingle; after all, in order to fight for "truth, justice, and the American way," the American science-fiction superhero re-quires fantastic powers, which may be internalized (Super-man) or externalized in high-tech paraphernalia (Batman). Indeed, the war cannot be fully comprehended unless it is seen in part as a form of American science fiction and fantasy.[1] For an introductory paradigm for the American self-images that helped engineer the war, just imagine Buck Rogers — as he uses his manly skills and twenty-fifth-century technology to lead the good fight against the Mongol hordes — sporting a green beret.

Science-fiction fans who tried escaping from the Vietnam War by diving into their favorite magazines in the spring of 1968 instead found themselves plunged right back into the conflict — in the form of two opposing advertisements about the war, each signed by scores of science-fiction writers, artists, and editors. The rival advertisements dramatize the deep fissure splitting not just the science-fiction community but also the American people and their culture.

Whereas the March issue of the *Magazine of Fantasy and Science Fiction* discreetly separated the foes with eighty-four pages of fiction and reviews, the June issue of *Galaxy Science Fiction* showcased the two ads on facing pages. Then came pages of anguished hand-wringing by editor Frederik Pohl, who chastised both groups for splitting what was supposedly a tight community, turning what he called "a choice of tactics" into a "polarized debate," thus making "opponents of people who should be friends" and threatening to protract the national debate, and hence the war, endlessly. Pohl, himself a major science-fiction author, pleaded for a unified vision that readers were supposed to be able to find in science fiction: "Look down the list of signers to the two divergent ads. . . . [F]rom their stories, you have an opportunity to judge of the kinds of worlds they would like for the future. . . . [T]here's not a pennyworth of difference between them. . . . [I]f these two groups were each constituted a committee for the construction of a World of Twenty-Sixty-Eight, and their optimum worlds were compared, they would be essentially the same world."[2]

Looking back at the rival camps, we may be puzzled by Pohl's inability to distinguish between either their ideologies or their conflicting roles in modern science fiction. For the prowar list reads like a roll call of champions of superscience and supermen, of manly and military virtue, indeed, some of those very values that helped shape the technowar being waged in Indochina. The antiwar list includes almost the entire vanguard of an emerging kind of science fiction, opposed to technocracy, militarism, and imperialism; originally called the New Wave, it evolved into new forms prominent in the 1970s, 1980s, and 1990s.[3] Yet Pohl's yearning for the vanished if not mythical community of science fiction also represented a wider national nostalgia. For the apparently unified, content, smiling-faced nation of the late 1950s — product of the post–World War II prosperity and repression that had

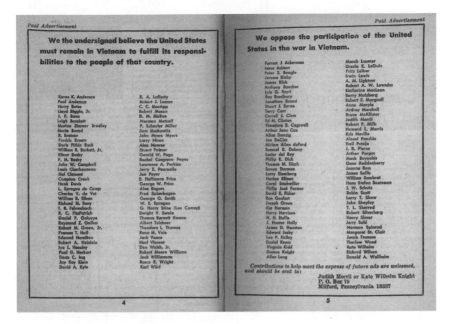

stifled almost all dissent — seemed in the process of being torn asunder by America's war in Vietnam.

Science-fiction authors Kate Wilhelm and Judith Merril had begun organizing the antiwar petition at the 1967 Milford Conference, an annual seminal event which aspiring science-fiction writers attended to learn the trade from established authors and editors. Wilhelm, then co-director of the conference, remembers the traumatic context:

> I recall perhaps too vividly the night we discussed and worded our protest over the Vietnam war. We planned for our discussion to take place after the Milford Conference was officially ended on Saturday night. We announced . . . that it had nothing to do with the writing conference, and we stated precisely that it was to discuss the wording of a protest against the war. Most of the attendees of the conference came, and it was clear that the whole thing would degenerate into yet another debate about the pros and cons of the war. I took the floor and repeated what we had stated earlier. This was not a meeting to debate the war, it was to form a nucleus of protestors who would sign a statement of protest and circulate it. I invited those who opposed such a statement to leave.
>
> It was the first time I ever had asked anyone to leave my house, and there was shock and dismay among those in opposition. I re-

member Doris Buck, a dear friend, who was very upset and said she supported the war effort; after all, she had a son in Vietnam. I said so did I.[4]

The late Judith Merril recalled that when she and Wilhelm began the petition, they had assumed that "95 percent" of the writers would sign because of the "global and anti-racist view" that supposedly guided science fiction. Blinded by this idealism, Merril was shocked when Robert Heinlein — often called "the Dean of Science Fiction" — was among those who responded with vociferous declarations of "America first" and "the U.S. must win."[5]

Perhaps the very first literary fantasy or science fiction to flow from America's war in Vietnam was Heinlein's *Glory Road,* serialized in the *Magazine of Fantasy and Science Fiction* way back in July, August, and September 1963. Written more than two years before the first official dispatch of American troops in February 1965, the novel presages ominous features of American culture of the late 1970s, 1980s, and 1990s.

The hero of *Glory Road* is full of resentment over the Korean War because "we weren't allowed to win."[6] So off he goes to fight as a "Military Adviser" in the jungles of Vietnam, where, he tells us, anyplace "you step it *squishes,*" and "the bushes are filled with insects and natives who shoot at you." Although boasting that there "I had killed more men in combat than you could crowd into a — well, never mind," he receives no GI educational benefits because the government was still pretending that it was not at war.[7] Indeed, when *Glory Road* was published, few Americans were aware that the United States was engaged in major combat in Vietnam and Laos.

Our hero comes to resemble a familiar figure in post-Vietnam American culture. Like Rambo, he is embittered by what he sees as government betrayal during the war and is thoroughly alienated from the domestic American society he finds when he returns. Unappreciated as a warrior, he is reduced to beating up a bearded poet who labels him a "mercenary" for fighting in Southeast Asia.[8] Here he is, "a hundred and ninety pounds of muscle and no fat," a fearless expert in martial arts, a hero in a society run by bureaucrats and dedicated to "single-minded pursuit of the three-car garage, the swimming pool, and the safe & secure retirement benefits."[9] Adroit in the arts of killing, and stripped of all ideals but those of the lone warrior, he seeks a destiny he can only hope to find in classified ads for mercenaries.

Thoroughly contemptuous of Third World peasants, our hero brags about having disemboweled "a pragmatic Marxist in the jungle," a man he sardonically refers to as "little brown brother."[10] His feelings foreshadow those of the Vietnam veterans later recruited through ads in *Soldier of Fortune* magazine to fight as mercenaries against peasants in Africa, Asia, and Latin America. The psychology of these warriors was well described in a 1979 *Wall Street Journal* report on the eighty to ninety U.S. veterans of Vietnam then fighting in the army of the white supremacist government of Rhodesia:

> Thus, Hugh McCall, a corporal in the Rhodesian army, describes the first man he killed in combat. "It's the most exciting goddam thing in the world. There's nothing else like it. The feeling you get when you come out of a contact — well, you bet your own life, and you know it." . . .
>
> "I went big-game hunting here once, but I haven't bothered again because it doesn't do that much for you," says one American who wants to remain anonymous. "After hunting men, hunting game is sort of tame."
>
> Liam Atkins, 34 years old, who fought as a captain with the green berets in Vietnam, says he has been here two years as a captain in the Rhodesian army [and] . . . "I like killing communists."[11]

The hero of *Glory Road* answers a classified ad which promises even more thrills: "We badly need a brave man . . . proficient with all weapons . . . indomitably courageous and handsome of face and figure. Permanent employment, very high pay, glorious adventure, great danger."[12] It turns out that the employer in search of a true hero is none other than "Star," the most beautiful, sexy, adoring, and exciting woman in "the Twenty Universes" — of which she is the Empress. So off he goes with her on "Glory Road," killing monsters, having sexual encounters even more amazing than his martial encounters, and achieving fabulous wealth and admiration.

The guiding political philosophy of Star's realm echoes an assumption underlying most American science fiction from the 1920s through the 1950s: "Democracy can't work. Mathematicians, peasants, and animals, that's all there is — so democracy, a theory based on the assumption that mathematicians and peasants are equal, can never work."[13] This view was also central to U.S. decision making in Vietnam. Two months after the final installment of *Glory Road,* the Kennedy administration directed the coup that killed Ngo Dinh Diem, the U.S.-installed puppet ruler of South Vietnam. President Kennedy was guided by this secret advice cabled in August 1963 from Henry Cabot Lodge, his ambassador to the Diem government:

> We are launched on a course from which there is no respectable turning back: the overthrow of the Diem government. . . . [T]here is no turning back because there is no possibility, in my view, that the war can be won under a Diem administration, still less that Diem or any member of the family can govern the country in a way to gain the support of the people who count, i.e., the educated class in and out of government service."[14]

If the peasants of Vietnam or other Third World nations contest the political philosophy shared by Heinlein and Lodge, it becomes necessary to find heroes, like the narrator of *Glory Road,* to kill as many of them as possible.

But in the midst of his romantic sword-and-sorcery adventures, the hero of *Glory Road* discovers that he is merely a character in a book, somebody else's fantasy.[15] For he comes at the tail end of the epoch of the bourgeois hero, who replaced the feudal hero with the rascal of the picaresque novel and then went on to metamorphose into Robinson Crusoe, Horatio Alger, Tom Edison, Jr., and Frank Reade, Jr., of the American dime novel, Edgar Rice Burroughs' John Carter and Tarzan, the detective, the cowboy, James Bond, Superman, Batman, Luke Skywalker — almost anyone but that alienated wage slave who pays some of his earnings for a piece of the fantasy. Now the bourgeois hero seeks happiness in the lost world of the romantically mythologized feudal past, where he can dwell forever, sword in hand and empress in bed.

The hero's lament that "we weren't allowed to win" the Korean War alludes to the decision not to drop nuclear bombs on Korea or China or both. The same kind of illusion informed one of the first U.S. government fantasies about Vietnam, which envisioned nuclear weapons as the magical power that would allow American will to reshape Indochinese reality. As early as April 5, 1954, while France teetered on the brink of defeat by the Democratic Republic of Vietnam, the U.S. National Security Council's plans for possible intervention stipulated: "Nuclear weapons will be available for use as required by the tactical situation and as approved by the President. The estimated forces initially to be supplied by the United States under the alternatives in this paper are based on the assumption of availability. . . . The political factors involved in the use of nuclear weapons are assessed under the various alternatives."[16]

Later that same month, Washington may have offered two nuclear bombs to be dropped on the forces besieging the French bastion of Dien Bien Phu.[17] A decade later, policy makers in Washington considered the use of nuclear weapons to support U.S. forces in Vietnam, even though officially these troops were not even there yet.[18] In 1968, with U.S. forces beleaguered throughout South Vietnam, their supreme commander, General Westmoreland, suggested to the Pentagon the use of nuclear weapons.[19] The antiwar movement and other political realities, however, evidently kept these fantasies, elaborated in the secret councils and plans of American military and political leaders, from bursting upon the world.

But reality had no such control over the fantasies of some of the signers of the 1968 prowar advertisement in the science-fiction magazines. Under the spell of technological fetishism, some imagined a final solution to the Vietnam problem in the form of that ultimate technological fix, nuclear weapons.

For example, one of those signers was Joe Poyer, who in 1966 had published "Challenge: The Insurgent vs. the Counterinsurgent" in the science-fiction magazine *Analog*, where he had confidently asserted that all guerrilla insurgencies were now doomed by the evolving technological wizardry commanded by counterinsurgent forces, such as spy satellites and people sniffers (electronic devices to detect the chemicals exuded by guerrillas).[20] Poyer's 1966 fantasies were shared by the generals and politicians running the war, who confidently predicted throughout 1966 and 1967 that the Vietnamese insurgency was on the verge of total collapse. But then came the stunning Tet offensive of early 1968, with its reduction of U.S. and puppet forces to a desperate defense of their own bases and the cities.

In July of that year, while the prowar ad he had signed was running, Poyer published a revealing story in *Analog*. Titled "Null Zone," this tale combines the two dominant American cultural images of what wins wars: superwarriors and techno-wonders. Its hero is Special Forces lieutenant Philip Schmittzer, a Rambo type who, stalking alone deep in the jungles of Indochina, ambushes and slays innumerable North Vietnamese soldiers who are tracking him, while taking pictures with an infrared camera to augment the computer-generated holograph map back at his base in Thailand. Echoing fantasies prevalent in the Pentagon and the White House, the story argues that America can win the war and secure Southeast Asia merely by blocking the Ho Chi Minh Trail: "Its importance to the North Vietnamese is such that their entire military efforts in South East Asia must collapse if this route is successfully interdicted." Poyer goes so far as to assert that the United States should never agree to a peace accord until this supply route is permanently nullified. So Lieutenant Schmittzer receives—and heroically carries out—his greatest mission: clearing the ground for an impenetrable "Null Zone" formed by airdrops of "deadly radioactive waste."[21]

Another signer of the 1968 prowar ad was Jerry Pournelle, who was to emerge from the 1970s through the end of the century as the loudest, most strident voice in science fiction exalting militarism and worshipping the complementary cults of the superweapon and the mercenary. Although his first outright science fiction would not appear until 1971, Pournelle in 1970 co-authored with right-wing ideologue Stefan Possony (then a colleague of mine on the faculty of Stanford University) a technowar apologia titled *The Strategy of Technology,* which may best be comprehended as science fiction. (In mid-1995 Pournelle was co-authoring with then–Speaker of the House Newt Gingrich a science-fiction novel about a future war based on weaponry proposed in *The Strategy of Technology,* a project that may have been abandoned because Gingrich's first science-fiction novel bombed when published that year.)[22]

Pournelle and Possony's prescription for victory in Vietnam bestows powers on nuclear weapons even more wondrous than those conjured up by Poyer. After claiming that the United States had held the remote outpost at Khe Sanh because "B-52s smashed the Communist positions and inflicted heavy casualties," they argue: "The B-52s dropped about 30 megatons of TNT munitions. If we had used some 3 megatons of small nuclear bombs with a strong neutron flux, we could have lifted the siege of Khe Sanh in one or two hours and we would have crippled the North Vietnamese divisions for a long while to come. We might have won the war in the Khe Sanh engagement."[23] The alleged "facts" on which the fantasy is based are themselves dubious: there is little evidence that "heavy casualties" were suffered by the besiegers; Khe Sanh was not held, but was evacuated under fire.[24] Pournelle and Possony's belief that B-52s dropped thirty megatons of munitions on the Khe Sanh besiegers reveals how far out of touch with material reality the technowarriors can soar. It would have taken almost a million B-52 sorties to drop thirty megatons of high explosives, which would have amounted to fifteen times the total tonnage dropped by the United States throughout World War II. So the imagined nuclear alternative is merely an expansion of the fantasy into a realm—like the magic empire in Heinlein's *Glory Road*—where one can simply dispense with such nuisances as facts and logic and probabilities. "We might have won the war" if we had dropped "some 3 megatons of small nuclear bombs with a strong neutron flux" near Khe Sanh is about as valid a proposition as the statement that we might have won the war if the Empress of the Twenty Universes had personally intervened. This technological mumbo-jumbo has the same function as the warp drives and phaser shields that allow science-fiction spaceships to travel faster than light and conquer alien evil empires.

If the technowarriors of the Pentagon, White House, and *Analog* were possessed by their fantasies, New Wave science fiction sought to exorcise them through alternative visions. Norman Spinrad, one of the signers of the antiwar ad, offered a splendid example of this contradictory mode of fantasy in his apocalyptic 1969 story "The Big Flash," which deeply probes the sources of the urge to use nuclear weapons to "win the war" in Vietnam.

In Spinrad's tale, a demonic rock group called the Four Horsemen bursts upon the late 1960s American scene. Sporting swastikas and "a shrunken head," garbed in the clothes of the counterculture, and peering from "eyes that looked something like a morgue," the Four Horsemen swiftly climb from a sleazy rock club called the Mandala to "a network-owned joint" named the American Dream. The Four Horsemen seem to offer the perfect solution to those who, like General Westmoreland and Jerry Pournelle, believed that they could win the war with tactical nuclear weapons if they were not hamstrung by public opinion.* Since the band's whole repertoire consists of orgiastic numbers that mesmerize their audience into lust for "the big flash," the administration and Pentagon plan to use them to remold public opinion into a clamor for nuclear weapons. Businessmen searching for new sales stimuli, promoters greedy for bucks, network executives groveling before big advertisers, a think tank guru who uses the pseudo-rational

---

*As opposed to strategic nuclear weapons, which are designed for annihilating cities and other "strategic" targets, tactical nuclear weapons, which merely have the destructive power of the Hiroshima and Nagasaki bombs, are intended for battlefield use.

technocratic discourse of a Possony or Pournelle — all become tools of the Four Horsemen's media blitz. The aerospace companies sponsor their huge televised concerts to win over "precisely that element of the population which was most adamantly opposed to nuclear weapons." The campaign succeeds — demonstrations fade away and zeal for nuclear weapons surges — though far beyond the dreams of the sponsors, who never do get to use their tactical nukes on Vietnam. Possessed by the Four Horsemen's overpowering beat and images and command to "Do it!" the missilemen in the ICBM silos and the SLBM-armed submarines launch their intercontinental strategic rockets armed with vastly more potent thermonuclear warheads, thus initiating the annihilation of the human species. Evidently America has been not using but being used by this demonic group, which is no mere rock band with a weird name but the actual Four Horsemen of the Apocalypse.[25]

Spinrad's story, by contrast, is using, not being used by, fantasy. Whereas Poyer, Pournelle, and Possony try to convince their readers that dropping nuclear weapons would *really* allow us to "win the war," Spinrad does not expect his readers to believe that the Four Horsemen of the Apocalypse might *really* appear in the guise of a rock band. But if they did, he suggests, isn't it plausible that the military-industrial-political powers would collude with them to make us stop worrying and love the bomb, thus helping them hurl us into thermonuclear apocalypse?

Combined with the illusions of technowar and Special Forces was yet another official U.S. fantasy, one glowing with liberal ideological colors. This was epitomized in the slogan "Winning Hearts and Minds," whose true meaning, soon recognized in GI jokes, was succinctly expressed by its acronym: WHAM.

"Winning Hearts and Minds" reached its climax in 1968 and 1969, when the CIA conducted a gigantic carrot-and-stick campaign aimed at reestablishing control in some of the countryside lost during the Tet offensive. The stick was Operation Phoenix, a massive program of torture and assassination designed to root out the insurgent infrastructure. U.S. intelligence officers subsequently testified before Congress that not one of the many "Viet Cong suspects" whose arrest they witnessed ever survived interrogation; the death toll from Phoenix ran well into the tens of thousands.[26] The carrot was a so-called land reform program that coopted Lenin's slogan "Land to the Tiller." It was designed and run by University of Washington law professor Roy L. Prosterman, who also drew up the document that asserted a legal basis for

Operation Phoenix.[27] In 1980, five years after the last U.S.-sponsored forces were overwhelmed in Vietnam, Prosterman, again functioning in a CIA operation, was given the job of implementing his "Land to the Tiller" program in El Salvador. In 1970, between these two attempts to impose his American fantasies on other peoples, Prosterman wrote a science-fiction story, "Peace Probe," which was published in the July 1973 issue of *Analog*, a few months after the U.S. agreed to withdraw all its combat forces from Vietnam and to pay $4 billion in war reparations to the Democratic Republic of Vietnam.[28]

Prosterman's tale expresses the overarching fantasy that was being frustrated by Vietnam, the vision of a world entirely subservient to American intentions, which, of course, are always purely benign. After two unnamed nations convulse the world in a 1978 nuclear and bacteriological war, the U.S. president, being "a very good and a very wise man," issues a "Unilateral Declaration" stipulating that "any nation, entity or person other than the United States" found to possess any "weapons of mass destruction" or "such other weapons, armies and armaments as the President of the United States shall from time to time designate" shall be utterly annihilated by the United States. To enforce this decree, he establishes the Unilateral Declaration Agency (UDA), which is authorized to use drugs and "other techniques" to "probe" the minds of "officials and citizens" throughout the world, "without limitation as to persons, times or places" so as to guarantee that the world will remain perpetually under the sway of this Pax Americana. This vision of a global Operation Phoenix is narrated by a heroic UDA agent who ferrets out a plot by some renegade Argentines to force the United States to deal with other nations "as 'equals.' " By using chemical interrogation to unmask the conspirators, he spares the entire population of Argentina in the nick of time from righteous thermonuclear incineration by the UDA.[29]

Just as Prosterman's "Peace Probe" reveals in the form of science fiction the interchangeability of "very good" U.S. intentions with genocidal U.S. practices, events in post-Tet Vietnam displayed to tens of millions of Americans how the benign appearance of "Winning Hearts and Minds" translated into rampant terror and slaughter. The most infamous example occurred in the province of Quang Ngai, an NLF stronghold, where U.S. forces by late 1967 had already destroyed 70 percent of the villages.[30] In the aftermath of Tet, units of the Americal Division were sent by their commanders on a rampage of arson, rape, and murder through the remaining rural settlements of Quang Ngai, including the village of My Lai. Because photographs of the My Lai massacre were sold to *Life* magazine, and because some U.S. soldiers testified to the atrocities, the American public learned that American soldiers had gone through the village murdering some five hundred unarmed civilians while systematically raping and sodomizing the women and girls, butchering the animals, and using babies and small children for target practice.[31]

Perhaps the finest work of art memorializing My Lai — and other devastated hamlets glimpsed on American TV — is Kate Wilhelm's short story "The Village." With dozens of volumes of fiction published since the early 1960s, Kate Wilhelm has long been a preeminent figure in science fiction, and her mainstream fiction has won an ever-widening audience and ever-increasing admiration. Her account of the writing and publication of "The Village" reveals much about the times: "When I heard the report on My Lai on the radio, I was so upset I couldn't sleep. I had an infant then. I paced the floor until near dawn. I vowed that the next day I would write *something* about this. Then I finally fell asleep. When I awoke, the story was just *there*. I wrote it in a passion, a white heat. I didn't edit it at all." Despite her prominence and success, Wilhelm ran into a stone wall when she tried to sell the story: "I couldn't get it published. I sent it around to everyone I could think of. The last one was an editor who said that the story certainly *should* be published but that he *could* not do it."[32] "The Village" was finally published almost five years later, when Tom Disch included it in his seminal 1973 New Wave anthology, *Bad Moon Rising*.

Comparable to Picasso's *Guernica* mural, which also used nonrealistic conventions to portray a reality deemed too atrocious for realism, "The Village" uses the science-fiction convention of transposing realistic surfaces into an unfamiliar time-space zone. The village of the title has two referents, one Vietnamese, the other American, and the story deftly crosscuts between the two scenes.

The tale opens in an all-American town which is experiencing a strange heat wave that makes festering problems and petty antagonisms leak through the placid surface of everyday life. There is a stink of dead fish from the local paper mill's pollution, plants seem unhealthy, inflation stalks the local market, the glare is more oppressive because maples have been cut down to widen the main street, and staid townspeople are appalled by some young people's marijuana, long hair, and lack of bras. Mildred Carey, whose son Mark is due back from the war in a few weeks, complains to her husband about some omnipo-

The Vietnamese scene interwoven with this domestic fabric is told
from the point of view of an American company ordered to conduct a
"search-and-clear" sweep through a village. Here too the heat is overwhelming, and the men begin to suspect that their own omnipotent
"they" don't know what they are doing: "They've got us lost, the bas-
tards. This fucken road ain't even on their fucken map" (153). But this
may not make much difference, because "one fucken village is just like
the others" (147), and their helicopters will give them lots of air cover.

The two scenes come together as green and brown helicopters—
"monstrous machines"—appear over the American village, gunning
down people in the street. Now the point of view shifts rapidly back and
forth between the American soldiers, who of course cannot comprehend a word spoken by the villagers whom they beat, rape, and ran-
domly shoot, and the American villagers, who are dismayed to discover
that the U.S.-uniformed soldiers who are beating, raping, and ran-
domly shooting them do not speak English but mouth some sort of incomprehensible "gibberish." "What are you doing here?" screams Mildred Carey, "You're American soldiers! What are you doing?" (155).
Trying to stop a gang rape, an old townsman futilely shouts that the
soldiers are brutalizing "the wrong town" (156).[34]

Wilhelm's fantasy of a time-space zone where America and Vietnam
merge poignantly expresses a growing consciousness that America's
war against Vietnam was coming home. Perhaps the most compressed
fantasy projecting what America's war against Vietnam was doing to
America is a fourteen-line poem by Steve Hassett, who served as an
infantryman and intelligence analyst in Vietnam:

> And what would you do, ma,
> if eight of your sons step
> out of the TV and begin
> killing chickens and burning
> hooches in the living room,
> stepping on booby traps
> and dying in the kitchen,
> beating your husband and
> taking him and shooting
> skag and forgetting in
> the bathroom?

would you lock up your daughter?
would you stash the apple pie?
would you change channels?[35]

Here American troops are both victimizers and victims, roles merged in the verb "shooting" which ends the ninth line. We first imagine them shooting "your husband," but it is themselves they are shooting with heroin as they try to forget their Vietnamese nightmare. The fantasy of America's sons stepping out of the TV to threaten ma and apple pie turns out to be the reality, which can be denied only by switching to fantasies on other channels.

In Ronald Anthony Cross's story "The Heavenly Blue Answer," a returning veteran discovers that America itself has somehow become "Orientalized." Amid all the "karate and kung fu and Thai boxing schools," Vietnamese restaurants, and "weird kids in orange robes [who] danced in the streets chanting Hindu mantras," he senses "the essence of Orientalism" as "a sort of melting of the borders, of all the borders, so that everything ran together." Haunted by the memory of the incomplete dying words of an old man he had killed in Vietnam, which sounded like "I am . . . ," he at last hears the final word from a Coke bottle in the gutter: "You. I am you."[36]

In Lewis Shiner's story "The War at Home," the protagonist has flashbacks of combat in which he never participated; his wife wears fashionable black pajamas and a conical straw hat; bamboo erupts in his garden; a supermarket massacre is carried out by a "gun nut" wielding an M-16 and shouting, "You're all fucking gooks' "; and finally America itself is transformed into a surrealist Vietnam:

> I walk through the haunted streets of my town, sweltering in the January heat. The jungle arches over me; children's voices in the distance chatter in their weird pidgin Vietnamese. The TV station is a crumbling ruin and none of us feel comfortable any more. We work now in a thatched hut with a mimeo machine.
>
> The air is humid, fragrant with anticipation. Soon the planes will come and it will begin in earnest.[37]

Alienation is taken even further in *The Forever War,* by wounded Vietnam combat engineer Joe Haldeman, perhaps the biggest best-seller of all novels about the Vietnam War. Despite widespread admiration among science-fiction critics and sales of well over a million copies, *The Forever War* is generally ignored by surveys and criticism of Vietnam

War literature.[38] The novel is a kind of autobiography in fantastic disguise (its protagonist is William Mandela, an anagram of William [H]aldeman, the author's middle and last names). It extrapolates both kinds of extreme alienation experienced by U.S. veterans — first as alien invaders of a foreign land, then as aliens returning to what no longer seems their own society — into the experience of becoming both extraterrestrial invaders of alien planets and exiles in time and space from planet Earth.

The Forever War fantasizes and extrapolates America's longest war into a 1,143-year intergalactic combat instigated by generals and politicians, waged for profit, and conducted as a devastating fiasco from beginning to end. A fabricated attack by the "Taurans" on a Terran spaceship, like the fabricated attack by North Vietnamese on U.S. ships in the Gulf of Tonkin, serves as the pretext for ordering attacks on Tauran ships and sending troops to invade an alien land, here a strange planet. When the Terrans encounter the inhabitants of the planet — harmless, possibly intelligent, telepathic vegetarians — they massacre them, recalling the U.S. campaign to slaughter all the elephants in Vietnam. Reflecting on the heartless carnage of these "aliens," Mandela begins to sense what he is becoming: "But they weren't aliens, I had to remind myself — we were."[39] The Terrans butcher every single Tauran they encounter in the first actual contact between the two species, mirroring the U.S. slaughter at My Lai and countless other Vietnamese villages. Most of the deaths suffered by the soldiers from Earth result from their traumatic revulsion against what the military and their government have made them do: "They conditioned us to kill anything that *moved,* once the sergeant triggered the conditioning with a few key words. When people came out of it, they couldn't handle the memory. Being a butcher" (104–5).

Haldeman explodes the pet practices and illusions of U.S. militarism by taking them to absurdly fantastic dimensions. The boot camp transformation of civilians into master killers, the officers molded by military academies into battlefield Clausewitzs, the Herculean feats of production and logistics, and unrestrained technowar all lead nowhere but to a convergence of Terran society with the civilization Earth has defined as its enemy. Haldeman delights in twisting the futuristic hardware and adventure formulas of old-fashioned militaristic science fiction into their opposite. Inventions such as a "one-microton" nuclear device (186) are described in the "Wow! Gosh!" style of combat fiction, inviting heedless bomb-loving readers — the personality type that craved nukes for Vietnam — to overlook the fact that they are being thrilled by an imaginary weapon with the force of one thirtieth of an ounce of TNT: a firecracker. The interface between human beings and the technology of devastation, so electrifying to technophiliacs, here serves to reduce people to killing machines, a fate foreshadowed when Mandela just before his first combat "dreamed that I was a machine, mimicking the functions of life" (48). Ultimately the greatest marvels of technowar create a "stasis field" on a remote, useless planet where Terrans and Taurans must slaughter one another with arrows and swords, not knowing that the war has long since ended. Whether flashing nova bombs or swords, this glory road leads to a renunciation of infantile fantasies such as Heinlein's, in which killing is the most gratifying human activity.

Ursula Le Guin wrote *The Word for World Is Forest* in 1968, the year her name appeared in the anti–Vietnam War advertisement in the science-fiction magazines, partly as an interpretation of the war's meaning.[40] The novella shifts at crucial points to the perspective of an extraterrestrial forest people subjected to global pillage and rape and genocide by men from Earth. From this point of view, the kinds of fantasies that governed U.S. political and military decision making in Vietnam appear as expressions of alienation not just from historical reality but also from humanity, nature, and sanity.

The Word for World Is Forest projects in the form of science fiction a quintessential vision of the Vietnam War as fantasy and science fiction. For it poses against each other the subconscious imperialist fantasies that dominated the U.S. war and the conscious anti-imperialist fantasies that developed in opposition to it.

In Le Guin's story the men from Earth, like the U.S. leaders of the Vietnam War, are possessed by fantasies of themselves as rational, civilized, self-controlled, superior beings, wielding irresistible technology which makes them masters of all other life forms, including not only the flora and fauna of the alien planet, but also the females of the human species and the images that appear in their own dreams. As Captain Don Davidson, who embodies the fantasy in its most unmitigated form, puts it, supremacy is all "a matter of will, skill, and weaponry."[41] This slogan could summarize the science fiction written by such apologists for the war as Jerry Pournelle, Joe Poyer, and Roy Prosterman.

Rather than denying and burying their unconscious, the small, green, furry Athsheans cultivate that part of life they spend in dream time, allowing the insights gained there to interpenetrate with those they derive from what they call "world time." Just as their word for "world" is also their word for "forest," their word for "dream" is also their word for "root." They embody harmony between the human and the natural, and a sane wholeness of the intellectual and emotional components of consciousness. To them, the colonists from Earth, possessed by their own uncontrolled dream selves, seeking escape from the prison of their own barren consciousness in hallucinogenic drugs, seem terminally sick: "The yumens poison themselves in order to dream. . . . But they couldn't call the dreams, nor control them, nor weave nor shape nor cease to dream; they were driven, overpowered" (104). Controlled by fantasies they are unable to shape, the invaders are so dangerously insane that the Athsheans must kill them to survive.

On another level, *The Word for World Is Forest* suggests that the nearest counterparts in our society to the Athshean dream weavers are the fantasists who seek to introduce a visionary dimension into our perception of daily and historical life, and into our conduct within that life. Thus fantasy and science fiction conceived in response to the Vietnam War are offered as an antidote to the science fiction and fantasies from which it materialized.

In the 1980s, as another Vietnam War seemed to be smoldering in Latin America while U.S. culture bubbled with militarist fantasies, some oppositional science fiction responded with increasingly apocalyptic visions of the war and its aftermath. A leading figure here is Lucius Shepard, whose special blend of science fiction and magic realism mixes the Vietnam War of the past, the Latin American "low-intensity conflict" of the 1980s, and a future combining the most grotesque elements of both.

In his 1987 story "Delta Sly Honey," one of Shepard's few works actually set in Vietnam, he portrays "a war twisted into a demonic exercise." "In Vietnam, with all its horror and strangeness," the narrator explains, "it was difficult to distinguish between the magical and the mundane, and it's possible that thousands of supernatural events went unnoticed as such." Yet "I'm certain," he confesses, "that I want there to have been some magic involved, anything to lessen my culpability, to shed a less damaging light on the perversity and viciousness of my brothers-in-arms."[42] This revelation suggests how and why Shepard uses the fantastic to mediate between us and a reality too appalling to handle.

The society left in the wake of the war is explored in Shepard's 1985 story "Mengele." The narrator, a former spotter pilot in Vietnam, has come home to find a postwar America that incarnates "the triumph of evil": "In the combat zones and shooting galleries, in the bombed-looking districts of urban decay, in the violent music and the cities teeming with derelicts and burned-out children, I saw reflected the energies that had created Vietnam."[43] If the bland, safe, prosperous society that so alienates the hero of *Glory Road* is a before-Vietnam picture of America, this is a picture of America after Vietnam.

Yet the narrator of "Mengele" is just as alienated as Heinlein's hero, and his first response is similar. Seized by a desire "to soar above decay," he goes into the business of ferrying small planes, no questions asked, "the farther away the better" (330). Forced to crash-land in the rain forest of Paraguay, he encounters what appears to be the fiendish Nazi experimenter of Auschwitz, Dr. Joseph Mengele, who has rejuvenated himself and created a legion of deformed monstrosities. In this modern version of "The Island of Dr. Moreau," the mad scientist differs from H. G. Wells's prototype in two respects: he embodies pure evil, and he exists in historical reality. Returning to New York, the narrator now understands that the society around him has succumbed to the most hideous fantasies of science and power gone insane, that "Mengele had won, that *his* principle, not ours, was in accord with the times" (342).

Shepard's extrapolation of the evolving Vietnam in Latin America into a future nightmare where devastating technology is under the control of unrestrained depravity is presented most succinctly in his 1984 story "Salvador." Here each member of the U.S. Special Forces trying to crush the revolution in El Salvador can instantly turn himself into a superwarrior like Rambo or the hero of Heinlein's *Glory Road*—just by popping a couple of ampules of standard-issue designer drugs. Under the influence of these magic chemicals, Dantzler, the protagonist, finds himself "marveling at his efficiency, at the comic-strip enthusiasm he felt for the task of killing."[44] His platoon leader "DT," who has painted the words "DIE HIGH" on his helmet, "collects trophies," "not just ears like they done in 'Nam," but dried testicles (65). As DT murders a teenage prisoner by pushing him out of a helicopter—a familiar scene from the Vietnam War—he makes a grotesque joke that suggests how the space-travel fantasies of mid-twentieth-century science fiction metamorphosed through *Star Trek* and the Apollo program into their bleakly sardonic sequels: " 'Space!' shouted DT, giving the kid a little shove. 'The final frontier!' " (67).

The Americans "waste" a village in Morazán Province, a place where "dreams afflicted everyone" (67). Possessed by guilt, paranoia, and the magical spirits that seem to haunt the mountain cloud forest through which they trek, Dantzler is soon popping combat drugs just to function. While on nighttime guard duty, his chemical fantasies and the phantasmagoric reality of El Salvador merge, as though the dreams of Le Guin's Athsheans — or her own morally controlled fantasy — could interpenetrate and dominate the murderous fantasies of these alpha male killers. Firing in every direction at the accusing apparitions around him, Dantzler blindly slaughters his sleeping platoon and then completes the operation by methodically killing the other sentries, including his crazed leader, DT.

Later, when Dantzler is back home, a friend who has been drafted implores him to come to a send-off party at a garish rock club to explain to him "what it's like, man" (81). At the end, ready to "explain about the war," Dantzler becomes its incarnation. As he prepares to enter the club, the explosive neon sign that spells out the club's name seems to recreate the hallucinations that had possessed him in the cloud forest, and the building itself merges with the enveloping blackness into which he had fired in his murderous panic. So he carefully adjusts the survival knife he has hidden in his boot and takes out two combat ampules he had secreted the night of his killing frenzy. The story ends with these words: "To be on the safe side, he popped them both." That old image of manly Buck Rogers fighting with futuristic technology against the alien hordes was giving way to this more up-to-date paradigm of post-Vietnam American warriors.

Indeed, in the decades after the war, legions of science-fiction superwarriors stormed forth amid the militaristic frenzy that sought to redeem American wonder weapons and American "manhood."[45] The heroic mercenary of Heinlein's *Glory Road* would no longer feel so lonely and alienated now that bestselling authors such as Jerry Pournelle and David A. Drake, a former U.S. Army interrogator in Vietnam, have created an entire science-fiction industry dedicated to glorifying mercenaries and their war making. At the same time, the opposing visions heralded during the Vietnam War by the New Wave have flowed into a vast sea of science fiction, including some of the more ambitious works of late twentieth-century American literature, filled with profound insights into possible human destinies in cosmic space and time — and fundamentally hostile to the militarist fantasies endemic to modern American culture.

Take, for example, Kurt Vonnegut, Jr., whose apocalyptic forebodings were intensified in the 1980s and 1990s by his sense of looming ecological disaster, deepening global poverty, proliferating superweapons, and the erasure of the truths of the Vietnam War. Each of his two major works of this period — *Galápagos* (1985) and *Hocus Pocus* (1990) — is a science-fiction novel narrated by a Vietnam veteran who has personally committed atrocities. Not merely complicit in American irrationality and destructiveness, these two narrators are for Vonnegut representatives of our epoch and our destiny.

After killing a toothless grandmother in Vietnam, the narrator of *Galápagos* joins with his platoon in burning down her village and massacring all its inhabitants, and then later deserts to Sweden. He narrates the novel as a ghost who oscillates between 1986, when the human species is almost annihilated, and a million years in the future, when we have evolved into furry seal-like creatures with flippers, webbed feet, and a brain too small to imagine much less implement the catastrophes that led to our demise.

Galápagos is a remorseless application of Darwinian logic. The large brains of our species turn out to be an evolutionary dead end, because they make us capable of inflicting so much devastation on one another and our environment. These brains bring about an apocalypse, with war, disease, and starvation cutting down all but ten survivors who chance to land on the Galápagos islands, the very place where Darwin began to construct his grand theory. Contrary to Darwin's vision of progressive evolution and to the techno-future projected in much science fiction, *Galápagos* offers our descendants, who flourish by catching their fishy dinners in their mouths, as ironic proof of the survival of the fittest. No longer having hands to do harm, they have lost the parts of the brain needed to control hands, thus making the human skull more streamlined, and "the more streamlined the skull, the more successful the fisher person."[46]

Set in the year 2001, *Hocus Pocus* offers a brooding reply to the movie *2001* and its conventional science-fiction vision of space travel and alien contact as the culmination of human destiny. The narrator of the novel, formerly a lieutenant colonel in the Vietnam War, imprisoned and racked with tuberculosis in the grimy near future, makes the comparison explicit when he tells us that while in Vietnam he twice saw "the movie *2001*, the very year in which I am writing and coughing now."[47]

That 1968 film projected the macrohistory of our species as an epic of progress from ape to cosmic voyager, aided at crucial stages by alien superbeings who stimulate our technology and guide us into space for the next phase of our upward evolution. In *Hocus Pocus,* the macrohistory of our species is a debacle of genocide and ecocide influenced by alien superbeings who see our extermination as a precondition for the evolution of cosmic voyagers. This history is sketched by "The Protocols of the Elders of Tralfamadore," an anonymous science-fiction story the narrator discovers in a soft-porn magazine. Some "intelligent threads of energy" want to concoct self-reproducing life forms that will spread throughout the Universe. Recognizing that only microorganisms would be capable of interstellar travel and knowing that no germs tough enough to withstand such trips had yet evolved, they decide to use a ferocious big-brained creature that had evolved on Earth to turn the planet into a laboratory for creating the cosmic superbugs. The purpose of human existence thus becomes making Earth into such a toxic lethal environment that the only surviving life forms will be microorganisms resistant to the worst vicissitudes of space travel.

By 2001, we seem to be well on our way to achieving our mission on this "whole ruined planet" (24). The narrator himself, who had ordered white phosphorus and napalm attacks on Vietnam and personally killed villagers and prisoners, tells one of many women he brags of seducing: "If I were a fighter plane instead of a human being, there would be little pictures of people painted all over me" (124). His own dismal fate is sealed when he is fired from his professorship at a college for stupid children of the ruling class because he has been undermining "the students' faith in the intelligence and decency of their country's leadership by telling them the truth about the Vietnam War" (230).

Those rival prowar and antiwar ads of 1968 have proved to be symptoms of deep cracks and splits, within science fiction and the society at large, that cannot be plastered over. The nostalgia for a lost community expressed back then by Frederik Pohl today seems hopelessly anachronistic if not downright myopic.

As for science fiction, it has become ever more central to American culture, as I have discussed at length in several books. One of the more obvious and revealing manifestations is the role of *Star Wars.* Whereas the Vietnam-era *Star Trek* series projected a future defined by space travel, the post-Vietnam *Star Wars* movies have abandoned this future for myths of the past: the films, set "long ago in a galaxy far, far away," have been consciously designed to evoke pre–World War II science fiction and World War II imagery, and center on a cult of "Jedi knights" endowed with supernatural powers. The billion-dollar *Star Wars* culture industry is dwarfed, however, by the billions of dollars spent each year on a bizarre science-fiction fantasy, the Star Wars shield designed to make America invulnerable to nuclear-armed missiles.

Meanwhile, the Vietnam War itself has been transformed into a direct source of fantasies central to American culture. The most outlandish does not appear in science fiction. It has been constructed by several presidents, ostensibly realistic movies, TV documentaries and soap operas, state legislatures, veterans' organizations, and every postwar Congress. It is a fantasy so potent that it has become virtually a national religion: the myth of Americans held captive in Vietnam after the war.

when the first missing man
walks alive out of that green tangle
of rumors and lies,
I shall lie
down silent as a jungle shadow
and dream the sound of insects
gnawing bones.
  W. D. Ehrhart, "POW/MIA"

CHAPTER NINE

Missing in Action in the Twenty-first Century

The red, white, and blue flag of the United States originated in the American Revolution, and its stars represent, in the words of the 1777 Continental Congress, "a new constellation." The Vietnam War has given the United States a second national flag, the black and white POW/MIA flag.

That flag is the only one besides the Star-Spangled Banner that has ever flown over the White House, where it has fluttered once a year since 1982. As visitors from around the world stream through the Rotunda of the U.S. Capitol, they pass a giant POW/MIA flag, the only flag that has ever been displayed amid the epic paintings and heroic statues, given this position of honor in 1987 by the Congress and president of the United States. Thanks to a law passed by Congress and signed by the president in 1997, the POW/MIA flag must fly several times a year over every U.S. post office (and many post offices fly it all year long). During the 1980s and 1990s, the legislatures and governors of each of the fifty states issued laws mandating the display of this flag over public facilities such as state offices, municipal buildings, toll plazas, and police headquarters. The POW/MIA flag also hangs over the trading floor of the New York Stock Exchange, waves at countless corporate headquarters, shopping malls, union halls, and small businesses. It is sewn onto the right sleeve of the official Ku Klux Klan white robe and adorns millions of bumper stickers, buttons, windows, motorcycle jackets, watches, postcards, coffee mugs, T-shirts, and Christmas tree ornaments.

The flag thus symbolizes our nation's veneration of its central image, a handsome American prisoner of war, his silhouetted head slightly bowed to reveal behind him the ominous shape of a looming guard tower. A strand of barbed wire cuts across just below his firm chin. Underneath runs the motto: YOU ARE NOT FORGOTTEN.

This colorless banner implies that the Vietnam War may never end. It demonstrates to the world both the official United States government position since 1973 and a profoundly influential national belief: Vietnam may still secretly hold American prisoners of war. This was the official reason why every postwar administration — Nixon, Ford, Carter, Reagan, Bush, and Clinton — reneged on the 1973 treaty pledge that the United States would help rebuild Vietnam and instead waged relentless economic and political warfare against that nation for decades. Even when President Clinton announced in 1995 that Washington was finally establishing diplomatic relations with Vietnam, he claimed the primary motive was to further "progress on the issue of Americans who were missing in action or held as prisoners of war."[1]

To begin to understand what this all means, it is first necessary to recognize that there is simply no rational basis or evidence for the belief that Americans are still imprisoned in Vietnam. Indeed, it runs counter to reason, common sense, and all evidence.

None of the armed forces has listed a single prisoner of war (POW) or even a single person missing in action (MIA) since 1994, when the only person still listed as a prisoner, for "symbolic" reasons, was reclassified as deceased at the request of his family. There are, it is true, 2,020 Americans listed as "unaccounted for" from the war in Vietnam, Laos, and Cambodia, but not one of these is classified as a prisoner, a possible prisoner, or even missing. Most of the "unaccounted for" were *never* listed as POW or even MIA because well over half were originally *known* to have been killed in action in circumstances where their bodies could not be recovered. Their official designation has always been "KIA/BNR": Killed in Action/Body Not Recovered. Crews of airplanes that exploded in flight or crashed within sight of their aircraft carrier, soldiers whose deaths were witnessed by others unable to retrieve their bodies, or men blown apart so completely that there were no retrievable body parts—all these are listed in the total of "unaccounted for." All that is missing is their *remains*. This KIA/BNR category was never included with the missing in action during the Vietnam War; it was lumped together with the POW/MIA category only after the 1973 Paris Peace Accords were signed.

The confusion thus created was quite deliberate. But this miasma was relatively mild compared to that generated by the "POW/MIA" concoction itself. Arguably the cagiest stroke of the Nixon presidency was the slash forever linking "POW" and "MIA." In all previous wars there was one category, "prisoners of war," consisting of those known or believed to be prisoners. There was an entirely separate and distinct category of those "missing in action." The Pentagon internally maintained these as two separate categories throughout the war and its aftermath. But for popular consumption, the Nixon administration publicly jumbled the two categories together into a hodgepodge called POW/MIA precisely in order *to make it seem that every missing person might possibly be a prisoner.* Because this possibility cannot be logically disproved, the POW/MIA invention perfectly fulfilled its original purpose: to create an issue that could never be resolved.

It also created an almost impenetrable fog of confusion that clouds the issue right up to the present. Although prisoners of war were not previously considered either missing or unaccounted for, once the MIAs became defined as possible POWs, then all the "POW/MIAs" could be dumped into the category "unaccounted for," which then became synonymous in the popular mind with "POW/MIA." So when it is reported that there are still more than two thousand "unaccounted for" from the Vietnam War, people assume that any or all of them might still be languishing in Vietnamese prisons. "MIA" and "POW" and "unaccounted for" have even become interchangeable terms, as manifested by a question I am frequently asked, usually in an incredulous tone, "Don't you believe there are MIAs?"—or, even more revealing, "Don't you believe in MIAs?"

In all major wars, many combatants die without being identified or having their bodies recovered. There are more than 8,100 unaccounted for from the Korean War and 78,794 still unaccounted for from World War II. So the total of 2,020 unaccounted for in the Indochina war is astonishingly small, especially since 81 percent of the missing were airmen mainly lost over the ocean, mountains, or tropical rain forest, many in planes that exploded. In fact, the proportion of unaccounted-for Americans to the total killed in action is far smaller for the Indochina war than for any previous war in the nation's history, even though this was its longest war and ended with the battlefields in the possession of the enemy. For World War II, after which the United States was free to explore every battlefield, those still unaccounted for represent 21.8 percent of the total killed in combat. For the Korean War, more than 24 percent of the combat dead were never found. In contrast, the unaccounted for from the Indochina war constitute only 3.4 percent of those killed in combat. To get another perspective on these numbers, consider the fact that on the other side there are between 200,000 and 300,000 Vietnamese missing in action.

During the war, the Pentagon listed as a POW anyone reported as *possibly* being held prisoner anywhere in Vietnam, Laos, Cambodia, or China at any time from 1963 to 1973, whether or not there was credible evidence of capture and even if there was evidence of subsequent death. After the 1973 Peace Accords, all but fifty-six prisoners on the Pentagon's internal lists were either released or reported to have died in captivity. In the following years, intensive analysis resolved each of these remaining cases. Except for one man who had defected, all had died. The one defector, Robert Garwood, is the only captured person who survived the war and was not returned to the United States during Operation Homecoming in 1973.

Despite many investigations by congressional committees, federal agencies, and private organizations, there has yet to be a shred of verifiable or even credible evidence that any American POWs were withheld by Vietnam. Debriefing of all the returning POWs, ongoing aerial and satellite reconnaissance, covert raids, as well as interrogations of thousands of Vietnamese refugees and defectors, including high-ranking military and intelligence officials, all point to one conclusion: except for Garwood, there were no surviving POWs. Even offers of huge rewards—currently amounting to well over $2 million—have produced nothing but waves of phony pictures, fake dog tags, and other bogus "evidence."

Then there is the question of motive. Why in the world would Vietnam keep U.S. prisoners for years and decades after the war?

To torture them, of course, a perfectly plausible motive, given the inscrutable cruelty of Asians—as depicted in a century and a half of Yellow Peril propaganda in American culture, including countless Hollywood images. Besides, these Asians are communists, so add half a century of Red Menace propaganda, and no further explanation is needed. One ostensibly more rational motive is offered by POW/MIA evangelists: the prisoners are being used as "hostages" or "bargaining chips." But what good are hostages to a nation that denies holding any? How can you bargain with a chip that you swear doesn't exist?

A belief that runs counter to reason, common sense, and all evidence but that is widely and deeply held by a society is a myth — in the fullest and most rigorous sense. A myth is a story of ostensibly historic events or beings crucial to the worldview and self-image of a people, a story that appears as essential truth to its believers, no matter how bizarre it may seem from outside that society or when subjected to rational analysis. Indeed, myths must defy commonplace plausibility and transcend everyday logic. Myths are often central to cultures, and may be their most distinctive feature, which is why many anthropologists and archaeologists find them so essential to understanding a society.

To comprehend the POW/MIA myth, we need to trace its history. For the first fifteen years of U.S. covert and overt combat in Vietnam — that is, from 1954 to 1969 — there was not even a POW/MIA concept. Its seeds were sown in 1968, the year of the Tet offensive and its aftermath, including President Johnson's withdrawal from the election campaign, the assassinations of Martin Luther King, Jr., and Robert Kennedy, the tidal wave of urban rebellion, the opening of peace negotiations in Paris, and the nomination of Richard Nixon as the Republican peace candidate. Remember that in his acceptance speech Nixon declared that "as we look at America, we see cities enveloped in smoke and flame," and then vowed that "if the war is not ended when the people choose in November," "I pledge to you tonight that the first priority foreign policy objective of our next Administration will be to bring an honorable end to the war in Vietnam."[2]

Richard Nixon had no intention of ending the Vietnam War without preserving a U.S. client government in Saigon. But how many Americans in 1968 could have predicted that he would be able to continue the war year after bloody year until 1973? Perhaps even fewer than those who remembered that back in 1954 as vice president he had been the first administration official openly to advocate sending American troops to fight in Vietnam, because, as he put it, "the Vietnamese lack the ability to conduct a war by themselves or govern themselves."

Nixon, however, now faced several formidable problems. Negotiations had already opened in Paris. The Tet offensive had convinced most Americans, and even much of his own Defense Department, that the war was unwinnable. The antiwar movement was growing ever more powerful, domestically and within the armed forces. There was certainly no enthusiasm for the war. What could he do?

What he needed was something to wreck the negotiations, shift the apparent goal of the war, counter the antiwar movement, and generate some zeal for continued combat. Soon after his inauguration, Nixon and an enterprising businessman named H. Ross Perot solved his problem by concocting a brand-new issue: demanding a "full accounting" for Americans missing in action and the release of American prisoners of war as a *precondition* of any peace accord.[3] This was truly a brilliant, albeit demonic, strategy.

The issue created, for the first time, sizable emotional support for the war. It deadlocked the Paris negotiations for four years. It counteracted the antiwar movement. It even provided a basis for continuing economic and political warfare against Vietnam for decades after the United States had conceded defeat.

The POW/MIA issue also neutralized another White House and Pentagon problem that had been building throughout 1968: American revulsion at the torture and murder of the prisoners held by U.S. and Saigon forces.

The fate of Saigon's prisoners had in fact been one of the root causes of the insurgency against the Diem government, whose infamous Law 10/59 (promulgated in 1959) branded those who had fought for independence against France as "Communists, traitors, and agents of Russia and China" and decreed the "sentence of death" for any person actively resisting Diem's rule.[4] The ensuing wholesale arrest, torture, and execution of hundreds of thousands, featuring portable guillotines and displays of victims' heads and intestines on stakes, helped lead in 1960 to the outbreak of organized armed struggle and the formation of the National Liberation Front.[5] As the war developed, anyone even suspected of loyalty to the "Viet Cong" was subject to torture and summary execution. Only in the last few years of the war were any captured combatants accorded a semblance of prisoner of war status.

Two books published in 1968 exposed the barbaric treatment of prisoners by U.S. and Saigon forces: *In the Name of America,* a documentary chronicle of U.S. war crimes in Vietnam by twenty-nine prominent American clergymen, with several sections devoted to the torture, mutilation, and murder of prisoners; and *Against the Crime of Silence,* the proceedings of the 1967 War Crimes Tribunal held in Denmark and Sweden, with extensive testimony by American veterans about their own participation in the systematic torture and execution of prisoners by both U.S. and Saigon soldiers and officials.[6] At the same time, the issue exploded into the consciousness of tens of millions of Americans as they actually watched, in their own homes, the chief of the Saigon national police execute a manacled NLF prisoner.

Americans were soon to witness even worse pictures and accounts of U.S. and Saigon soldiers torturing and slaughtering prisoners, both combatants captured in battle and civilians rounded up in sweeps through hamlets and villages. As early as May 1968 came the first published descriptions of the My Lai massacre of March.[7] The CIA's Phoenix program, designed to wipe out the insurgent infrastructure by imprisoning and assassinating tens of thousands of suspects, was launched in mid-1968; U.S. intelligence officers attached to Phoenix later testified that they never saw any of its prisoners survive interrogation.[8] In violation of the 1949 Geneva Convention Relative to the Treatment of Prisoners of War, soldiers captured by U.S. forces were turned over to the Saigon government, whose appalling prison camps were gradually being exposed to American readers and viewers, most dramatically in Tom Harkin's photographs of the notorious tiger cages of Con Son Island, where the few survivors were almost all permanently disfigured and severely crippled by torture.[9]

The Saigon government's tiger cages would soon be transfigured by American media magic into images of the prison conditions of captured Americans, thus reversing the direction of popular outrage. But neutralizing protest about what was being done to Vietnamese prisoners by Washington and Saigon was merely a bonus from turning American "POW/MIAs" into the main bone of contention with Hanoi.

The first goal was to deadlock the Paris peace talks. Accordingly, five days after Richard Nixon's inauguration, his representative at the talks introduced the POW/MIA issue. A month later, the Defense and State departments began laying the groundwork for a massive campaign at home.

Domestically, the issue was a masterly stroke. After all, how else could any deeply emotional support for the war be generated? Certainly not by holding out the old discredited promises of military victory. And who would be willing to fight and die for the notoriously corrupt generals ruling Saigon? But supporting our own prisoners of war and missing in action was something no loyal American would dare oppose. It also seemed easy to understand, requiring no knowledge of the history of Vietnam and the war. One measure of the campaign's success was the sale of more than 50 million POW/MIA bumper stickers during the next four years.[10]

The Nixon administration's "go public" campaign, designed to "marshal public opinion" for "the prompt release of all American prisoners of war," was initiated on March 1, 1969, and officially launched on May 19.[11] It was immediately and enthusiastically promoted by the media, which, in the relatively restrained language of the *New York Times* editorial staff, denounced "the Communist side" as "inhuman," asserted that "at least half of the 1,300 Americans missing in action in Vietnam are believed to be alive," and insisted that "the prisoner-of-war question is a humanitarian, not a political issue."[12]

Perot was put in charge of building mass support, and he was soon rewarded. Thanks to White House intervention, his EDS Corporation was awarded 90 percent of the computer work on Medicare claims, enabling Perot to become what one writer in 1971 dubbed "the first welfare billionaire."[13]

Perot was to buy "full-page ads in the nation's 100 largest newspapers" and run "United We Stand," a heartwrenching program about POWs, on television stations in fifty-nine cities.[14] Meeting with Perot in the Oval Office, President Nixon approved his plan "to mobilize massive popular support" for the war, including, according to a White House memorandum, a "charter plane to transport to Paris approx. 100 wives and children of American POWs," where they would stage a Christmas vigil "with heavy press and television coverage" to embarrass Hanoi's delegation; appearances by Perot on *Meet the Press,* the *Today Show,* the *Mike Douglas* show and so on; and a major conference to launch the National League of Families.[15]

On November 6, Congress unanimously passed and President Nixon signed a bill declaring November 9 a National Day of Prayer for U.S. prisoners of war in Vietnam. Right on schedule, on November 9 Perot's United We Stand ran full-page advertisements featuring a picture of two small children praying, "Bring our Daddy home safe, sound and soon." Headlined "The Majority Speaks: Release the Prisoners," the ads demanded the immediate release of all American POWs. On November 13 and 14, the House Subcommittee on National Security Policy of the Committee on Foreign Affairs held hearings to denounce "the ruthlessness and cruelty of North Vietnam" and to provide a pep rally for a congressional resolution demanding the release of American POWs.[16] The resolution was passed unanimously by both the Senate and House in December; it was immediately exploited by U.S. negotiators in Paris.[17] Perot soon was off to Vientiane with two chartered jets filled with Christmas presents for the POWs and, according to presidential assistant Alexander Butterfield's report to the president, "reporters from *Time, Life, Newsweek,* AP, UPI, *Los Angeles Times, Reader's Digest, Look, New York Times, Washington Post, Dallas Morning News,* and some five–six other publications." Butterfield then explained how "we were able to give Ross a good bit of behind-the-scenes assistance."[18]

During the campaign's formative months in early 1969, officials from the State and Defense departments flew all over the country to build an organization of family members under the leadership of Sybil Stockdale, whose husband was the highest-ranking naval officer imprisoned in Vietnam, and who herself had been working closely with Naval Intelligence since May 1966.[19] By June, Stockdale had made herself the national coordinator of an organization she christened the National League of Families of American Prisoners in Southeast Asia.[20] With Henry Kissinger advising that our "propaganda offensive in the POW issue" required an ostensibly independent citizens' movement and stressing the need to make it appear that "there is no U.S. Government involvement with the ladies," the White House meticulously choreographed every step in building and using this organization.[21]

In the spring of 1970, Sybil Stockdale received a phone call from Republican senator Robert Dole, who asked whether she could "deliver 1,000 family members" to a POW/MIA "extravaganza" he was planning for May 1 in Constitution Hall if he were to arrange government transportation for them. Dole pledged to orchestrate political support, putting Vice President Spiro Agnew and a bipartisan lineup of senators and representatives on the stage, and having Democratic representative Clement Zablocki turn his Subcommittee on National Security Policy into a publicity forum just prior to the event.[22] Dole, Stockdale, and Perot collaborated in organizing the festivities, aided by a host of senators and representatives, including such prominent Democrats as Senate Majority Leader Mike Mansfield and Senator Edmund Muskie.[23] The Zablocki committee devoted days of hearings to doing publicity work for Senator Dole's May 1 POW/MIA rally, as exemplified by this exchange:

MR. ZABLOCKI. Just a final question, Senator Dole. What arrangements are being made for national television coverage, which could be used, then, worldwide?

SENATOR DOLE. We are contacting the networks, and there will be press conferences Friday with Mrs. Stockdale and Mr. Perot and others. I will be on the "Today Show" tomorrow with reference to this program. . . . We have talked to Peter Kenney at NBC, he is working on it; we have talked to Mr. Galbraith of CBS, and ABC has been most helpful, and generally they are coming around.[24]

The day after the rally, Stockdale presided in Washington over the constitutional convention that transformed her network into the National League of Families of American Prisoners and Missing in Southeast Asia. Its structure and bylaws had been defined three days earlier by Stockdale, a handful of wives chosen by her, and attorney Charles Havens, with whom she had worked when he was in the Office of International Security Affairs of the Defense Department. Within three weeks of its incorporation, the National League received its IRS tax-exempt status as a "non-partisan, humanitarian" organization.[25]

From then on the National League of Families would play a changing but always crucial role in the evolution of the POW/MIA issue. Almost all its principal organizers and activists were wives or parents of career officers, not draftees, mainly because the vast majority of missing and captured men were flight officers. Sponsored in its early years by the White House, the Department of Defense, and the Republican National Committee, the League would become in the 1980s the official liaison between the Department of Defense and the American public on all POW/MIA matters.[26] The League designed the POW/MIA flag and gets much of its current income from selling it to the U.S. government, the fifty state governments which have mandated its display, and private organizations and citizens.

Meanwhile, Congress obediently placed in the Rotunda of the Capitol a POW exhibit designed and financed by Perot. On June 4, 1970, House Speaker John McCormack was the featured speaker during the televised ceremony inaugurating Perot's display, with figures of two POWs besieged by huge cockroaches and rats.[27] By the end of the year, this tableau was being set up in state capitols across the country, the "Steve Canyon" cartoon strip was featuring POW/MIA relatives in its daily sagas, the ABC television network had presented a "POW/MIA Special," President Nixon had created a national Prisoner of War Day, the *Ladies' Home Journal* had published an article with a tear-out letter for readers to mail, and the U.S. Post Office, amid special fanfare by the president, had issued 135 million POW/MIA postage stamps.[28]

America's vision of the war was being transformed. The actual photographs and TV footage of massacred villagers, napalmed children, Vietnamese prisoners being tortured and murdered, wounded GIs screaming in agony, and body bags being loaded by the dozen for shipment back home were being replaced by simulated images of American POWs in the savage hands of Asian communists.

Second only to the POW/MIA flag in inculcating the POW/MIA myth is the POW/MIA bracelet. It was devised by the militant prowar organization known as VIVA (originally Victory in Vietnam Association).

Applauded by the right-wing press for counterdemonstrating in 1965 against "peaceniks," VIVA soon got an important patron. By October 1966, Gloria Coppin, wife of Los Angeles industrialist Douglas Coppin, whose Hydro-Mill Corporation manufactured airplane parts for major military contractors, was providing a headquarters and contacts with wealthy and influential members of southern California society. In March 1967 the Victory in Vietnam Association received a state charter from California as an educational institution, and less than two months later the IRS granted it tax-exempt status as a "charitable and educational" organization.[29] VIVA was now able to hold the first of its lucrative annual Salute to the Armed Forces formal dinner dances, organized by its Ladies Auxiliary (made up of wives of wealthy business, military, and political leaders), which allowed the guests—including Barry Goldwater, Alexander Haig, H. Ross Perot, Bob Hope, Los Angeles mayor Sam Yorty, and California governor Ronald Reagan—to receive tax deductions for their contributions.[30] With brimming coffers, VIVA expanded rapidly and planned ever more ambitious campaigns to thwart the antiwar movement.

But meanwhile the Tet offensive, as well as ensuing offensives mounted by the insurgents throughout 1968 and 1969, had made talk of U.S. "victory" in Vietnam ring hollow and become politically embarrassing. By the time of the November 1968 elections, "peace," not "victory," had become the catchword, as the nation bet on Nixon's secret peace plan. So in 1969 VIVA ceased to be the Victory in Vietnam Association and became Voices in Vital America.

A few months later, members of VIVA and Robert Dornan, later a Republican representative from California, then a right-wing Los Angeles TV talk show host and close friend of Gloria Coppin, contrived

idea of selling bracelets engraved with the names of POWs and
As to promote and fund the POW/MIA campaign. In addition to
ria Coppin, who was chair of VIVA's board of directors from its
founding until 1974, one of the prime movers in VIVA's bracelet man-
ufacturing was Carol Bates, who was to take over the directorship of the
National League of Families in 1976 and then in 1984 become a princi-
pal coordinator of the POW/MIA issue for the Defense Intelligence
Agency.[31] The prototype bracelets were produced just in time for the
May 9, 1970, Salute to the Armed Forces Ball, where Governor Ronald
Reagan was the keynote speaker, Bob Hope and Martha Raye were
made co-chairs of the bracelet campaign, and H. Ross Perot was named
Man of the Year.[32]

The bracelet idea quickly mushroomed into a propaganda coup and
financial bonanza for the POW/MIA campaign, especially for VIVA,
which was soon wholesaling bracelets to the National League, Perot's
United We Stand, and Junior Chambers of Commerce across the country. By mid-1972 VIVA was distributing more than ten thousand bracelets a day. Bracelets were prominently worn by such luminaries as President Nixon, General William Westmoreland, Billy Graham, George
Wallace, Charlton Heston, Bill Cosby, Pat Boone, Cher and Sonny
Bono, Fred Astaire, Johnny Cash, Steve Allen, Princess Grace of Mo-
naco, and Bob Hope, who personally distributed more than a thousand. The bracelet also became a kind of fetish for sports stars such as
Willie Shoemaker, Don Drysdale, Lee Trevino (who claimed it saved his
golf game), and Jack Kramer (who swore it cured his tennis elbow).[33]

Before American combat in Vietnam ended, perhaps 10 million
Americans were wearing POW/MIA bracelets.[34] The influence on the
national imagination cannot be calculated. Each person who wore a
bracelet vowed never to remove it until his or her POW/MIA was either
found to be dead or returned home from Vietnamese imprisonment.
Millions of people thus developed profound emotional bonds with the
man on their wrist. Countless American schoolchildren went through
their formative years linked to these amulets. How could they not continue to believe that their POW/MIAs were alive?

With growing popular and almost unanimous congressional support
on the POW/MIA issue, the Nixon administration was able to stale-
mate the Paris talks for almost four years by demanding that Hanoi
must account for America's missing in action and negotiate the release
of American prisoners separately from the question of U.S. withdrawal.
Throughout 1969 the other side insisted that the release of prisoners

of war could not be considered separately from a resolution of the war itself. Although this was the customary position of warring powers, it was denounced by the administration and the media as "unprecedented," "inhuman," and "barbaric." What the Vietnamese wanted to talk about was ending the war and the U.S. occupation of half their country. But the more Hanoi and the insurgents refused to negotiate separately about the POW issue, the more Washington made it the central issue of the negotiations. In the final negotiating session of the year, the head of the U.S. delegation "scarcely mentioned the question of peace, devoting his formal remarks to the prisoner problem."[35]

Nixon had in fact carried out a brilliant propaganda coup. At first Hanoi and the PRG* simply denounced the POW/MIA issue as a "perfidious maneuver to camouflage the fact that the United States is pursuing the war . . . and misleading public opinion, which demands that the United States end the war and withdraw its troops."[36] When they became more flexible and suggested that they would set a date for the release of all prisoners of war if the United States would set a date for withdrawal from their country, the administration accused them of "ransoming" the POWs and using them as "hostages" and "bargaining chips." The administration's line was echoed by the media. For example, the *Christian Science Monitor* ran a five-part series that labeled Hanoi's position "a cruel ploy" and concluded with this bizarre argument: "Never before, in any other war . . . have prisoners been held as international hostages, ransomed to a political and military settlement of the war."[37]

This dizzying inversion of history conveniently ignored the fact that the United States, like most nations, had never been involved in a war in which either side released all its prisoners prior to an agreement to end the war. But through the strange logic of the administration's negotiating position and its masterly public relations campaign, the American prisoners of war had indeed been successfully transformed — in the public mind — into "bargaining chips" and "hostages" held for "ransom." These metaphors not only would increasingly influence the debates about negotiations to end the war, but also would eventually become central to the postwar POW/MIA myth.

*The Provisional Revolutionary Government, formed in 1969, subsumed the National Liberation Front and was in 1973 one of the four signatories of the Paris Peace Accords (along with the United States, the Democratic Republic of Vietnam, and the Republic of Vietnam).

How is it possible to comprehend this truly astonishing position, by which the United States seemed ready to trade countless American and Vietnamese lives for several hundred prisoners who would presumably be released anyhow at the conclusion of the war? By early 1971, President Nixon could explicitly declare that U.S. ground and air forces would remain in Vietnam "as long as there is one American prisoner being held prisoner by North Vietnam." Since North Vietnam was making the release of the prisoners contingent on U.S. withdrawal, the logic of Nixon's position could be, as Tom Wicker put it, that "we may keep both troops and prisoners there forever."[38] If that seems absurd, what would follow if it could be made to appear that North Vietnam was concealing some of its prisoners? Since it could never be proved that some missing American was not "being held prisoner by North Vietnam," and since more Americans would be missing as long as the fighting continued, the war could literally go on forever.

Rationality, however, has never been a component of the POW/MIA issue. As Jonathan Schell observed, by 1972 "many people were persuaded that the United States was fighting in Vietnam in order to get its prisoners back," and the nation's main sympathy was no longer for "the men fighting and dying on the front," who "went virtually unnoticed as attention was focused on the prisoners of war," who had become "the objects of a virtual cult." Schell probed to the core of the growing obsession: "Following the President's lead, people began to speak as though the North Vietnamese had kidnapped four hundred Americans and the United States had gone to war to retrieve them."[39]

Perhaps the most startling and penetrating judgment came years later from Gloria Coppin, VIVA's longtime chair. Although remaining a fervent believer in the existence of living POWs, she had come to a painful realization of how she and many others may have been manipulated. As she put it in a 1990 interview: "Nixon and Kissinger just used the POW issue to prolong the war. Sometimes I feel guilty because with all our efforts, we killed more men than we saved."[40]

The Nixon administration's four-year campaign to secure the release of American prisoners of war separate from U.S. withdrawal from Vietnam was doomed, along with its other war goals, by the Peace Accords signed in Paris on January 27, 1973. The agreement called for the complete withdrawal of all U.S. forces from Vietnam within sixty days and the return of all prisoners of war to be "carried out simultaneously with and completed not later than the same day" as the U.S. withdrawal.[41]

Hanoi had already delivered to Washington a complete list of its prisoners of war and those who had died in captivity. Within the stipulated two months, all the living prisoners on the list were repatriated. Both Vietnam and Laos returned or accounted for *more,* rather than *fewer,* than those listed by the Pentagon and State Department as probably captured in each country. The return of the prisoners was staged as Operation Homecoming, an event transformed by an awesome media blitz into a public relations coup for President Nixon, who boasted at his formal White House dinner party for the ex-POWs that he had achieved "the return of all of our prisoners of war" as part of his successful conclusion of the war in Vietnam.[42]

Article 21 of the Peace Accords guaranteed that "the United States will contribute to healing the wounds of war and to postwar reconstruction of the Democratic Republic of Viet-Nam." On February 1, Richard Nixon wrote a secret letter to Prime Minister Pham Van Dong in Hanoi pledging that this reconstruction aid would amount to at least $3.25 billion.[43] But when national security adviser Henry Kissinger brought this document to Hanoi in early February, he simultaneously confronted the Hanoi government with "some 80 files of individuals who we had reason to believe had been captured," as he testified during Senate hearings in September to confirm him as secretary of state. Because "we are extremely dissatisfied" with Hanoi's accounting for these MIAs, Kissinger concluded, "we cannot proceed in certain other areas such as economic aid."[44] In other words, Kissinger and Nixon were using the MIA issue to renege on Nixon's secret pledge, whose very existence was denied by the White House until 1976.

Why did Kissinger's list contain eighty names? The *highest* number of such "discrepancy" cases (men unaccounted for and deemed by the Pentagon as likely to have been captured or whose fate would be known by the Vietnamese) either publicly claimed or secretly listed by the government at that time was fifty-six. The truth finally came out in 1992, when Roger Shields, who had been head of Pentagon POW/MIA affairs in 1973, acknowledged that Washington had deliberately included on Kissinger's list a number of cases that the Vietnamese could not possibly have accounted for.[45] Thus the Nixon administration created an issue that could never be resolved.

Having no intention of honoring the U.S. pledge of aid, Nixon made *accounting* for the *MIAs* the issue. But accounting is a meaningless issue unless there is some belief in the possibility of living *POWs.* Hence each postwar administration has tried to exaggerate this *possibility* of living

POWs. But no administration could afford to claim that there actually *were* POWs,, because then it would be expected to rescue them. True believers, however, knew that reconnaissance, espionage, and the debriefing of defectors would have to reveal the existence of POWs to U.S. intelligence. Hence by the late 1970s the POW myth was beginning to incorporate belief in a government conspiracy precisely the opposite of the real one: while the government was pretending that there might be POWs, the POW/MIA myth saw the government pretending that POWs might not exist.

Not all the machinations of the Pentagon, political opportunists, scam artists, the media, and presidents can create a true myth, however, unless that myth resonates with deep psychocultural needs of a society. There are some fairly obvious needs being met by the images of American POWs tortured year after year by sadistic Asian communists. We, not the Vietnamese, become the victims as well as the good guys. The American fighting man becomes a hero betrayed by his government and the antiwar movement, especially by unmanly types such as the bureaucrats in control of the government, "peaceniks," cowards, and those who would rather make love than war. This stab-in-the-back theme, with its loud echoes of the myth of national betrayal central to the rise of Nazism, is one way of convincing ourselves that *we* didn't really lose the war. It also suggests that American manhood itself is threatened and must be rescued if we are to restore America's military might and determination. So it is no surprise that the POW/MIA myth has been functioning as a potent agent of militarism.

Yet the POW/MIA myth expresses even deeper psychocultural cravings. Sometimes it is hard to see what is most peculiar about something in one's own culture because the culture is, after all, also inside one's own head. So I remained only dimly conscious of another level of meaning of the POW/MIA myth until I had a startling encounter in 1991 while I was a visiting professor at Meiji University in Tokyo. Several Japanese scholars of American Studies expressed their keen interest in the POW/MIA myth. They said that on some levels they thought they understood the myth, that from their study of the POW movies and other cultural artifacts they could see that the prisoner of war was functioning in American society as an icon of militarism. "But," one said, "that's what we find so puzzling. When militarism was dominant in Japan, the last person who would have been used as an icon of militarism was the POW. What did he do that was heroic? He didn't fight to the death. He surrendered." I was flabbergasted. Here I had been studying the POW/MIA myth for years and had missed its most essential and revealing aspect. Only then did I realize that this is a myth of imprisonment, a myth that accumulates deep emotional power by displacing onto Vietnam the source of the imprisonment, powerlessness, and alienation felt by many Americans in an epoch when alien economic, technological, and bureaucratic forces dominate much of their lives.

What these Japanese scholars made me realize in 1991 was driven home dramatically in 2000 when John McCain seemed close to winning the Republican nomination for president. Month after month throughout the immense media coverage, McCain was portrayed as a hero of the Vietnam War not for his exploits as a pilot bombing North Vietnam but as a prisoner of war. Indeed, his main qualifications for the presidency were presented not as those of such victorious military leaders as George Washington, Andrew Jackson, Zachary Taylor, Ulysses S. Grant, Theodore Roosevelt, and Dwight D. Eisenhower, or even those of brave warriors like PT-boat commander John F. Kennedy and fighter pilot George Bush, but rather those of a victim who had endured captivity.

Because the postwar POWs are, unlike McCain, imaginary beings, elaborating the POW/MIA myth and implanting it deep in America's collective imagination has been the job of art forms specializing in imaginary beings: novels, comic books, television soap operas, video games, and, of course, movies. Although the story of American prisoners abandoned in Southeast Asia could not become a major American myth until the dream factory geared up its assembly line for mass production of the essential images, Hollywood was actually involved in creating bits of the history that its POW rescue movies would soon fantasize.

The character central to the POW/MIA story as mythologized in the 1980s was retired Special Forces colonel James ("Bo") Gritz, who organized raids into Laos to rescue POWs he imagined as captives of Asian communists. Gritz claimed that he had to accept this mission because the two other men capable of such intense "action" were unavailable: "Both Teddy Roosevelt and John Wayne are dead."[46]

But other men of action were at least available to help: Captain Kirk of the Starship *Enterprise*, Dirty Harry, and the Hollywood star who had just moved into the White House. William Shatner put up $10,000 and received movie rights to the Gritz story. Clint Eastwood contributed $30,000 and was assigned a crucial role in the adventure.[47] And Ronald Reagan's administration was secretly arranging funding and logistics.[48]

By 1980 the POW myth envisioned a conspiracy high in the government to deny the existence of American prisoners. The villains were government bureaucrats, devious CIA operatives, and liberal politicians, personified by President Jimmy Carter. With the inauguration of Reagan in early 1981, the myth evolved a new twist: the good president walled off by a cabal of scheming bureaucrats and liberals now known collectively as the "gatekeepers." There could be no doubt about the president's sincerity. After all, Ronald Reagan had been active with POW issues ever since he himself had actually been a POW of Asian communists during the Korean War—as the star of the 1954 movie *Prisoner of War.*

There was one man in America who could get by the all-powerful gatekeepers and bring the truth to the good president: Clint Eastwood. Gritz's plan hinged on two tête-à-têtes between Eastwood and Reagan. On the night of November 27, 1982, after receiving confirmation that Gritz's team had crossed the Mekong River into Laos, Eastwood was to fly from his Shasta, California, ranch to a prearranged meeting at Reagan's Santa Barbara ranch to inform the president about the raid. When the raiders had actually released living American POWs, they would relay the message to Eastwood, who would once again fly to see his old friend Reagan, who would then have to do what he had wanted to do all along: send U.S. aircraft and military forces to rescue the POWs.[49] When the raiders returned from Laos to Thailand on December 3, they found this message from a team member in California: "CLINT AND I MET WITH PRESIDENT ON 27TH. PRESIDENT SAID: QUOTE, IF YOU BRING OUT ONE U.S. POW, I WILL START WORLD WAR III TO GET THE REST OUT. UNQUOTE."[50]

Gritz's raids, however, did not turn out like a Hollywood production. The American heroes did not ambush and wipe out hordes of Asian communists. In fact, almost as soon as they arrived in Laos they were ambushed, routed, and forced to flee back to Thailand.[51] The raiders of course encountered no POWs. Yet three days before the news of Gritz's first raid burst on the public, and while he was conducting an unsuccessful second raid, President Reagan, who had been kept closely informed, publicly declared that from now on "the government bureaucracy" would have to understand that the POW/MIA issue had become "the highest national priority."[52]

Reagan had been preparing for this since early 1981, when his administration had sent Congressmen Billy Hendon and John LeBoutillier to Laos, partly to prepare for the raids that Gritz was organizing.[53] LeBoutillier, working closely with White House liaisons and National League of Families head Ann Mills Griffiths, set up Skyhook II, an organization that raised large sums of money, ostensibly to free POWs. Griffiths set up covert bank accounts in Bangkok to receive the funds. Carol Bates (wartime coordinator of VIVA's bracelet campaign) and Griffiths, operating with White House help, then moved Skyhook II funds through the Bangkok accounts to mercenary forces in Laos known as the "Lao resistance."[54] This byzantine, illegal funding of covert operations outdid the Iran-Contra scheme, for it included a self-sustaining mechanism. The "Lao resistance" produced a stream of phony evidence of living POWs for LeBoutillier to use in his Skyhook II propaganda to raise more funds for the "Lao resistance," which was then able to supply still more phony evidence of living POWs to raise still more funds, and so on.[55] Reagan would soon make Griffiths co-equal with the State and Defense Department representatives in his POW/MIA Interagency Group, and in 1984 he placed Bates in a key position in his expanded POW/MIA section of the Defense Intelligence Agency.

The first POW rescue movie began shooting amid the media hoopla about the Gritz raids. Starring Gene Hackman as a thinly veiled counterpart to Gritz, *Uncommon Valor* made it to the screen in time for the Christmas season of 1983. Reviewers, who at first dismissed it as a "grind actioner" and a "bore" featuring "comic-strip-level heroism," were soon trying to comprehend the startling audience response to what turned out to be the "biggest movie surprise" of the 1983–84 season. The best explanation seemed to come from "an ordinary moviegoer who said with satisfaction of the bloody ending in which dozens of the enemy are mowed down by the Americans, 'We get to win the Vietnam War.' "[56]

Uncommon Valor presents a tableau of a nation run by bureaucrats, politicians, and shadowy secret agents in business suits who revile and betray its true warrior heroes. Hackman is a retired colonel whose efforts to rescue his MIA son are continually menaced by "the politicians" and omnipresent government agents equipped with high-tech spy mikes and phone taps. The idealism, virility, martial prowess, and heroism of men who dedicate their lives to rescuing their abandoned comrades, sons, and fathers are presented as the alternative to a weak, decadent America subjugated by materialism, hedonism, and feminism. This perspective is a familiar element in the culture of fascism and Nazism.[57]

In the film, Hackman's character reestablishes patriarchal order by recruiting a team composed of Vietnam veterans who have all been victimized by an American society that castrates military and manly virtue. Their rescue mission also rescues them from the corrupting and degrading bonds of civilian life. The most revealing salvations are for two team members liberated from women.[58]

One, an expert on conducting ambushes, has been kept from expressing his true identity by a wife who now persuades him to hide from Hackman, whom she tries to block physically as she shrieks, "It's taken me ten years to get that goddamn war out of his head!" Shoving her aside, Hackman rends these enfeebling domestic fetters, shouting: "What did you send your wife out here for? Don't you have the guts to come out here and talk to me yourself?" The second example is a helicopter pilot who has become an even more miserable prisoner of peace, permanently shut in from the world behind sunglasses and headset, and married to a blond floozy whom we see about to traipse out to happy hour at a local club. Embodying the fusion of American women with hedonism and materialism, she finally asks Hackman, "If he did go, how much would he be paid?"

Hackman himself is called to his mission by the memory of his son as a young boy coming to his parents' bedroom for help. While his wife lies oblivious in sleep, he reaches out to clutch his son's hand, a bond that becomes the pivotal symbol of the movie. His sleeping wife (who never speaks a word in the film) personifies women's irrelevance to the ties between warriors and between fathers and sons.[59] Hackman explicitly articulates the central message: "There's no bond as strong as that shared by men who have faced death in battle."

The bonding among the men is first consummated in their training camp, a world without women where they regain their killing skills. The pleasures of this buddy-buddy society are ritualized as the men dance with one another, some holding their assault rifles at upright angles from the groin as they bump bottoms. Thus primed, these rugged heroes are ready to slaughter hordes of puny little Asians, rescue their enslaved comrades, give the Vietnam War a noble ending, and redeem America.

The following year brought *Missing in Action,* with Chuck Norris as retired Special Forces colonel James Braddock, a fantasy version of retired Special Forces colonel James ("Bo") Gritz. Here the myth took more potent shape, with Norris as lone superhero — incarnate in a fetishized male body — replacing Hackman's team of manly warriors and graphically dramatizing how much more erotically exciting it is to make war, not love. There is no secret about the meaning and tremendous popular allure of *Missing in Action,* which were expressed in full-page ads showing Chuck Norris, headband half restraining his savage locks, sleeves rolled up to reveal bulging biceps, and a huge machine gun seeming to rise from his crotch, which is blackened by its great shadow. Beneath ran the message: "THE WAR'S NOT OVER UNTIL THE LAST MAN COMES HOME!"[60]

Because the power of these movies flows from some of the deepest elements of American culture, they were able to transform the POW/MIA *issue* into a true *myth.* After all, one foundation of American culture is the mythic frontier, with its central images of white captives tortured by cruel nonwhite savages until they are rescued by the first great American hero, the lone frontiersman who abandons civilized society to merge with the wilderness. The movies that transmuted what had been a fringe right-wing political issue of the mid-1970s into a central national myth did so precisely by using these primal cultural materials.[61] Hollywood moves us from seeing American POWs in Vietnam as quintessential symbols of betrayed American manhood in *The Deer Hunter* (1978) through the formative POW rescue movies *Uncommon Valor* (1983) and *Missing in Action* (1984) to the apotheosis of the myth in *Rambo: First Blood Part II* (1985). *The Deer Hunter* explicitly calls attention to its use of the mythic frontier and frontiersman, fleshed out in the early nation-state by James Fenimore Cooper's Deerslayer. But it was *Rambo* that used the old mythic elements to turn Sylvester Stallone, as muscled as the giant he-men in Nazi propaganda posters, into the true American superhero of the post-Vietnam epoch.

At the beginning of the movie, Rambo himself is a prisoner in America. Thoroughly alienated from civil society by his experience in the Vietnamese wilderness — what GIs called "Injun country" — he is the only one who can rescue the tortured white captives from their savage captors. Rambo can do this by merging with the wilderness even more completely than the Vietnamese can. Why? Because he, like the mythic frontiersman, has coalesced with the Indian and the wilderness. Rambo is of "German-Indian descent," we're told, "a hell of a combination." His long, dark hair restrained by a headband, a necklace dangling above his bare muscled chest, armed with a huge caricature of a bowie knife and a bow that shoots exploding arrows, Rambo conceals himself behind trees and waterfalls and literally rises out of the mud and water to ambush the savages in their own primitive land.

Rambo's vast powers — over both his enemies and his audiences — derive also from other American mythic heroes. America's most popular author, Edgar Rice Burroughs, created two of Rambo's forebears: a veteran of a defeated army who uses his expertise in martial arts to fight for good causes in alien lands against seemingly insurmountable odds (John Carter); and a bare-chested muscular he-man who merges completely with the tropical jungle to carry out spectacular deeds of heroism (Tarzan). Rambo also incorporates one of America's most distinctive cultural products, the comic book hero who may seem to be an ordinary human being but really possesses superhuman powers that allow him to fight, like Superman, for "truth, justice, and the American way" and to personify national fantasies, like Captain America. No wonder Rambo can stand invulnerable against the thousands of bullets fired at him, many from point-blank range, by America's enemies.

Like the mythic frontiersman, Rambo confronts his antithesis not in the Indian but in feminized, devious, emasculating civil society as embodied by Murdock, the arch-bureaucrat who represents the Washington administration and those who manipulate the computerized technology used to control the lives of ordinary men. The climax comes when Rambo, after rescuing the POWs, hurls himself on top of the prostrate Murdock and forces this fake man to whimper and moan in terror of our hero's gigantic phallic knife.

Thus *Rambo* projects a fantasy in which the audience gets to violate the enemies of everyday life: the boss and his computerized control over work life, the bureaucrats and politicians who conspire to emasculate America's virility and betray the American dream. American men find their surrogates both in the POWs who embody humiliated, betrayed, enslaved American manhood and in the warrior hero who can rescue them when he escapes the imprisonment of post-Vietnam America.[62]

Six weeks after the opening of *Rambo*, President Reagan projected himself into its star role — while hyping the film with a presidential plug — as he declared (ostensibly as a microphone test before his national address on the release of U.S. hostages in Beirut): "Boy, I saw *Rambo* last night. Now I know what to do the next time this happens."[63] Two weeks later, members of Congress "signaled a new tough-minded attitude" on foreign relations by invoking the image of Rambo a dozen times in debating a foreign aid bill.[64] Rambo's political repercussions ricocheted around the world. For example, in 1990 President Saddam Hussein of Iraq defiantly responded to the U.S. threat of war with his own bluster in the guise of cultural criticism: "The Americans are still influenced by Rambo movies, but this is not a Rambo movie."[65]

As *Rambo* packed theaters with audiences who howled with pleasure and wildly cheered every slaying of a Vietnamese or Russian by its invulnerable hero, the nation was flooded with Rambo "action dolls," watches, walkie-talkies, water guns, bubble gum, pinball machines, sportswear for all ages, TV cartoons, and even "Rambo-Grams," messages delivered by headbanded musclemen sporting bandoliers across their bare chests. A *Rambo* TV cartoon serial, designed by Family Home Entertainment "for ages 5–12," transformed Rambo into "liberty's champion," a superman engaged in global struggles against evil. And for "adult" audiences there were the pornographic video spinoffs such as *Ramb-Ohh!* (1986), *Bimbo: Hot Blood Part I!* (1985), and *Bimbo 2: The Homecoming!* (1986).

The advent of *Rambo* helped make the MIA religion not only a prominent feature of American culture but also a lucrative market. Rescuing POWs from the evil Vietnamese communists now became almost a rite of passage for Hollywood heroes, as the formula degenerated through *P.O.W.: The Escape,* the 1986 Israeli production starring David Carradine, to *Operation Nam,* a 1987 Italian production starring John Wayne's son Ethan Wayne, which might be called the first spaghetti rescue movie. In 1987 there appeared the first issue of *Vietnam Journal,* a comic book prominently displaying on the cover of every number the POW/MIA logo next to a banner about an MIA feature. In 1985 Jack Buchanan published *M.I.A. Hunter,* a mass-market POW rescue novel featuring Mark Stone, a former Green Beret who "has only one activity that gives meaning to his life—finding America's forgotten fighting men, the P.O.W.'s the government has conveniently labeled M.I.A.'s, and bringing them back from their hell on earth."[66] By 1991 Buchanan had published fourteen more volumes in what had become the immensely popular *M.I.A. Hunter* series, each promising more blood than the last, including *M.I.A. Hunter: Cambodian Hellhole* (1985), *M.I.A. Hunter: Hanoi Deathgrip* (1985), *M.I.A. Hunter: Mountain Massacre* (1985), *M.I.A. Hunter: Exodus from Hell* (1986), *M.I.A. Hunter: Blood Storm* (1986), *M.I.A. Hunter: Saigon Slaughter* (1987), and *Back to Nam* (1990).

The cultural products that disseminate the MIA mythology and give it potent forms in the popular imagination have tended increasingly to project a vast government cover-up and conspiracy. *Vietnam Journal,* for example, in 1990 ran a three-part series titled "Is the U.S. Hiding the Truth about Missing Soldiers?" (numbers 11, 12, and 13). The answer of course was yes. In the 1989 TV movie *The Forgotten,* starring Keith Carradine and Stacy Keach, high government officials actually conspire to torture and assassinate POWs held by Vietnam until 1987 to keep them from revealing that these officials had colluded with North Vietnam to sabotage a POW rescue mission. Jack Buchanan's "M.I.A. Hunter" constantly battles against "Washington" and its sinister operatives; in *M.I.A. Hunter: Cambodian Hellhole* he can pursue his quest only "after demolishing a C.I.A. hit team sent to arrest him."

By the end of the 1980s, the POW/MIA myth had emerged from American popular culture in the shape of an ominous Frankenstein's monster beginning to haunt its ingenious creators in Washington. The monster became a more serious problem as corporations from Europe and Asia staked out major investments in Vietnam, barred to American corporations by the U.S. embargo. Pressure was building for normalization of relations.

On April 9, 1991 — one month after declaring, "By God, we've kicked the Vietnam syndrome once and for all!" — President George Bush handed Vietnam a "Road Map" toward normalizing relations within two years — contingent on Vietnam's making what Washington deemed satisfactory progress in resolving "all remaining POW/MIA cases."[67] Instantly the smoldering POW/MIA issue was fanned into a firestorm.

In May, Senator Jesse Helms released, in the name of all Republicans on the Senate Foreign Relations Committee, a hundred-page pseudo-history alleging that thousands of U.S. POWs had been abandoned in Indochina, and that some were still alive, betrayed by a vast Washington conspiracy. Although at no time during the war did the Pentagon or White House believe that there could be more than a few hundred U.S. POWs, Helms's treatise claimed that Hanoi had held "5000" U.S. POWs.[68] Where did Helms get the figure five thousand? From a 1973 *New York Times* story. However, the figure five thousand in the *Times* story referred not to U.S. POWs but to the number of prisoners Hanoi was demanding from Saigon.[69] The report's principal author was later exposed as having falsified much of its "evidence" about abandoned POWs.[70] Nevertheless, well over a hundred thousand copies of the

Helms volume continued to be mailed out by the Senate Foreign Relations Committee.

Senator Bob Smith, who helped engineer the Helms document, next tried to set up a Senate committee to ballyhoo its thesis. But Smith's efforts seemed doomed because the Senate was due to recess on August 2, 1991.

Suddenly on July 17 began one of the most spectacular media coups in U.S. history, orchestrated largely by Smith and his associates. A photograph purportedly showing three U.S. POWs from the Vietnam War still being held captive in Indochina burst as the lead story onto the TV and radio network news. Newspapers across the country front-paged the picture under banner headlines. The "prisoners" were identified as three pilots shot down over Vietnam and Laos between 1966 and 1970. Within a week, photographs ostensibly showing two more POWs in Indochina — identified as Daniel Borah, Jr., and Donald Carr — hit the media. According to a *Wall Street Journal*/NBC News poll, 69 percent of the American people now believed that American POWs were being held in Indochina and 52 percent were convinced that the government was derelict in not getting them back.[71] A headline in the August 2 *Wall Street Journal* read "Bring on Rambo." The same day a stampeded Senate unanimously passed Bob Smith's resolution to create a Senate Select Committee on POW/MIA Affairs, along with a resolution to fly the POW/MIA flag over federal buildings.

The photos that launched the Senate committee later proved as bogus as all other "evidence" of postwar POWs. "Daniel Borah" turned out to be a Lao highlander who had happily posed because he had never had his photograph taken before.[72] "Donald Carr" was a German bird smuggler photographed in a Bangkok rare bird sanctuary.[73] The picture of the three other alleged POWs was a doctored version of a 1923 photograph reproduced in a 1989 Soviet magazine; the three men were actually holding a poster extolling collective farming (mustaches had been added and a picture of Stalin subtracted).[74]

All the photographs were the handiwork of notorious scam artists. Each was used to blitz the media and the public — and thus help create the Senate Select Committee. Senator Smith displayed the "Daniel Borah" pictures on the *Today* show.[75] The picture of the threesome had been released by Captain Red McDaniel, head of the right-wing American Defense Institute, who has been promising the faithful since 1986 that as soon as they contributed enough money, he would produce living POWs. McDaniel got the photo from Jack Bailey, head of a crooked POW/MIA fundraising scheme known as Operation Rescue. Bailey, who had conspired to fake the "Donald Carr" photos, assaulted two ABC reporters on camera when they confronted him in the rare bird sanctuary where the pictures had been shot.[76]

Bob Smith was made vice chairman of the Senate committee. The chairman was John Kerry, who may have been unaware how the POW/MIA issue had been used back in 1971, when he joined hundreds of other antiwar Vietnam veterans to throw their medals at the Capitol. Panic-stricken by these actions and the growing antiwar movement among POW/MIA wives, Nixon aide H. R. Haldeman had then ordered the White House staff "to be doubly sure we are keeping the POW wives in line."[77]

Ironically, Kerry now accepted the spurious history of the POW/MIA issue promulgated by those bent on continuing the conflict, including the preposterous notion that the government during the war and ever since had been minimizing and perhaps concealing the possibility of prisoners being kept after the U.S. withdrawal. The committee refused to permit testimony about how the POW/MIA issue had been created and used by the government to legitimize hostilities against Vietnam from 1969 on. The only witnesses allowed to testify were either government apologists or POW/MIA movement partisans.[78] Although the Select Committee found not a shred of credible evidence of postwar POWs, its final report asserted that the POW/MIA issue should continue to have the "highest national priority."[79]

While the Select Committee had the media spotlighting the POW/MIA issue in 1992, President Bush was fighting for his political life. The very man who had boasted about healing America's Vietnam wounds was now trying to win reelection by reopening them, turning what Bill Clinton had or hadn't done during the Vietnam War into the Republicans' main campaign issue. Meanwhile, Ross Perot was campaigning as the wartime champion of the POWs and a Rambo-like hero who would rescue the dozens allegedly still alive in Indochina, and by extension the nation itself.

Unlike Bush and Clinton, Perot had no national party apparatus. What he used as a remarkably effective substitute was a ready-made national infrastructure, a network of activists motivated by religious fervor and coordinated by grassroots organizations: the POW/MIA movement. Perot chose ex-POW James Stockdale, husband of the founder of the National League of Families, as his running mate and ex-POW Or-son Swindle as his campaign manager. Typically at his campaign rallies Perot would sit with former POWs and their family members on a stage bedecked with POW flags. POW activists and organizations were central to the petition campaigns that got Perot on the ballot in every state.[80]

Portraying himself as the lone outsider from Texas ready to ride into Washington to save us from its sleazy bureaucrats and politicians who had betrayed the POWs and the American people, Perot cut deeply into President Bush's constituency. Without the Perot candidacy, Bush probably would have beaten Bill Clinton in a one-on-one race. The POW/MIA issue was thus central to the election's outcome.

In the closing days of the campaign, George Bush claimed that he was on the verge of ending hostilities by forcing Vietnam into resolving the POW/MIA issue. He now presented himself as the man who was about to lead the nation to "begin writing the last chapter of the Vietnam War."[81]

In doing so, the president was responding to two developments. One was Vietnam's all-out effort to resolve the POW/MIA issue, including actions utterly unprecedented between hostile states, such as opening its military archives to U.S. inspection, conducting joint searches throughout the country, and allowing short-notice U.S. inspection of suspected prison sites. The other was the pressure from U.S. corporations anxious not to lose lucrative business opportunities to foreign competitors already swarming into Vietnam.[82]

But neither corporate anxiety nor Vietnamese cooperation could overcome the potent forces wielding the POW/MIA issue, forces still including its original engineer, Richard Nixon. On December 30, 1992, Nixon sent a judiciously leaked memo to the Senate Select Committee, insisting that "it would be a diplomatic travesty and human tragedy to go forward with normalization" of relations until Hanoi "fully accounts for the MIAs." As the *Los Angeles Times* observed, "Nixon's written statement provides the strongest evidence so far that he and officials of his former Administration constitute a powerful and determined, though largely hidden, lobby against normalization."[83]

So instead of following his own "Road Map," Bush merely allowed U.S. enterprises to begin negotiating for future business. This left the Clinton administration in a curious position in its early months, as U.S. corporate interests, which had supported and profited from the Vietnam War, furtively leaned on the former antiwar demonstrator to end the war. Even the *Wall Street Journal*, for decades one of the master builders of the POW/MIA myth, ran a major editorial headlined "President Clinton, Normalize Ties with Vietnam," and arguing that "by any account, the Vietnamese have more than met" all the conditions of the "Road Map," including the requested "help in resolving the fate of American MIAs."[84] The Clinton administration began tiptoeing toward normalization. "Bill Clinton may be on the verge of finally ending the Vietnam War," declared the *Wall Street Journal* on April 12, 1993, but went on to warn of "an orchestrated campaign" to stop him.[85]

Right on cue, the same day's *New York Times* featured a sensational front-page story about a "top secret" document "discovered" in Moscow by "Harvard researcher" Stephen Morris and "authenticated by leading experts" (unnamed) as a Russian translation of a 1972 report to Hanoi's Politburo. This "smoking gun," the article said, "proves" that Vietnam withheld "hundreds" of American POWs. For an "expert" opinion, the *Times* turned to Zbigniew Brzezinski, who in 1978 had persuaded Jimmy Carter not to normalize relations with Vietnam. Since, as Brzezinski knew, there had never been any credible evidence of postwar POWs held in Vietnam, he offered an explanation that was sooner or later destined to become part of the POW/MIA mythology: "The Vietnamese took hundreds of American officers out and shot them in cold blood."[86]

In a replay of the phony photo gambits of 1991, the "smoking gun" now exploded as the lead story on every TV network, including PBS, whose balanced coverage showcased a *MacNeil/Lehrer Newshour* panel on April 13 consisting of three disinterested "experts" — Brzezinski, Kissinger, and Morris himself. Brzezinski's massacre scenario was repeated in newspaper editorials across the country. Headlines blared "North Vietnam Kept 700 POWs after War: 'Smoking Gun' File Exposes '20 Years of Duplicity' "; "POWs: The Awful Truth?"; and "We Can't Set Up Ties with Killers of Our POWs."[87]

Not one of the "facts" about POWs in this spurious document conforms to the historical record.[88] Yet this clumsy hoax helped maintain the trade embargo for almost a year. And when President Clinton finally did call off the embargo in 1994, he claimed that he was doing so to get more "answers" about the MIAs, because "any decisions about our relationships with Vietnam should be guided by one factor and one factor only — gaining the fullest possible accounting for our prisoners of war and our missing in action."[89]

A 1993 poll indicated that two thirds of Americans believed that U.S. POWs "are still being held in Southeast Asia."[90] The poll did not measure how many of the remaining third believed Brzezinski's fable about hundreds of American officers being massacred in "cold blood." Though conveniently disposing of the belief in living POWs—which would eventually become biologically impossible anyway—this scenario has become a fantasy that may allow the POW/MIA myth to endure indefinitely.

When diplomatic relations with Vietnam were finally established in 1995, President Clinton deftly undercut the POW/MIA lobby by naming as the first U.S. ambassador Douglas ("Pete") Peterson, a former air force fighter pilot who had spent six and a half years as a POW in Hanoi. In the years that have followed, joint U.S.-Vietnamese search teams have combed every accessible site for possible remains; swarms of U.S. visitors, including many veterans as well as businesspeople, have toured all parts of Vietnam; American veterans have disclosed the sites of mass burials, enabling the Vietnamese to recover the remains of some of their hundreds of thousands of missing compatriots; and Hanoi has opened its secret records of those captured to American researchers. We know with as much certainty as could ever be possible that there are not now, and never have been, American prisoners held in Vietnam after the war. So why are the POW/MIA flags still flying all over America?

NOTES

PROLOGUE: ON "DIFFERING PERCEPTIONS OF REALITY"

1. For my view of the Stanford affair, see "Perceptions of Stanford: Or 'Can We Have Quiet Please,' " in my political autobiography *Back Where You Came From* (New York: Harper's Magazine Press, 1975), and "The Real Issues in My Case," *Change* 4 (June 1972), 31–39. Steven Choi's "The Case of Bruce Franklin" is a well-researched reexamination of the proceedings done as a Stanford senior honors thesis in 1998. The many other writings about the case range from boxes of documents produced during eight years of legal proceedings to Paul Levitt's play *The Trial of Benedict Spinoza, Melville Scholar.* See also chapter 3, note 17.
2. "In the Matter of H. Bruce Franklin: Decision," Advisory Board, Stanford University, January 5, 1972, 11–12.
3. Ibid., 12.
4. Philip D. Beidler, *Re-writing America: Vietnam Authors in Their Generation* (Athens: University of Georgia Press, 1991), 2.

CHAPTER 1. FROM REALISM TO VIRTUAL REALITY

1. William A. Frassanito, *Antietam: The Photographic Legacy of America's Bloodiest Day* (New York: Charles Scribner's Sons, 1978), 27–28.
2. Alan Trachtenberg, *Reading American Photographs: Images as History, Matthew Brady to Walker Evans* (New York: Hill and Wang, 1989), 74.
3. *Collected Poems of Herman Melville*, ed. Howard P. Vincent (Chicago: Hendricks House, 1947), 39–40.
4. William C. Davis, "Finding the Hidden Images of the Civil War," *Civil War Times Illustrated* 21 (1982, no. 2), 9.
5. "Brady's Photographs: Pictures of the Dead at Antietam," *New York Times,* October 20, 1862.
6. Oliver Wendell Holmes, "Doings of the Sunbeam," *Atlantic Monthly* 12 (July 1863), 11–12.
7. Amy Kaplan, "The Spectacle of War in Crane's Revision of History," in *New Essays on the Red Badge of Courage*, ed. Lee Clark Mitchell (Cambridge: Cambridge University Press, 1986), 77–108. Although Crane continued to use realism, that literary analogue of Civil War photography, in his own reporting about wounds and death in combat, he also included his own romantic glorification of war, especially in his dispatches from Cuba in 1898. For example, in articles published in the *New York World* in July, he called the charge up San Juan Hill "the best moment of anybody's life" and proclaimed that "the soldier of the regular army is the best man standing on two feet on God's

green earth." *The War Dispatches of Stephen Crane,* ed. R. W. Stallman and E. R. Hagemann (New York: New York University Press, 1968), 176, 188.

8. Stephen Crane, *The Red Badge of Courage: An Episode of the American Civil War,* ed. Henry Binder (New York: Avon Books, 1983), 37.

9. See H. Bruce Franklin, "From Empire to Empire: *Billy Budd, Sailor,*" in *Herman Melville: Reassessments,* ed. A. Robert Lee (London and Totowa, N.J.: Vision Press and Barnes & Noble, 1984), 199–216.

10. Mark Twain, *A Connecticut Yankee in King Arthur's Court,* ed. Bernard L. Stein (Berkeley: University of California Press, 1979), 466; hereafter cited by page in the text.

11. During the Spanish-American War, the Edison Company recorded some motion pictures of the embarking troops but was unable to obtain any battle footage. Later the company recreated battle scenes at a mountain reservation near Edison's headquarters in Essex County, New Jersey. See "Historian Remembers the Maine, Spain-America Conflict," *Star-Ledger* (Newark), February 11, 1992.

12. Larry Wayne Ward, *The Motion Picture Goes to War: The U.S. Government Film Effort during World War I* (Ann Arbor: UMI Research Press, 1985), 55–56. This volume is an excellent source of information on U.S. government and commercial filmmaking during World War I.

13. Ibid., 56.

14. Quoted in Burke Davis, *The Billy Mitchell Affair* (New York: Random House, 1967), 16.

15. *Voli sulle ambe* (Florence, 1937), a book Vittorio Mussolini wrote to convince Italian boys that they should all try war, "the most beautiful and complete of all sports"; as quoted in Denis Mack Smith, *Mussolini's Roman Empire* (New York: Viking, 1976), 75.

16. For extended analyses of the significance of this event, see Clinton Burhans, Jr., "Spindrift and the Sea: Structural Patterns and Unifying Elements in *Catch-22,*" *Twentieth-Century Literature* 19 (1973), 239–250; and H. Bruce Franklin, *War Stars: The Superweapon and the American Imagination* (New York: Oxford University Press, 1988), 123–27.

17. Joseph Heller, *Catch-22* (New York: Dell Publishing, 1962), 334–37.

18. When the Korean War began in mid-1950, there were fewer than 10 million television sets in the United States. Americans' principal visual images of the war came from newsreels shown before feature films in movie theaters and from still photos in magazines.

19. Stephen Wright, *Meditations in Green* (New York: Bantam, 1984), 39; hereafter cited by page in the text.

20. "How Helicopter Dumped a Viet Captive to Death," *Chicago Sun-Times,* November 29, 1969; "Death of a Prisoner," *San Francisco Chronicle,* November 29, 1969.

21. See Jacqueline Sharkey, *Under Fire: U.S. Military Restrictions on the Media from Grenada to the Persian Gulf* (Washington, D.C.: Center for Public Integrity, 1991).

22. "Two Embassies Ringed in Noriega Search," *Star-Ledger* (Newark), December 22, 1989.

23. Everette E. Dennis, David Stebenne, et al., *The Media at War: The Press and the Persian Gulf Conflict* (New York: Gannett Foundation Media Center, 1991), 14.
24. Ibid., 17–18.
25. Dana L. Cloud, "Operation Desert Comfort," in *Seeing Through the Media: The Persian Gulf War,* cd. Susan Jeffords and Lauren Rabinovitz (New Brunswick: Rutgers University Press, 1994), 160–63; Douglas Kellner, *The Persian Gulf TV War* (Boulder, Colo.: Westview Press, 1992), 82–85.
26. Dennis, Stebenne, et al., *The Media at War,* 20–22.
27. This subject is insightfully explored in depth by Kellner, *The Persian Gulf TV War;* Jeffords and Rabinovitz, *Seing Through the Media;* and Hamid Mowlana, George Gerbner, and Herbert I. Schiller, eds., *Triumph of the Image: The Media's War in the Persian Gulf—A Global Perspective* (Boulder, Colo.: Westview Press, 1992).
28. Kellner, *The Persian Gulf TV War,* 68. As Lynda Boose points out in "Techno-Muscularity and the 'Boy Eternal': From the Quagmire to the Gulf," in *Cultures of United States Imperialism,* ed. Amy Kaplan and Donald E. Pease (Durham: Duke University Press, 1993), 593, the tens of millions of Americans outraged by this bogus story of Kuwaiti infants being killed seemed oblivious to the actual deaths of some 170,000 Iraqi infants resulting from the 1991 U.S. bombing of urban infrastructure and hospital facilities.

CHAPTER 2. PLAUSIBILITY OF DENIAL

1. *The Pentagon Papers: The Defense Department History of United States Decisionmaking in Vietnam,* Senator Gravel edition, 4 vols. (Boston: Beacon Press, 1971), 3:141.
2. Christian G. Appy, *Working-Class War: American Combat Soldiers and Vietnam* (Chapel Hill: University of North Carolina Press, 1993), 9.
3. This 1990 text written by George Donelson Moss and published by Prentice-Hall, a subsidiary of Viacom, had gone through three editions by 1998. Among the important studies that have explored how the war has been transformed into a trauma inflicted not by America on Vietnam but by Vietnam on America, see Susan Jeffords, *The Remasculinization of America: Gender and the Vietnam War* (Bloomington: Indiana University Press, 1989); Fred Turner, *Echoes of Combat: The Vietnam War in American Memory* (New York: Doubleday Anchor, 1996); and Keith Beattie, *The Scar That Binds: American Culture and the Vietnam War* (New York: New York University Press, 1998).
4. "Kicking the 'Vietnam Syndrome,' " *Washington Post,* March 4, 1991.
5. Ronald Reagan, press conference, February 18, 1982, in *Public Papers of the Presidents of the United States: Ronald Reagan, 1982,* vol. 1 (Washington, D.C.: U.S. Government Printing Office, 1983), 184–85. Reagan kept repeating this revision of Vietnamese history. For example: "The settlement of French Indochina created two nations—South Vietnam and North Vietnam. They were two separate nations. In fact, back through history they had pretty much been separate countries" (April 4, 1984, in *Public Papers of the Presidents of the United*

States: Ronald Reagan, 1984, [Washington, D.C.: U.S. Government Printing Office, 1985], 467).

6. Turner, *Echoes of Combat,* 63; Arnold R. Isaacs, *Vietnam Shadows: The War, Its Ghost, and Its Legacy* (Baltimore: Johns Hopkins University Press, 1997), 49.

7. The texts of the agreement between France and the DRV as well as the Final Declaration of the conference are reprinted in *Vietnam and America: A Documented History,* ed. Marvin E. Gettleman, Jane Franklin, Marilyn Young, and H. Bruce Franklin (New York: Grove Press, 1995), 66–76.

8. *Pentagon Papers,* 1:247, 287, 448. In *Mandate for Change: The White House Years, 1953–1956* (Garden City, N.Y.: Doubleday, 1963), 372, Eisenhower wrote, "I have never talked or corresponded with a person knowledgeable in Indochinese affairs who did not agree that had elections been held at the time of the fighting, possibly 80 percent of the population would have voted for the Communist Ho Chi Minh."

9. U.S. Department of State, *A Threat to the Peace: North Vietnam's Effort to Conquer South Vietnam,* Publication 308, Far Eastern series 110 (Washington, D.C.: U.S. Government Printing Office, 1961), 3.

10. *Pentagon Papers,* 1:247.

11. See "Lansdale Team's Report on Covert Saigon Mission in 1954 and 1955," in *Pentagon Papers,* 1:573–83; reprinted in Gettleman et al., *Vietnam and America,* 81–92.

12. David G. Marr, "The Rise and Fall of 'Counterinsurgency': 1961–1964," in *Pentagon Papers,* 5:202–10; reprinted in Gettleman et al., *Vietnam and America,* 205–15.

13. The NLF's ten-point program, Nixon's eight-point response, and the Paris Peace Accords are reprinted in Gettleman et al., *Vietnam and America,* 430–34, 472–86.

14. Robert S. McNamara, James G. Blight, and Robert K. Brigham, *Argument without End: In Search of Answers to the Vietnam Tragedy* (New York: Public Affairs, 1999), 178–83, 205–12, and passim.

15. Jim Neilson, *Warring Fictions: Cultural Politics and the Vietnam War Narrative* (Jackson: University Press of Mississippi, 1998), 143 and passim.

16. Ibid., 163; James C. Wilson, *Vietnam in Prose and Film* (Jefferson, N.C.: McFarland, 1982), 44, 45.

17. W. D. Ehrhart, "Making the Children Behave," in *The Vietnam War in American Stories, Songs, and Poems,* ed. H. Bruce Franklin (Boston: Bedford Books, 1996), 251.

18. W. D. Ehrhart, *Passing Time: Memoir of a Vietnam Veteran Against the War* (Amherst: University of Massachusetts Press, 1995), 172, 175; originally published as *Marking Time* (New York: Avon, 1986). The 1995 edition contains my extended introduction to the book, including a discussion of the utterly astonishing impact it has on students.

19. Eric James Schroeder, "Two Interviews: Talks with Tim O'Brien and Robert Stone," *Modern Fiction Studies* 30 (Spring 1984), 146. O'Brien personally reviewed and corrected the transcript of this interview.

20. W. D. Ehrhart, *Vietnam-Perkasie* (Amherst: University of Massachusetts Press, 1995), 9; originally published by McFarland & Co., 1983.

21. Tim O'Brien, "The Vietnam in Me," *New York Times Magazine*, October 2, 1994, 52; hereafter cited by page in the text.

22. Tim O'Brien, *If I Die in a Combat Zone Box Me Up and Ship Me Home* (New York: Dell/Laurel, 1979), 66, 73; originally published by Delacorte Press/Seymour Lawrence, 1973.

23. Tim O'Brien, *Going After Cacciato* (New York: Dell, 1979), 377. O'Brien revised this paperback version from the original hardback published in 1978 by Delacorte Press/Seymour Lawrence.

24. Tim O'Brien, *The Things They Carried* (New York: Penguin Books, 1991), 43, 54, 63.

25. Tim O'Brien, *In the Lake of the Woods* (New York: Penguin, 1995), 298; hereafter cited by page in the text. This paperback edition was revised by O'Brien from the original hardback published by Houghton Mifflin/Seymour Lawrence in 1994.

26. By 1968, tens of millions of Americans and hundreds of millions of people elsewhere on the planet were convinced that the U.S. war in Southeast Asia, with its massive use of chemical warfare, wholesale slaughter of the civilian population, intentional devastation of the countryside, and conscious destruction of food supplies, constituted genocide. Two widely read volumes documenting this view were *In the Name of America: A Study Commissioned and Published by Clergy and Laymen Concerned about Vietnam, January 1968* (New York: E. P. Dutton, 1968) and John Duffett, ed., *Against the Crimes of Silence: Proceedings of the International War Crimes Tribunal, Stockholm-Copenhagen* (New York: Simon and Schuster, 1968), which included Jean-Paul Sartre's essential work "On Genocide."

27. Jonathan Schell, *The Military Half: An Account of Destruction in Quang Ngai and Quang Tin* (New York: Alfred A. Knopf, 1968); originally published in the *New Yorker.*

28. Ronald Reagan, February 24, 1981, in *Public Papers of the Presidents of the United States: Ronald Reagan, 1981* (Washington, D.C.: U.S. Government Printing Office, 1982), 155.

29. Ronald Reagan, April 18, 1985, in *Public Papers of the Presidents of the United States: Ronald Reagan, 1985,* vol. 1 (Washington, D.C.: U.S. Government Printing Office, 1985), 464.

30. As quoted in the *Fresno Bee,* October 10, 1965. In subsequent years, variant forms of Reagan's statement have been widely disseminated.

31. Adolf Hitler, *Mein Kampf,* trans. Ralph Manheim (Boston: Houghton Mifflin, 1943), 186, 190, 243, 273, 275.

32. David Halberstam, *The Making of a Quagmire* (New York: Random House, 1965), 38, 322.

33. *Pentagon Papers,* 1:x–xii.

34. As reproduced here, this table comes from a revealing source: Samuel P. Huntington, "The United States," in Michael Crozier, Samuel P. Huntington and Joji Watanuki, *The Crisis of Democracy: Report on the Governability of Democracies to the Trilateral Commission* (New York: New York University Press, 1975), 79. Formed in 1973, the year the United States agreed to end its war in Vietnam, the Trilateral Commission consisted of political and economic elites

from North America, western Europe, and Japan; it had a profound influence on policy in the 1970s and beyond.

CHAPTER 3. THE ANTIWAR MOVEMENT WE ARE SUPPOSED TO FORGET

1. "Public Likes Carter, Survey Finds, More for His Style Than Programs," *New York Times,* July 29, 1977.

2. One instructive document is "The Real Indo-China" by First Lieutenant R. Shaw, a twenty-one–page handwritten account filled with admiration for the Viet Minh who rescued him. Declassified in 1987, the document is available through the National Archives; a copy, together with a typed manuscript, was furnished to me by Tara McAuliff. Former OSS agent Charles Fenn describes how Ho Chi Minh personally arranged for Shaw's liberation in *Ho Chi Minh* (New York: Charles Scribner's Sons, 1973), 73, 75, 78.

3. The classic text is by the former head of OSS operations in Indochina, Archimedes L. A. Patti, *Why Viet Nam? Prelude to America's Albatross* (Berkeley: University of California Press, 1980).

4. Reprinted in *Vietnam and America,* ed. Marvin Gettleman, Jane Franklin, Marilyn Young, and H. Bruce Franklin (New York: Grove Press, 1995), 26–28.

5. "History of the Vietnam-USA Society" (typescript published in the late 1990s by the Vietnam-USA Society, 105A Quan Thanh Street, Hanoi). An account of General Gallagher's speech at the first meeting of the Vietnam-American Friendship Association on October 17, 1945, in Hanoi appears in *V.A.F.A. Monthly Magazine* (Hanoi) (November 1945), 1–2. Both these documents were provided to me by Tara McAuliff.

6. The information about these early protests comes from Michael Gillen's invaluable Ph.D. dissertation, "Roots of Opposition: The Critical Response to U.S. Indochina Policy, 1945–1954" (New York University, 1991).

7. "Transcript of the Proceedings at the Meeting in Celebration of the Second Anniversary of the Independence of the Republic of Viet-Nam, 1947," typescript, Cornell University Library. Tara McAuliff unearthed this document and provided me with a copy.

8. Reprinted in Gettleman et al., *Vietnam and America,* 52.

9. Senator Ernest Gruening and Herbert Wilton Beaser, *Vietnam Folly* (Washington, D.C.: National Press, 1968), 100–105.

10. Ibid., 105.

11. Gillen, "Roots of Opposition," 379–83, 402. As Gillen notes, some sources incorrectly attribute this speech to Lyndon Johnson.

12. Ibid., 402.

13. Paul M. Sweezy and Leo Huberman, "What Every American Should Know about Indo-China," *Monthly Review* 6 (June 1954), 1–23.

14. See the 1955 report of Colonel Edward Lansdale in Gettleman et al., *Vietnam and America,* 82–92.

15. See Gettleman et al., *Vietnam and America,* 241–42.

16. Harlan Hahn, "Dove Sentiments among Blue-Collar Workers," *Dissent* 17

(May–June 1970), 202–5; Richard F. Hamilton, "A Research Note on the Mass Support for 'Tough' Military Initiatives," *American Sociological Review* 33 (June 1968), 439–45; Jim O'Brien, "The Anti-War Movement and the War," *Radical America* 8 (May–June 1974), 57; William L. Lunch and Peter W. Sperlich, "American Public Opinion and the War in Vietnam," *Western Political Quarterly* 32 (March 1979), 21–44.

17. This poll was the central theme of the main speech for which I was fired from Stanford; given in February 1971, the speech is reprinted in "In the Matter of H. Bruce Franklin: Decision," Advisory Board, Stanford University, January 5, 1972, 13–14. The poll is cited in Lunch and Sperlich, "American Public Opinion," 33–34.

18. James W. Loewen, *Lies My Teacher Told Me* (New York: New Press, 1995), 297–99.

19. For an excellent analysis of the Chicano antiwar movement and a detailed description of what was evidently the deliberate police murder of Salazar (who was actively exposing police terror against the Chicano community), see George Mariscal, *Aztlán and Viet Nam* (Berkeley: University of California Press, 1999), 187–212. This marvelous anthology by Mariscal, himself a Vietnam veteran, provides rich literary and other materials from the Chicano experience in the Vietnam War.

20. Because Jackson State was a black college, the slaughter there, where Mississippi highway patrolmen fired with shotguns, rifles, and submachine guns into a women's dormitory and an unarmed crowd, has been largely wiped from memory. Or it has been written off as occurring "during a protest unrelated to the war." See Nancy Zaroulis and Gerald Sullivan, *Who Spoke Up? American Protest against the War in Vietnam, 1963–1975* (Garden City, N.Y.: Doubleday, 1984), 329. But in fact one of the main targets of the students' protest was the campus ROTC building, as described by Tim Spofford, "Lynch Street: The May 1970 Slayings at Jackson State University," *Kent and Jackson State, 1970–1990*, a special issue of *Vietnam Generation* 2, no. 2 (1990), 59–64.

21. Martin Luther King, Jr., "Declaration of Independence from the War in Vietnam," in Gettleman et al., *Vietnam and America*, 312.

22. See Clyde Taylor, *Vietnam and Black America: Anthology of Protest and Resistance* (New York: Anchor, 1973).

23. *Malcolm X Speaks: Selected Speeches and Statements*, edited with prefatory notes by George Brietman (New York: Grove Press, 1966), 219.

24. "The War in Vietnam" (leaflet), in *Black Protest*, ed. Joanne Grant (New York: Fawcett, 1979), 416.

25. "Statement on Vietnam," ibid., 416.

26. Commander George L. Jackson, "Constraints of the Negro Civil Rights Movement on American Military Effectiveness," *Naval War College Review* (January 1970), 100–107; reprinted in Gettleman et al., *Vietnam and America*, 321–26.

27. "Army Deserters Nobody Looks For," *San Francisco Chronicle*, January 17, 1972.

28. "Issue of Granting Amnesty Echoes Division over War," *New York Times*, August 20, 1974.

29. Ibid.

30. Richard Moser, *The New Winter Soldiers: GI and Veteran Dissent during the Vietnam Era* (New Brunswick, N.J.: Rutgers University Press, 1996), 77; Richard De-Camp, "The GI Movement in Asia," *Bulletin of Concerned Asian Scholars* 4 (Winter 1972), 110. Also see Terry Whitmore, *Memphis Nam Sweden* (Jackson: University Press of Mississippi, 1997), the fascinating memoir of a wounded soldier who deserted in Japan, traveled in a Russian fishing boat to the Soviet Union, and eventually made his way to Sweden, where he was still living in the late 1990s; the book was originally published by Doubleday in 1971. Many more deserters, of course, simply walked or drove across the border to Canada; see "The Flow of GI Deserters to Canada," *San Francisco Chronicle*, October 10, 1969.

31. "Déserteurs américains en France," *L'événement* (Paris) (March 1967), 13–14; "De nombreux jeunes Américains fuient la guerre du Vietnam," *Le Monde*, May 5, 1967; "Leaflets Urge GIs to Desert," *International Herald Tribune,* May 29, 1967; "How Anti-Vietnam Deserters Go Underground," *The Times* (London), August 17, 1967; "1,000 GIs in Europe Said Planning Protest Desertion," *International Herald Tribune*, August 18, 1967; "À travers l'Europe, un mystérieux réseau, celui des déserteurs américains," *Paris Match,* September 2, 1967, 5–6; "The Resister/Deserter Underground," *The Nation* (November 1967), 487–91; "GI Deserter Tells Why He Opposes the War: Recounts 'Resistance inside Army' In U.S., Vietnam, Western Europe," *International Herald Tribune*, December 11, 1967; "American Deserters Explain Their Motives," *The Times* (London), February 12, 1968; "U.S. Deserters Plan to Step Up Their Campaign in Europe," *International Herald Tribune*, February 12, 1968; "The New Men without a Country: Why GIs Defect — Report on a Strange Stockholm Colony," *San Francisco Sunday Examiner & Chronicle*, March 31, 1968; "Tomi Schwaetzer" (Max Watts), mimeographed pamphlet on history of deserter underground, Heidelberg, ca. 1969; Max Watts, *US-Army — Europe: Von der Desertion zum Widerstand in der Kaserne oder wie die U-Bahn zur RITA fuhr* (West Berlin: Harald Kater Verlag, 1989); personal experience in the deserter support movement in France, 1967. Max Watts, then using the name Tomi Schwaetzer, was the most important organizer of the deserter underground.

32. Watts, *U.S. Army — Europe,* 54–60; E-mail from Watts, April 7, 1999 (in author's possession). Although the April 1967 upheaval was almost completely blocked from U.S. media, vivid glimpses of it are available in the 1967 film *Loin du Vietnam* (English version released as *Far from Vietnam*), made by such leading cinéastes as Jean-Luc Godard, Joris Ivens, Alain Resnais, William Klein, Agnes Varda, and Chris Marker. I was a participant in the deserter underground, the demonstration, and the making of the film.

33. "1000 GIs in Britain Stage Vietnam Protest," *San Francisco Chronicle*, June 1, 1971.

34. A taste of this can be got from *FTA! Songs of the GI Resistance Sung by Barbara Dane with Active-Duty GIs*, Paredon P1003, Paredon Records, 1970.

35. The importance of GIs and veterans in the antiwar movement in Vietnam and at home has been richly documented in works such as Larry G. Waterhouse and Mariann G. Wizard, *Turning the Guns Around: Notes on the GI Movement*

(New York: Praeger, 1971); Matthew Rinaldi, "The Olive Drab Rebels: Military Organizing during the Vietnam Era," *Radical America* (May–June 1974), 17–51; David Cortright, *Soldiers in Revolt* (Garden City, N.Y.: Doubleday, 1975); Moser, *The New Winter Soldiers;* Jerry Lembcke, *The Spitting Image: Myth, Memory, and the Legacy of Vietnam* (New York: New York University Press, 1998).

36. See chapter 5.

37. *Only the Beginning* is available for rent or purchase from Third World Newsreel, 545 Eighth Avenue, New York, NY 10018; or on-line at twn@twn.org; http://www.twn.org.

38. Lembcke, *The Spitting Image*, chap. 5. See also Lynda Boose's insightful analysis of the myth of the spat-upon vet, "Techno-Muscularity and the 'Boy Eternal': From the Quagmire to the Gulf," in *Cultures of United States Imperialism*, ed. Amy Kaplan and Donald E. Pease (Durham: Duke University Press, 1993), 581–616.

39. Barry Romo, a former infantry platoon leader in Vietnam, has spent three decades tracking down veterans who claim they were spat upon. Many then tell him, "Well, it wasn't actually me, but my buddy told me about it." But some do believe it happened to them—until he explores the incidents with the supposed victims. They then discover that the "remembered" spitting incidents are a product of the collective belief system. "Seventy-five percent of these guys were amazed to discover they didn't get off in San Francisco or Los Angeles," Romo reports, but at military air bases. They remember flying home on civilian airlines, with stewardesses serving meals, and this memory fits their image of arriving at civilian airports. Indeed, they did fly back on civilian airlines—airlines under military charter that landed at Travis Air Force Base, thirty-five miles northeast of Oakland, or, much less frequently, at Norton Air Force Base near San Bernardino. From Travis, the returnees were bused directly to the Oakland Army Terminal (army) or Treasure Island (navy and marines) to complete their discharge procedures, which usually took one to three days. Romo has found only one veteran who remained convinced that he had been spat upon. A former platoon sergeant who was then staying at Romo's home, he at first insisted that he had been spat upon without provocation. After three hours of discussing what actually happened, he recalled that he had berated a teenager passing out antiwar leaflets in a tunnel at the Los Angeles airport; they started fighting, and during the fight the youth spat on him. (Telephone interview with Barry Romo, April 4, 1999.)

40. Lembcke, *The Spitting Image*, 78–79, 106.

41. *New York Times*, November 28, 1969; Lynda Van Devanter, *Home before Morning: The True Story of an Army Nurse in Vietnam* (New York: Warner Books, 1984), 184; Moser, *The New Winter Soldiers*, 57.

42. "The Troops Trick the General," *San Francisco Chronicle*, December 23, 1968.

43. For extensive accounts and documentation, see the books by Moser, Waterhouse and Wizard, Cortright, and Lembcke cited in notes 30 and 35; also Shelby L. Stanton, *The Rise and Fall of an American Army: U.S. Ground Forces in Vietnam, 1965–1973* (Novato, Calif.: Presidio Press, 1985); and "Cincin-

natus," *Self-Destruction: The Disintegration and Decay of the U.S. Army during the Vietnam Era* (New York: Norton, 1981).

44. "Des militaires américains refusent de combattre," *L'Humanité*, April 6, 1967; "Le Vietcong fait état d'une rébellion de soldats Américains," *Le Monde*, April 27, 1967.

45. Horst Faas and Peter Arnett, "The Fighting Men Who Had Enough," *San Francisco Chronicle*, August 26, 1969.

46. Cortright, *Soldiers in Revolt*, 35–39; Moser, *The New Winter Soldiers*, 44–47; Richard Boyle, *The Flower of the Dragon: The Breakdown of the U.S. Army in Vietnam* (San Francisco: Ramparts Press, 1972), 216–53.

47. "The GI Targets of U.S. Grenades," *San Francisco Chronicle*, January 8, 1971; Ron Ridenhour, " 'Fragging' the Officers in Vietnam," *San Francisco Chronicle*, February 21, 1971; "Mansfield's Story of a Fragging," *San Francisco Chronicle*, April 21, 1971; Cortright, *Soldiers in Revolt*, 43–47.

48. Moser, *The New Winter Soldiers*, 48–52.

49. Colonel Robert D. Heinl, Jr., "The Collapse of the Armed Forces," *Armed Forces Journal* (June 1971), 30–37; reprinted in Gettleman et al., *Vietnam and America*, 326–35.

50. "Navy May Charge 3 in Sabotage," *San Francisco Chronicle*, June 14, 1970.

51. See Cortright, *Soldiers in Revolt*, 110–13, for an excellent history of this movement and its ties to the civilian antiwar movement.

52. "Midway's Bay Spill Called 'Deliberate,' " *San Francisco Chronicle*, May 24, 1972.

53. "Ship Engine Damaged," *Palo Alto Times*, July 15, 1972; "Suspect in Navy Sabotage," *San Francisco Chronicle*, August 6, 1972; "Sailor Accused of Carrier Sabotage," *San Francisco Chronicle*, November 7, 1972; "Sailor Charged with Sabotage Asks Out on Bail," *Palo Alto Times*, November 11, 1972; "Carrier Ranger Hit by Fire," *Palo Alto Times*, December 13, 1972; "Fire Aboard the Ranger," *San Francisco Chronicle*, December 14, 1972; "Incidents on the Ranger (Naval Investigative Service List)," unsigned pamphlet, San Francisco, November 1972; "Sabotage Immobilizes USS Ranger," pamphlet issued by Eric Seitz (attorney for sailor accused of deliberately damaging the engine), San Francisco, November 6, 1972, showing that incidents of sabotage continued after his client was jailed.

54. "Suspect in Carrier Fire," *San Francisco Chronicle*, July 18, 1972; "Sailor Accused of Carrier Sabotage," *San Francisco Chronicle*, November 7, 1972.

55. "Stop Our Ship," leaflet, San Francisco, October 1972 (in author's possession); Moser, *The New Winter Soldiers*, 86–87.

56. Cortright, *Soldiers in Revolt*, 114–15.

57. "10 Marines Charged in Racial Fight," *San Francisco Chronicle*, January 10, 1973.

58. "Sailor Accused of Carrier Sabotage," *San Francisco Chronicle*, November 7, 1972; "10 Marines Charged in Racial Fight," *San Francisco Chronicle*, January 10, 1973; Cortright, *Soldiers in Revolt*, 120–21; "Kitty Hawk Arrives Here for Refitting," *San Francisco Chronicle*, January 10, 1973.

59. *Report on Disciplinary Problems*, House Armed Services Committee, 17670, 17674, 17684, quoted in Cortright, *Soldiers in Revolt*, 125.

60. "Sailors' Shipside 'Strike,'" *San Francisco Chronicle,* November 10, 1972; "Strife-Torn Constellation Resumes Duties," *San Francisco Chronicle,* January 6, 1973; Cortright, *Soldiers in Revolt,* 121–22, 124. Henry P. Leifermann's article in the *New York Times Magazine,* February 18, 1973, 17–32, never mentions the antiwar movement on board and presents this "first mass mutiny in the history of the U.S. Navy" as a purely racial event.

61. "Strife-Torn Constellation Resumes Duties," *San Francisco Chronicle,* January 6, 1973.

62. Gareth Porter, *A Peace Denied: The United States, Vietnam, and the Paris Agreement* (Bloomington: Indiana University Press, 1975), 161–62; Gabriel Kolko, *Anatomy of a War* (New York: Pantheon Books, 1985), 440; James William Gibson, *The Perfect War: Technowar in Vietnam* (Boston: Atlantic Monthly Press, 1986), 416–17; Marilyn Young, *The Vietnam Wars 1945–1990* (New York: HarperCollins, 1991), 278–79; Jeffrey Kimball, *Nixon's Vietnam War* (Lawrence: University Press of Kansas, 1998), 365.

63. Cortright, *Soldiers in Revolt,* 135.

64. Seymour M. Hersh, *The Price of Power: Kissinger in the Nixon White House* (New York: Summit Books, 1983), 628–29.

65. The text of the Paris Accords, along with the text of Nixon's secret promise of reparations, can be found in Gettleman et al., *Vietnam and America,* 472–78; compare the text of the ten-point program, 430–33. As a key Kissinger aide put it, "We bombed the North Vietnamese into accepting our concessions." See Young, *The Vietnam Wars 1945–1990,* 269–79.

66. Ralph McGehee, *Deadly Deceits: My Twenty-Five Years in the C.I.A.,* (New York: Sheridan Square Publications, 1983; reprinted Melbourne, Australia: Ocean Press, 1999). Since 1991, McGehee has continued to publish CIABASE, a very useful electronic database on the CIA available at http://www/webcom/com/~pinknoiz/covert/ciabase.html.

67. Philip Agee, *Inside the Company: CIA Diary* (Harmondsworth: Penguin Books, 1975), 563.

68. In the film *Hearts and Minds,* directed by Peter Davis, Warner Brothers/Columbia, 1974.

CHAPTER 4. BURNING ILLUSIONS

1. See my discussion of Douhet and his importance in *War Stars: The Superweapon and the American Imagination* (New York: Oxford University Press, 1988), 87–90.

2. "Barcelona Horrors," *Time,* March 28, 1938, 13; quoted in George E. Hopkins, "Bombing and the American Conscience during World War II," *Historian* 28 (May 1966), 451–73. For a history of strategic bombing in American culture, see Franklin, *War Stars,* chaps. 4–7.

3. Franklin D. Roosevelt, "The President Appeals to Great Britain, France, Italy, Germany, and Poland to Refrain from Air Bombing of Civilians," in *The Public Papers and Addresses of Franklin D. Roosevelt: 1939* (New York: Macmillan, 1941).

4. This description and other information about the history of napalm and strategic bombing is taken from Chapter 6 of my *War Stars*, where full documentation can be found.

5. Ronald Reagan with Richard G. Hubler, *Where's the Rest of Me?* (New York: Elsevier-Dutton, 1965), 118–19.

6. Bruce Cumings, *The Origins of the Korean War*, vol. 2, *The Roaring of the Cataract, 1947–1950* (Princeton: Princeton University Press, 1990), 705–7, 753–55; Cullum A. MacDonald, *Korea: The War before Vietnam* (New York: Free Press, 1986), 234–36; I. F. Stone, *The Hidden History of the Korean War* (New York: Monthly Review Press, 1971), 256–57.

CHAPTER 5. 1968; OR, BRINGING THE WAR HOME

1. Robert J. Glessing, *The Underground Press in America* (Bloomington: Indiana University Press, 1970), 120.

2. Abe Peck, *Uncovering the Sixties: The Life and Times of the Underground Press* (New York: Pantheon Books, 1985), xv. In addition to the books by Glessing (see note 1) and Peck, two other useful histories are Laurence Leamer, *The Paper Revolutionaries: The Rise of the Underground Press* (New York: Simon and Schuster, 1972), and Roger Lewis, *Outlaws of America; The Underground Press and Its Context: Notes on a Cultural Revolution* (Harmondsworth: Penguin Books, 1972).

3. David Cortright, *Soldiers in Revolt: The American Military Today* (Garden City, N.Y.: Doubleday, 1975), 283. Cortright gives a detailed list of 259 GI newspapers he personally was able to locate.

4. Jerry Lembcke, *The Spitting Image: Myth, Memory, and the Legacy of Vietnam* (New York: New York University Press, 1998), 43.

5. Peter Braestrup, *Big Story: How the American Press and Television Reported and Interpreted the Crisis of Tet 1968 in Vietnam and Washington* (Boulder, Colo.: Westview Press and Freedom House, 1977).

6. *Reporting Vietnam*, 2 vols. (New York: The Library of America, 1998). For a valuable critique of the narrowly conventional nature of this collection, see Tom Engelhardt, "Vietnam: A Reportorial DMZ," *The Nation*, November 16, 1998, 50–53.

7. Clarence Wyatt, *Paper Soldiers: The American Press and the Vietnam War* (Chicago: University of Chicago Press, 1995); William Hammond, *Reporting Vietnam: Media and Military at War* (Lawrence: University Press of Kansas, 1998). Neither of these books nor the Library of America's *Reporting Vietnam* nor Braestrup's *Big Story* even mentions the widely influential publication by perhaps the most perspicacious reporter on the war, *I. F. Stone's Weekly*.

8. "Westmoreland Says Ranks of Vietcong Thin Steadily," *New York Times*, November 22, 1967.

9. James Reston, "Washington: Why Westmoreland and Bunker Are Optimistic," *New York Times*, November 22, 1967.

10. Hanson W. Baldwin, "Vietnam Report: Foe Seeks to Sway U.S. Public," "Vietnam Report: The Foe Is Hurt," "Report on Vietnam: Sanctuaries Viewed as a Major War Factor," *New York Times*, December 26, 27, 28, 1967.

11. Wilfred Burchett narrates his six-month epic journey through the liberated areas of South Vietnam in *Vietnam: Inside Story of the Guerilla War* (New York: International Publishers, 1965).

12. *The Pentagon Papers: The Defense Department History of United States Decisionmaking in Vietnam,* Senator Gravel edition, 4 vols. (Boston: Beacon Press, 1972), 4: 232, 234–35, 539, 548, 604; David Hunt, "Remembering the Tet Offensive," in *Vietnam and America,* ed. Marvin Gettleman, Jane Franklin, Marilyn Young, and H. Bruce Franklin (New York: Grove Press, 1995), 366.

13. "Saigon under Fire," CBS News Special Report, January 31, 1968.

14. Robert Pisor, *The End of the Line: The Siege of Khe Sanh* (New York: Ballantine, 1983), is a perceptive and readable account.

15. "Survivors Hunt Dead of Ben Tre, Turned to Rubble in Allied Raids," *New York Times,* February 8, 1968; based on AP story, February 7, 1968. See Braestrup, *Big Story,* 254–60, for a history of the quotation.

16. Art Buchwald, "We Have the Enemy on the Run, Says General Custer," *Washington Post,* February 6, 1968.

17. *New York Times,* April 7, 1968. Westmoreland gives his analysis of the Tet offensive, riddled with bogus statistics and glaring contradictions, in William C. Westmoreland, *Report on the War in Vietnam (as of 30 June 1968),* sec. 2, *Report on Operations in South Vietnam, January 1964–June 1968* (Washington, D.C.: U.S. Government Printing Office, 1968); an annotated version is available in Gettleman et al., *Vietnam and America,* 342–59.

18. None of the foregoing is meant to imply that the NLF did not suffer very heavy casualties. For a helpful overview, see Marilyn Young, *The Vietnam Wars 1945–1990* (New York: HarperCollins, 1991), 216–25. For a detailed military and political history, see Gabriel Kolko, *Anatomy of a War: Vietnam, the United States, and the Modern Historical Experience* (New York: Pantheon, 1985), 303–37. An important corrective to most U.S. scholarship comes from Ngo Vinh Long's on-the-scene interviews with NLF participants, who reported that their severest casualties came in the May and August offensives: "The Tet Offensive and Its Aftermath," *Indochina Newsletter,* no. 49 (January–February 1988), 1–5; no. 50 (March–April 1988), 2–10; no. 60 (November–December 1989), 1–10. To compare contradictory arguments and evidence on the Tet offensive, see Don Oberdorfer, *Tet!* (New York: Da Capo, 1984); Gettleman et al., *Vietnam and America,* 339–400; and Marc Jason Gilbert and William Head, eds., *The Tet Offensive* (Westport, Conn.: Praeger, 1961), which includes a version of Ngo Vinh Long's analysis.

19. *Pentagon Papers,* 4: 232. Some relevant sections of the *Pentagon Papers* are reprinted in Gettleman et al., *Vietnam and America,* 378–97.

20. *Pentagon Papers,* 4: 539.

21. Ibid., 4: 238.

22. Ibid., 4: 547. This statement is from General Earle Wheeler, chairman of the Joint Chiefs of Staff, who had been one of the most optimistic voices among the decision makers.

23. Ibid., 4: 604.

24. Robert Buzzanco, *Masters of War: Military Dissent and Politics in the Vietnam Era* (Cambridge: Cambridge University Press, 1996), 311–40; reprinted as "The

Myth of Tet: Military Failure and the Politics of War," in Gilbert and Head, *The Tet Offensive,* 231–58.

25. See, for example, the remarkably prescient article "Gold, Dollars, and Empire," *Monthly Review* 19 (February 1968), 1–9.

26. "The Democratic Convention: A Challenge to Organizers," *The Movement* 4 (February 1968), 4.

27. See "Washington Explodes," *LNS* (journal of the Liberation News Service), April 6, 1968; and "Black Rebellion around the U.S.," *LNS,* April 8, 1968.

28. "The Death of the American Press: How the Media Plans to Cover Revolts," *The Movement* 3 (July 1967), 5. Excerpts of this article were widely reprinted in 1967 and 1968.

29. For a representative example, see "Either/or in 1968," *Guardian,* March 30, 1968.

30. Mark Lane, "Is Bobby Silent Because Central Intelligence Agency Killed His Brother?" *Los Angeles Free Press,* April 19, 1968, 1, 16, 24, 26.

31. *Guardian,* August 31, 1968.

32. Thorne Dreyer, "Know Your Enemy," *LNS,* August 30, 1968. Other reports indicated that more than 160 Fort Hood soldiers had "refused to take part in riot control operations in Chicago" (*Great Speckled Bird,* August 30–September 12, 1968). The resistance by these soldiers was important news in the GI antiwar press; see *Vietnam GI* (September 1968).

33. Wilfred Burchett, "The Lies Crumble," *National Guardian,* February 10, 1968.

34. David Hunt, "Remembering the Tet Offensive," *Radical America* 12 (February 1978), 95–96; reprinted in Gettleman et al., *Vietnam and America,* 377. Hunt's quotation is from a February 4 *New York Times* account.

35. Mary Lou Greenberg, "Does Double Standard Exist in the Movement?" *Midpeninsula Observer,* February 19–March 4, 1968, 1, 9 (the name of this paper was changed to *Peninsula Observer* in August 1968). See also Bernardine Dohrn, "The Liberation of Vietnamese Women," *LNS,* November 1, 1968.

36. *Peninsula Observer,* December 9, 1968.

37. *New Left Notes,* December 4, 1968.

38. Harvey Wasserman, "1968: Year of the Heroic Guerilla MEDEA," *LNS,* July 10, 1968, 2–3. The slogan appears on issues from July 17 on.

39. *The Movement* 3 (November 1967).

40. *LNS,* February 16, 1968; "Slaughter in South Carolina," *The Movement* 4 (April 1968), 12.

41. *CAW!* May–June 1968; *New Left Notes,* May 6, 1968.

42. Alex Foreman, "San Francisco Police State College," *The Movement* 4 (January 1969), 13.

43. "Why Latin America?" *Viet-Report* 3 (April–May 1968), 3.

44. Editors' Foreword, "Colonialism and Liberation in America," *Viet-Report* 3 (Summer 1968), 3.

45. Joanne Grant, ed., *Black Protest* (New York: Fawcett, 1979), 416; Martin Luther King, Jr., "Declaration of Independence from the War in Vietnam," *Ramparts* (May 1967), 33–37; reprinted in Gettleman et al., *Vietnam and America,* 310–18.

46. *The Black Panther* 2, no. 1 (March 16, 1968), 1, 5, 20.

47. Bob Riche, "Proposal: A Peace Riot," *LNS*, January 26, 1968.

48. *Pentagon Papers*, 4: 564, 583.

49. *Vietnam Veterans Stars & Stripes for Peace* 1 (September 1967). The February 1968 issue of this paper carries a front-page picture of a confrontation between Veterans for Peace and MPs at the October 1967 Pentagon demonstration. For samples of reports on organized desertions and demonstrations within the army, see *Midpeninsula Observer*, December 11–25, 1967, 12.

50. "G.I.'s Warned Not to Speak Out," *LNS*, January 5, 1968.

51. *LNS*, February 5, 14, 15, 1968.

52. "Defense Dept. Up-Tight over Servicemen's Union," *LNS*, May 12, 1968.

53. *Midpeninsula Observer*, March 14–18, 1968, 12; April 8–12, 1968, 4; *New Left Notes*, April 20, 1968, 4.

54. "G.I. Organizing," *New Left Notes*, June 24, 1968, 7.

55. *Vietnam GI*'s publication history is discussed in an interview with the paper's editors, "The New Left and the Army: Let's Bridge the Gap!" *The Movement* 4 (October 1968), 10–11. Its Vietnam circulation figures appeared in ads in the movement press; see, for example, the back page of *New Left Notes*, May 13, 1968.

56. *LNS*, "Special Issue on Soldiers," Mid-July 1968.

57. Harvey Stone, "Summer of Support: GI Coffee Houses for Peace," *LNS*, July 17, 1968. The singer Barbara Dane describes her work at the Oleo Strut in "The Army Can't Have Our Minds," *Guardian*, July 20, 1968, 1, 8.

58. Thorne Dreyer, "Know Your Enemy," *LNS*, August 30, 1968; *Great Speckled Bird*, August 30–September 12, 1968; *Vietnam GI* (September 1968).

59. Tom Cleaver, "Texas GIs Join Antiwar Rally," *Guardian*, October 26, 1968.

60. "GIs Hold Teach-In," *The Ally* (September 1968).

61. "Support GI Week: SDS Gets Drafted," *New Left Notes*, October 18, 1968, 4.

62. Carrie Iverson, "GIs 'bout face," *Peninsula Observer*, October 7–13, 1968, 7.

63. *LNS*, October 21, 1968.

64. Tom Cleaver, "Texas GIs Join Antiwar Rally," *Guardian*, October 26, 1968.

65. Mary Hamilton, "U.S. Military Is Target for GI Week," *Guardian*, October 19, 1968.

66. Bernardine Dohrn, "Revolution in the Army," *New Left Notes*, January 22, 1969.

67. See, for example, Commander George L. Jackson, "Constraints of the Negro Civil Rights Movement on American Military Effectiveness," *Naval War College Review* (January 1970), 100–107; and Colonel Robert D. Heinl, Jr., "The Collapse of the Armed Forces," *Armed Forces Journal*, June 7, 1971, 30–37; both essays are reprinted in Gettleman et al., *Vietnam and America*, 321–35. For fuller treatments of the insurrection in the armed forces and its effect on the military history of the war, see Larry G. Waterhouse and Mariann G. Wizard, *Turning the Guns Around: Notes on the GI Movement* (New York: Delta Books, 1961); Richard Boyle, *Flower of the Dragon: The Breakdown of the U.S. Army in Vietnam* (San Francisco: Ramparts Press, 1972); Cortright, *Soldiers in Revolt;* and Richard R. Moser, *The New Winter Soldiers: GI and Veteran Dissent during the Vietnam Era* (New Brunswick, N.J.: Rutgers University Press, 1996).

68. Among the many fine books documenting the growth of corporate media monopolies, see Ben Bagdikian, *The Media Monopoly,* 5th ed. (Boston: Beacon Press, 1997), and Robert W. McChesney, *Rich Media, Poor Democracy: Communication Politics in Dubious Times* (Champaign: University of Illinois Press, 1999).

69. James McGrath Morris, *Jailhouse Journalism: The Fourth Estate behind Bars* (Jefferson, N.C.: McFarland & Co., 1998), 187.

70. Matthew Lasar, "The Crisis That Wouldn't Go Away: A Short History of Pacifica Radio's 50th Anniversary War," http://www.savepacifica.com, January 2000; Frank Ahrens, "Tiny Pacifica's Big Troubles," *Washington Post,* February 8, 2000; "Free-Lancers on Strike at Pacifica News: Radio Reporters Call for End to Gag Rule," *San Francisco Chronicle,* February 1, 2000; Media Alliance Press Release, "Leadership Shake-up at Pacifica Foundation," http:www.media-alliance.org, February 28, 2000; "Leadership Meeting Frustrates Local Rep," *Berkeley Daily Planet,* February 29, 2000; "New Faces for Top Spots at Pacifica," *Berkeley Daily Planet,* February 29, 2000; "Chairman, Director to Leave Pacifica; Both Had Roles in Labor Strife at KPFA," *San Francisco Chronicle,* February 29, 2000. For background, see Matthew Lasar, *Pacifica Radio: The Rise of an Alternative Network* (Philadelphia: Temple University Press, 1999).

71. "B-52's to Carry Less Accurate Gravity Bombs," *New York Times,* April 30, 1999.

CHAPTER 6. THE VIETNAM WAR AND THE CULTURE WARS

1. Quoted in "With Populist Themes, Surging Buchanan Puts Squeeze on Own Party," *Wall Street Journal,* February 14, 1996.

2. Quoted in Frank Rich, "Love It or Leave It," *New York Times,* February 13, 1999.

3. Speech to the New Hampshire legislature, February 13, 1996, as quoted in "With Populist Themes, Surging Buchanan Puts Squeeze on Own Party," *Wall Street Journal,* February 14, 1996.

4. Dorothy Canfield Fisher, *Why Stop Learning?* (New York: Harcourt, Brace, 1927), 5–6.

5. J. J. Janeway, *Report to the Synod of New Jersey on the Subject of Parochial Schools* (Philadelphia, [1845]), 5.

6. "An Argument against Public Schools," *Philadelphia National Gazette,* July 10, 1830; quoted in Edgar W. Knight and Clifton Hall, *Readings in American Educational History* (New York: Appleton-Century-Crofts, 1951), 149.

7. Cited in Knight and Hall, *Readings in American Educational History,* 664.

8. G. Stanley Hall, president of Clark University, quoted ibid., 722.

9. A. L. Smith, "Higher Education of Women," *Popular Science Monthly* 66 (March 1905), 467, 469. I am indebted to Joan Hedrick for bringing this article to my attention.

10. Quotation from the 1820 *Western Review* (Cincinnati) in Frank Luther Mott, *A History of American Magazines, 1741–1850* (Cambridge, Mass.: Harvard University Press, 1930), 146.

11. Gerald Graff, *Beyond the Culture Wars: How Teaching the Conflicts Can Revitalize*

American Education (New York: W. W. Norton, 1992), 95. For excellent histories of the teaching of literature in American higher education, see Richard Ohmann, *English in America* (New York: Oxford University Press, 1976), and Gerald Graff, *Professing Literature: An Institutional History* (Chicago: University of Chicago Press, 1987).

12. Louis Untermeyer, ed., *American Poetry from the Beginning to Whitman* (New York: Harcourt, Brace, 1931).

13. Louis Untermeyer, ed., *Modern American Poetry,* 5th ed. (New York: Harcourt, Brace, 1936).

14. Paul Lauter lists the following in *Canons and Context* (New York: Oxford University Press), 41–42: Robert T. Kerlin, *Contemporary Poetry of the Negro* (1921) and *Negro Poets and Their Poems* (Washington, D.C.: Associated Publishers, 1923); James Weldon Johnson, ed., *The Book of American Negro Poetry* (New York: Harcourt, Brace, 1922); Newman Ivey White and Walter Clinton Jackson, eds., *An Anthology of Verse by American Negroes* (Durham, N.C.: Trinity College Press, 1924); Countee Cullen, ed., *Caroling Dusk* (New York: Harper & Row, 1927); Alain Locke, ed., *Four Negro Poets* (New York: Simon & Schuster, 1927); V. F. Calverton, ed., *An Anthology of American Negro Literature* (New York: Modern Library, 1929); and Otelia Cromwell, Lorenzo Dow Turner, and Eva B. Dykes, eds., *Readings from Negro Authors* (New York: Harcourt, Brace, 1931). It is interesting to note that the one college publisher in this list, Trinity College Press, was an organ of a southern institution shortly to be renamed Duke University, a school that would not admit its first African American student for decades.

15. For example, not a single work by a person of color can be found in the 1,396 pages of the 1959 edition of *Masters of American Literature,* edited by Leon Edel, Thomas H. Johnson, Sherman Paul, and Claude Simpson, or the 1,119 pages of Perry Miller's 1962 edition of *Major Writers of America,* or the 1,246 pages of the 1965 edition of *American Poetry,* edited by Gay W. Allen, Walter B. Rideout, and James K. Robinson. For more evidence and analysis of the academy's whitening of American literature, see my *Prison Literature in America: The Victim as Criminal and Artist,* expanded ed. (New York: Oxford University Press, 1989), xxiii–xxxii, 5–7.

16. Herman Melville, *Typee: A Peep at Polynesian Life* (Evanston: Northwestern University Press, 1968), 125.

17. Ho Chi Minh's 1919 and 1945 appeals are reprinted in *Vietnam and America,* ed. Marvin E. Gettleman, Jane Franklin, Marilyn Young, and H. Bruce Franklin (New York: Grove Press, 1995), 18–20, 46–47.

18. See W. B. Carnochan, *The Battleground of the Curriculum: Liberal Education and American Experience* (Stanford: Stanford University Press, 1993), chap. 6.

19. See Lauter, *Canons and Context,* 25 and 42, n. 6, for information on the contents of many standard anthologies after the 1930s. Lauter argues that the process of whitening the anthologies began in the 1920s, but his main examples of all-white anthologies or anthologies that eliminated previously included black writers were almost all published in the 1940s and 1950s.

20. Allen Tate, *Reactionary Essays on Poetry and Ideas* (New York: Charles Scribner's Sons, 1936), 155–56.

21. For a fuller exposition of the role of New Criticism in shaping American literary culture prior to the late 1960s, see Franklin, *Prison Literature in America,* xxvi–xvii, 27–28.

22. Aimeé Césaire, *Discourse on Colonialism* (New York: Monthly Review Press, 1972), 14–15; originally published as *Discours sur le colonialisme* by Présence Africaine in 1955. Césaire quotes from an 1883 French newspaper account of how "we amused ourselves counting the dead" Vietnamese (19) and later argues that "the barbarism of Western Europe" is "being only surpassed — far surpassed, it is true — by the barbarism of the United States" (26).

23. See chapter 4. For a history and cultural analysis of "strategic" bombing, see my *War Stars: The Superweapon and the American Imagination* (New York: Oxford University Press, 1988), 81–130.

24. Washington Irving, "The Men of the Moon," from *A History of New York by Diedrich Knickerbocker* (1809), reprinted in H. Bruce Franklin, *Future Perfect: American Science Fiction of the Nineteenth Century* (New Brunswick, N.J.: Rutgers University Press, 1995), 252, 254.

25. *New York Times,* August 9, 1968.

26. Two friends and associates of mine, one a Chicano paratrooper veteran from Vietnam and the other a Filipino former police officer himself, never recovered psychologically from these tortures.

27. Louis Kampf and Paul Lauter, eds., *The Politics of Literature: Dissenting Essays on the Teaching of English* (New York: Random House, 1972). The introduction to this volume includes an invaluable account of the events at the MLA convention and their role in the cultural battles and transformations then emerging.

28. Richard M. Nixon, speech delivered at General Beadle State College, Madison, South Dakota, June 3, 1969, in *Public Papers of the Presidents of the United States: Richard Nixon, 1969* (Washington, D.C.: U.S. Government Printing Office, 1971), 429.

29. Spiro Agnew, "Threat to Educational Standards," speech at Republican fundraising dinner, Des Moines, Iowa, April 14, 1970, in *The University Crisis Reader: The Liberal University under Attack,* ed. Immanuel Wallerstein and Paul Starr (New York: Vintage Books, 1971), 320.

30. "Professor Sees Peril in Education," *San Francisco Chronicle,* October 30, 1970.

31. Two excellent analyses of the fight over free tuition and open admissions at CUNY are Michael Harrington, "Keep Open Admissions Open," *New York Times Magazine,* November 2, 1975, 16–17, 94–102; Deborah Davis, "Free Tuition Is Dead — And Who Killed It," *Village Voice,* December 8, 1975, 13.

32. Speech by Gerald Ford to the National Press Club, October 29, 1975, reported in *New York Times,* October 30, 1975.

33. Ron Nessen, statement to the press, October 17, 1975.

34. Ira Shor, *Culture Wars: School and Society in the Conservative Restoration, 1969–1984* (Chicago: University of Chicago Press, 1992), 7.

35. Brent Staples, "The Politics of Remedial Education at CUNY," *New York Times,* September 7, 1998. On November 24, 1999, the New York State Board of Regents approved a plan to phase out remedial courses at CUNY by the year 2001.

36. See Elihu Rosenblatt, ed., *Criminal Injustice: Confronting the Prison Crisis* (Bos-

ton: South End Press, 1996); Elliott Currie, *Crime and Punishment in America* (New York: Metropolitan Books, 1998); Daniel Burton-Rose, Dan Pens, and Paul Wright, eds., *The Celling of America* (Monroe, Maine: Common Courage Press, 1998); Scott Christianson, *With Liberty for Some* (Boston: Northeastern University Press, 1998); Eric Schlosser, "The Prison-Industrial Complex," *Atlantic Monthly* 282 (December 1998), 51–77.

37. As demonstrated by Andrew L. Shapiro in "Challenging Criminal Disenfranchisement under the Voting Rights Act: A New Strategy," *Yale Law Journal* 103 (November 1993), 537–66, the explicit purpose of most of the state laws that stripped the vote from convicted felons was to disenfranchise the black electorate. Many of these laws were bundled in legislation mandating poll taxes, literacy tests, and other devices to curtail or eliminate black voting, and their framers sometimes declared that criminal disenfranchisement would be the only one to resist constitutional challenges.

38. Typical are a lengthy editorial titled "Politically Correct" (November 26, 1990) and "The Dumbing Down of Higher Education" (March 19, 1996), a half-page op-ed piece by William Simon, secretary of the treasury in the Nixon and Ford administrations and then president of the John M. Olin Foundation, calling for a return to the curriculum of "only a generation ago, built around English literature, the history of Western civilization," and "timeless fundamentals, built around the study of Western thought and literature."

39. For details on funding of the culture wars by right-wing organizations such as the Olin Foundation, the American Enterprise Institute, and the Hudson Institute, see Jon Wiener, "The Olin Money Tree: Dollars for Neocon Scholars," *Nation,* January 1, 1990, 12–14; Donald Lazere, "Political Correctness Left and Right," *College English* 54 (March 1992), 79–88; Barbara Foley, "What's at Stake in the Culture Wars," *New England Quarterly* 68 (September 1995), 458–79; and Eric Alterman, "The 'Right' Books and Big Ideas," *Nation,* November 22, 1999, 16–21.

CHAPTER 7. *STAR TREK* AND KICKING THE VIETNAM SYNDROME

1. "Magellan Sends First Images of Venus; Now Flawless Spacecraft Begins Mapping Surface of Elusive Planet," *Washington Post,* September 25, 1990.
2. "Venus Spacecraft Finds Signs of Active Volcano," *Washington Post,* October 30, 1991.
3. "The 'Enterprise' Turns 25," *Entertainment Weekly,* September 27, 1991, 21–22, gives figures on 1991 broadcasts and indicates that the original series had never been higher than fiftieth in the Nielsen ratings.
4. For an analysis of the *Star Trek* industry, see Gary Westfahl, "Where No Market Has Gone Before: 'The Science-Fiction Industry' and the Star Trek Industry," *Extrapolation* 37 (Winter 1996), 291–301. On K/S fiction, see Patricia Frazer Lamb and Diana L. Veith, "Romantic Myth, Transcendence, and *Star Trek* Zines," in *Erotic Universe: Sexuality and Fantastic Literature,* ed. Donald Palumbo (New York: Greenwood Press, 1986), 235–55; and Henry Jenkins III, "*Star*

Trek Rerun, Reread, Rewritten: Fan Writing as Textual Poaching," *Critical Studies in Mass Communication* 5 (June 1988), 85–107.

5. See Daniel Leonard Bernardi, *Star Trek and History: Race-ing toward a White Future* (New Brunswick, N.J.: Rutgers University Press, 1998).

6. Rick Worland, "From the New Frontier to the Final Frontier: *Star Trek* from Kennedy to Gorbachev," *Film & History* 24 (February–May 1995), 19–35.

7. Much of the analysis that follows is adapted from the script that I wrote for portions of the 1991 exhibit "*Star Trek* and the Sixties" at the National Air and Space Museum in Washington, D.C., especially the Vietnam section. As co-author of the full script, Mary Henderson, art curator of the museum and curator of the exhibit, also contributed to the Vietnam section.

8. In the fall of 1963, before U.S. troops were officially supposed to be fighting in Vietnam, *Twilight Zone* opened its final season with "In Praise of Pip," a tale of a mortally wounded soldier in Vietnam and his guilt-ridden father, who pleads with God to take his life rather than his son's.

9. Marvin E. Gettleman, Jane Franklin, Marilyn Young, and H. Bruce Franklin, eds. *Vietnam and America* (New York: Grove Press, 1995), 227–42; see chapters 3 and 5 for a fuller discussion of these and subsequent events.

10. Allan Asherman, *The Star Trek Compendium* (New York: Pocket Books, 1989), 9.

11. The scripts of May 13 and June 3, 1966, are in the Gene Roddenberry Collection, Arts Library/Special Collection, UCLA; I examined them while they were on loan to the National Air and Space Museum in 1991–92. The June 3 script is reprinted in Harlan Ellison, *Harlan Ellison's The City on the Edge of Forever* (Clarkston, Ga.: White Wolf Publishing, 1996), which includes a 30,000-word denunciation of Roddenberry by Ellison, two earlier treatments, and afterwords by eight of the participants involved in rewriting, producing, and staging the episode.

12. Interview with Robert Justman, February 26, 1992.

13. *New York Times*, November 22, 1967.

14. Hanson W. Baldwin, "Vietnam Report: Foe Seeks to Sway U.S. Public," "Vietnam Report: The Foe Is Hurt," "Report on Vietnam: Sanctuaries Viewed as a Major War Factor," *New York Times*, December 26, 27, 28, 1967; James Reston, editorial, *New York Times*, November 22, 1967.

15. Quote in Worland, "From the New Frontier to the Final Frontier," 33. Worland insightfully analyzes in detail these letters, which he examined in the Gene Roddenberry Collection, Box 18, Folder 2, "A Private Little War," UCLA Theater Arts Library (renamed Arts Library/Special Collection in 1991).

16. Quoted ibid., 33.

17. Rick Worland, "Captain Kirk: Cold Warrior," *Journal of Popular Film and Television* 16 (Fall 1988), 109–17. My own analysis owes a considerable debt to Worland's exceptionally insightful essay.

18. See chapter 5 for a discussion of the role of the antiwar media.

19. See chapter 8 for a fuller discussion of these ads and their significance.

20. *Nixon Speaks Out: Major Speeches and Statements by Richard Nixon in the Presidential Campaign of 1968* (New York: Nixon-Agnew Campaign Committee, 1968), 235.

21. David Gerrold, *The World of Star Trek,* rev. ed. (New York: Bluejay Books, 1984), 117–18; Westfahl, "Where No Market Has Gone Before," 294.

22. David Perlman, "Losing Sight of Space," *San Francisco Chronicle,* September 6, 1981; Richard D. Lyons, "Military Planners View the Shuttle as Way to Open Space for Warfare," *New York Times,* March 29, 1981; "Air Force Forms Space Command on Military Uses," *Wall Street Journal,* June 22, 1982; "Allen to Head Jet Propulsion Lab," *New York Times,* July 23, 1982.

23. Quoted in Karl Grossman, "Master of Space," *The Progressive* 64 (January 2000), 28.

24. Ibid., 27. This vote received hardly any media coverage.

25. Editorial, *Wall Street Journal,* January 21, 1991.

26. Gregg Easterbrook, "Robowar," *New Republic,* February 11, 1991, 17–20.

27. "Excerpts from U.N. Report on Need for Humanitarian Assistance to Iraq," *New York Times,* March 23, 1991; "Critic of Patriot Missile Says It Was 'Almost Total Failure' in War," *New York Times,* January 9, 1992; "Patriot Games: What *Did* We See on Desert Storm TV?" *Columbia Journalism Review,* July/August 1992, 13; "Patriot Missile's Success a Myth, Israeli Aides Say," *New York Times,* November 21, 1993.

28. By 1995 the estimate was half a million. See "Iraq Sanctions Kill Children, U.N. Reports," *New York Times,* December 1, 1995.

29. This imaging is explored in chapter 1. For book-length discussions of the media's presentation of the Gulf War, see chapter 1, notes 23, 25, and 27.

30. See the excellent collection of essays, *History Wars: The "Enola Gay" and Other Battles for the American Past,* ed. Edward T. Linenthal and Tom Engelhardt (New York: Metropolitan Books, 1996).

31. "New Space Museum Head," *New York Times,* November 25, 1999.

CHAPTER 8. THE VIETNAM WAR AS AMERICAN SCIENCE FICTION AND FANTASY

1. James William Gibson in *The Perfect War: Technowar in Vietnam* (New York: Atlantic Monthly Press, 1986) analyzes the ideological basis of U.S. technowar in Vietnam as a self-enclosed universe of discourse, essentially a mode of fantasy. The role of science fiction in the development of U.S. military discourse and war making, especially in relation to techno-wonders, is discussed in depth in my *War Stars: The Superweapon and the American Imagination* (New York: Oxford University Press, 1988), and relations between the superwarrior in U.S. science fiction and John F. Kennedy's sponsorship of the Green Berets is discussed in my *Robert A. Heinlein: America as Science Fiction* (New York: Oxford University Press, 1980).

2. Frederik Pohl, "On Inventing Futures," *Galaxy Science Fiction* (June 1968), 7.

3. The conflicting tendencies in the rival ads are noted by Richard Lupoff in "Science-Fiction Hawks and Doves: Whose Future Will You Buy?" *Ramparts* 10 (February 1972), 25–30, who argues that "the 'peace' ad carried more names than the 'war' ad even though it was signed exclusively by professionals while the other was padded with the signatures of fans," that "*every* author or

editor who signed the 'war' ad was a traditionalist," and that "these traditionalists" were "united by their engineering mentality, and its preference for violent, repressive solutions to the political problems posed in its novels" (26–27).

4. Letter from Kate Wilhelm to the author, March 5, 1994.

5. Telephone interview with Judith Merril, August 19, 1988.

6. Robert A. Heinlein, *Glory Road,* three-part serial, *Magazine of Science Fiction and Fantasy* (July, August, September 1963); quotation (July 1963), 23.

7. Ibid. (July 1963), 9, 16.

8. Ibid. (September 1963), 87.

9. Ibid. (July 1963), 13–14.

10. Ibid. (July 1963), 11.

11. "Ex-GIs in Rhodesia Provide Slang Terms and Zest for Combat," *Wall Street Journal,* April 30, 1979.

12. Heinlein, *Glory Road* (July 1963), 27.

13. Ibid. (September 1963), 69.

14. Cablegram from Ambassador Henry Cabot Lodge to Secretary of State Dean Rusk, August 29, 1963, in *The Pentagon Papers,* Senator Gravel edition, 4 vols. (Boston: Beacon Press, 1971), 2:738; reprinted in *Vietnam and America,* ed. Marvin E. Gettleman, Jane Franklin, Marilyn Young, and H. Bruce Franklin (New York: Grove Press, 1995), 227.

15. Heinlein, *Glory Road* (July 1963), 50.

16. *Pentagon Papers,* 1:466–67.

17. French foreign minister Georges Bidault describes such an offer from Secretary of State John Foster Dulles in an interview recorded in the documentary film *Hearts and Minds* (BBS Productions, 1974).

18. *Pentagon Papers,* 3:65, 175.

19. Herbert Y. Schandler, *The Unmaking of a President: Lyndon Johnson and Vietnam* (Princeton: Princeton University Press, 1977), 89–90; Robert Pisor, *The End of the Line: The Siege of Khe Sanh* (New York: Ballantine, 1982), 153–54; William Westmoreland, *A Soldier Reports* (Garden City, N.Y.: Doubleday, 1976), 338.

20. Joe Poyer, "Challenge: The Insurgent vs. the Counterinsurgent," *Analog* (September 1966), 69–90; (October 1966), 72–91.

21. Joe Poyer, "Null Zone," *Analog* (July 1968), 63, 70.

22. See my discussion of this novel in relation to science fiction and U.S. politics in "Only the Hardware Is Erotic," *Nation,* August 14–21, 1995, 174–75.

23. Stefan T. Possony and J[erry] E. Pournelle, *The Strategy of Technology: Winning the Decisive War* (Cambridge, Mass.: University Press of Cambridge, 1970), 149.

24. Even the official body count of 1,602 killed was labeled by the marine commander General Rathvon McCall Tompkins "a bunch of poop." Pisor, *The End of the Line,* 237. In July, U.S. troops retreated from the base, which was then turned into an enemy surface-to-air missile site.

25. Norman Spinrad, "The Big Flash" in *Orbit 5,* ed. Damon Knight (New York: G. P. Putnam's Sons, 1969), 199, 211.

26. Gettleman et al., *Vietnam and America*, 403–4; "U.S. Assistance Programs in Vietnam," *Hearings before a Subcommittee of the Committee on Government Operations*, House of Representatives, 92nd Cong., 1st sess., 321, 357.

27. Philip Wheaton, "Agrarian Reform in El Salvador: A Program of Rural Pacification," in *Revolution in Central America*, ed. Stanford Central America Action Network (Boulder, Colo.: Westview Press, 1983), 260.

28. Prosterman summarizes the story, and says that he wrote it in late 1970, in Roy L. Prosterman, *Surviving to 3000: An Introduction to the Study of Lethal Conflict* (Belmont, Calif.: Duxbury Press, 1972), 343–44, a book that offers a revealing display of his ideological assumptions and fantasies.

29. Roy L. Prosterman, "Peace Probe," *Analog* (July 1973), 98–101.

30. See Jonathan Schell, *The Military Half: An Account of Destruction in Quang Ngai and Quang Tin* (New York: Alfred E. Knopf, 1968), for a detailed account of this genocidal campaign.

31. The official investigation of the My Lai massacre was headed by three-star general William Peers, who concluded that "war crimes" had been committed, including "individual and group acts of murder, rape, sodomy, maiming, and assault on noncombatants" and recommended courts-martial against over two dozen officers, including the commanding and assistant commanding generals of the Americal Division. See *Report of Department of Army Review of Preliminary Investigations into My Lai Incident* (Washington, D.C.: U.S. Government Printing Office, 1976), 12-1–12-5. Only one junior officer, Lieutenant William Calley, was ever tried and convicted.

32. Telephone interview with Kate Wilhelm, May 31, 1994.

33. Kate Wilhelm, "The Village," in *Bad Moon Rising*, ed. Thomas M. Disch (New York: Harper & Row, 1973), 147; hereafter cited by page in the text.

34. In British science fiction the Vietnam War has generated similar images of American troops as alien invaders, dating at least from J. G. Ballard's 1966 "The Killing Ground" through Brian Aldiss's 1987 "My Country 'Tis Not Only of Thee," each of which imagines England as another Vietnam. Ballard's story is told from the point of view of an officer of the British National Liberation Army, whose ragged, half-starved guerrilla band, "living for months in holes in the ground," desperately resists an overwhelming force of American invaders, armed with a technology "so sophisticated that even the wrist-watches stripped off dead prisoners were too complicated to read." Despite a U.S. "puppet regime in London," the British insurgents can maintain their struggle because, "thirty years after the original conflict in south-east Asia, the globe was now a huge insurrectionary torch, a world Viet Nam" in which England is merely a "remote backwater" for the American's "global war against dozens of national liberation armies." J. G. Ballard, "The Killing Ground," in *The Day of Forever* (London: Panther Books, 1967), 139, 140, 142. Aldiss's story projects a British civil war between a communist north and a capitalist south, which U.S. intervention degrades to a puppet nation of "slimeys," the GIs' equivalent of "gooks." Brian Aldiss, "My Country 'Tis Not Only of Thee," in *In the Field of Fire*, ed. Jeanne Van Buren Dann and Jack Dann (New York: T. Doherty Associates, 1987), 372–92.

35. Steve Hassett, "And what would you do, ma," in *The Vietnam War in American Stories, Songs, and Poems,* ed. H. Bruce Franklin (Boston: Bedford Books, 1996), 258.

36. Ronald Anthony Cross, "The Heavenly Blue Answer," ibid., 152.

37. Lewis Shiner, "The War at Home," ibid., 180.

38. For example, the novel is not mentioned or even listed in the bibliographies of Nancy Anisfield's *Vietnam Anthology: American War Literature* (Bowling Green, Ohio: Bowling Green State University Popular Press, 1987); John Hellman's *American Myth and the Legacy of Vietnam* (New York: Columbia University Press, 1986); and Philip D. Beidler's *American Literature and the Experience of Vietnam* (Athens: University of Georgia Press, 1982), though Beidler does give half a sentence to Haldeman's more overtly autobiographical *War Year.* The novel is very briefly mentioned in Timothy J. Lomperis, *"Reading the Wind": The Literature of the Vietnam War,* with bibliographic commentary by John Clark Pratt (Durham: Duke University Press, 1987). Science-fiction scholars and critics, however, have frequently discussed *The Forever War* as a major Vietnam War novel; such discussions include Joan Gordon, *Joe Haldeman* (Mercer Island, Wash.: Starmont House, 1980); Patrick L. McGuire, "The Forever War," in *Survey of Science Fiction Literature,* ed. Frank N. Magill (Englewood Cliffs, N.J.: Prentice-Hall 1979), 2:813–18; Darrell Schweitzer, "An Interview with Joe Haldeman," *Science Fiction Review* 20 (February 1977), 26–30; Ellen R. Weil, "From Autobiography to Fantasy: Joe Haldeman's *War Year* and *The Forever War,"* paper delivered at the Conference on the Fantastic in the Arts, Fort Lauderdale, March 17, 1989; and Tim Blackmore, "Warring Stories: Fighting for Truth in the Science Fiction of Joe Haldeman," *Extrapolation* 34 (Summer 1993), 131–46.

39. Joe Haldeman, *The Forever War* (New York: Ballantine Books, 1976), 47; hereafter cited by page in the text. This is the bestselling and most familiar text of the novel, which was originally serialized in *Analog* as "Hero" (June 1972), 8–59; "We Are Very Happy Here" (November 1973), 104–47; "This Best of All Possible Worlds" (November 1974), 137–49; and "End Game" (January 1975), 66–103. Haldeman has extensively revised the novel in its several editions since its first publication as a book in 1975. Robert Stone gives a stunning account of the "Great Elephant Zap" in *Dog Soldiers* (New York: Penguin, 1987), 41–42.

40. Ursula Le Guin, "Introduction to *The Word for World Is Forest,"* in *The Language of the Night: Essays on Fantasy and Science Fiction,* ed. Susan Wood (New York: G. P. Putnam's Sons, 1979), 151; this introduction was originally published in Ursula Le Guin, *The Word for World Is Forest* (London: Gollancz, 1977).

41. Ursula Le Guin, *The Word for World Is Forest,* in *Again, Dangerous Visions,* ed. Harlan Ellison (New York: New American Library, 1973), 112; hereafter cited in the text.

42. Lucius Shepard, "Delta Sly Honey," in *In the Field of Fire,* ed. Jeanne Van Buren Dann and Jack Dann (New York: T. Doherty Associates, 1987), 34.

43. Lucius Shepard, "Mengele," in *The Jaguar Hunter* (Sauk City, Wis.: Arkham House, 1987), 329; hereafter cited by page in the text. Originally published in *Universe 15,* ed. Terry Carr (New York: Random House, 1985).

44. Lucius Shepard, "Salvador," in *The Jaguar Hunter,* 65; hereafter cited by page in the text. Originally published in *The Magazine of Fantasy and Science Fiction* (April 1984).

45. For an indispensable exploration of other forms of militarism in post-Vietnam popular culture and politics, see James William Gibson, *Warrior Dreams: Paramilitary Culture in Post-Vietnam America* (New York: Hill and Wang, 1994).

46. Kurt Vonnegut, Jr., *Galápagos* (New York: Delacorte Press/Seymour Lawrence, 1985), 185.

47. Kurt Vonnegut, Jr., *Hocus Pocus* (New York: G. P. Putnam's Sons, 1990), 167; hereafter cited by page in the text.

CHAPTER 9. MISSING IN ACTION IN THE TWENTY-FIRST CENTURY

1. "Clinton on Vietnam's Legacy," *New York Times,* July 12, 1995.

2. *Nixon Speaks Out: Major Speeches and Statements by Richard Nixon in the Presidential Campaign of 1968* (New York: Nixon-Agnew Campaign Committee, 1968), 235.

3. Memorandum from Peter Flanigan, June 30, 1969, Nixon Presidential Materials Project, National Archives and Records Administration, White House Special Files, Haldeman Box 133, Perot Folder. For a more extensive account with additional documentation, see H. Bruce Franklin, *M.I.A. or Mythmaking in America* (New Brunswick, N.J.: Rutgers University Press, 1993), 50–56, 188–92.

4. Law 10/59, in *Vietnam and America,* ed. Marvin E. Gettleman, Jane Franklin, Marilyn Young, and H. Bruce Franklin (New York: Grove Press, 1995), 157–61.

5. The NLF estimated that prior to its formation, the Diem government had killed 90,000 and imprisoned 800,000, including 600,000 crippled by torture. *South Vietnam: From the NLF to the Provisional Revolutionary Government,* Vietnamese Studies 23, ed. Nguyen Khac Vien (Hanoi, 1970), 12. For primary documents on the formation of the NLF, see Gettleman et al., *Vietnam and America,* 165–92.

6. *In the Name of America: A Study Commissioned and Published by Clergy and Laymen Concerned about Vietnam, January 1968* (New York: E. P. Dutton, 1968); John Duffett, ed., *Against the Crimes of Silence: Proceedings of the International War Crimes Tribunal, Stockholm-Copenhagen* (New York: Simon and Schuster, 1968).

7. Howard Zinn, *A People's History of the United States* (New York: Harper Colophon Books, 1980), 469–70, discusses these early accounts. The classic description is Seymour Hersh, *My Lai 4* (New York: Random House, 1970).

8. Gettleman et al., *Vietnam and America,* 403–4.

9. Article 12 of the Geneva Convention stipulates: "Prisoners of war may only be transferred by the Detaining Power to a Power which is a party to the Convention and after the Detaining Power has satisfied itself of the willingness and ability of such transferee Power to apply the Convention"; South Vietnam was not a party to the Convention. For a description of South Vietnam's Con Son

Island prison, see Don Luce, "Behind Vietnam's Prison Walls," *Christian Century,* February 19, 1969, 261–64. Luce, who speaks Vietnamese, later led William Anderson and Representative Augustus Hawkins through the secret access to the tiger cages, which were photographed for *Life* by Tom Harkin (later elected to the U.S. Senate). The chief American adviser to the South Vietnamese prison system, Frank "Red" Walton (former police commander of the Watts district of Los Angeles), had first told the visiting congressional delegation that Con Son was like "a Boy Scout recreational camp"; after they found the cages, Walton angrily told them, "You aren't supposed to go poking your nose into doors that aren't your business" ("The Tiger Cages of Con Son," *Life,* July 17, 1970, 27–29).

10. *Final Report of the House Select Committee on Missing Persons in Southeast Asia,* 94th Cong., 2nd sess., December 13, 1976, 136.

11. Ibid., 106, 135; "Laird Appeals to Enemy to Release U.S. Captives," *New York Times,* May 20, 1969; Captain Douglas L. Clarke, *The Missing Man: Politics and the MIA* (Washington, D.C.: National Defense University, 1979), 32.

12. Editorial, "Inhuman Stance on Prisoners," *New York Times,* May 29, 1969.

13. Memorandum from Arthur Burns, April 9, 1969, and memorandum from Peter Flanigan, June 30, 1969, White House Special Files, Haldeman Box 133, Perot Folder; Robert Fitch, "H. Ross Perot: America's First Welfare Billionaire," *Ramparts* (November 1971), 42–51.

14. "Projects Proposed by Ross Perot," memorandum from Butterfield to Haldeman, Ehrlichman, Kissinger, and Harlow, October 24, 1969, White House Special Files, Haldeman Box 133, Perot Folder.

15. White House Special Files, Haldeman Box 55, John Brown folder.

16. *American Prisoners of War in Vietnam: Hearings before the Subcommittee on National Security Policy and Scientific Developments of the Committee on Foreign Affairs,* House of Representatives, 91st Cong., 1st sess., November 13, 14, 1969, 2, 6.

17. *American Prisoners of War in Southeast Asia, 1970: Hearings before the Subcommittee on National Security Policy and Scientific Developments of the Committee on Foreign Affairs,* House of Representatives, 91st Cong., 2nd sess., April 29; May 1, 6, 1970, 2.

18. "Message from Perot," memorandum for the president from Alexander Butterfield, President's Handwriting Files, Box 4. Nixon has written a big, double-underlined "Good!" on this memo.

19. "Wives Organizing to Find 1,332 G.I.'s Missing in War," *New York Times,* July 31, 1969; Joseph Lelyveld, " 'Dear Mr. President'—The P.O.W. Families," *New York Times Magazine,* October 3, 1971, 56; Jim and Sybil Stockdale, *In Love and War* (New York: Harper & Row, 1984), 133–46, 206–8, 210–13, 230–31, 306–7.

20. Stockdale and Stockdale, *In Love and War,* 310–11; testimony of Sybil Stockdale, in *American Prisoners of War in Southeast Asia, 1970,* 61.

21. "POW Policy in Vietnam," memorandum for the president from Henry A. Kissinger, October 2, 1969, White House Special Files, President's Office Files, Series A: Documents Annotated by the President, Box 3. The first major media event using the wives was a methodically planned meeting to be held on December 12 between the president and a carefully selected delegation

led by Sybil Stockdale. "Dick Capen and his people have worked hard to put together the package," Alexander Butterfield wrote to fellow White House staffer Colonel James D. Hughes on December 4, but "a final decision has been made that there will be no fathers among those invited so wives and mothers must be substituted for the 2 sets of parents," the "demographic spread" must be widened, and "there must be at least 1 and preferably 2 more enlisted men represented, without exceeding a total of 23 ladies" (memorandum from Butterfield to Colonel Hughes, December 4, 1969, White House Special Files, Haldeman Box 55, Hughes folder). Lyn Nofziger, director of communications for the Republican National Committee, asked Butterfield for "a brief bit on each POW wife we might be able to make use of . . . on the Hill" (Nofziger to Butterfield, December 4, 1969, White House Special Files, Butterfield, Box 8). Butterfield asked Hughes to forward the president's preplanned answers to possible questions from the press "so that I can complete the required scenario" (Butterfield to Hughes, December 8, 1969, White House Special Files, Haldeman Box 55, Hughes Folder).

22. Stockdale and Stockdale, *In Love and War,* 373.
23. *American Prisoners of War in Southeast Asia, 1970,* 20.
24. Ibid., 27.
25. Stockdale and Stockdale, *In Love and War,* 375–76; Clarke, *Missing Man,* 32; Iris R. Powers, "The National League of Families and the Development of Family Services," in *Family Separation and Reunion: Families of Prisoners of War and Servicemen Missing in Action,* ed. Hamilton I. McCubbin, Barbara Dahl, et al. (Washington, D.C.: U.S. Government Printing Office, [1974]), 5.
26. See Clarke, *Missing Man,* 34–35, on early government connections with the League; Representative Les Aspin introduced into the *Congressional Record* of January 22 and January 31, 1972, letters proving that the Republican National Committee was actually managing the fundraising campaign of the National League and that Senator Robert Dole of the Republican National Committee had placed "advisers" in the League's structure who coordinated its activities and public statements with his own.
27. *American Prisoners of War in Southeast Asia, 1970,* 66–79; "Exhibit to Stir Opinion on P.O.W.'s Open in Capitol," *New York Times,* June 5, 1970.
28. Jon M. Van Dyke, "Nixon and the Prisoners of War," *New York Review of Books,* January 7, 1971, 35; Richard A. Falk, "Pawns in Power Politics," reprinted in *American Prisoners of War in Southeast Asia, 1971: Hearings before the Subcommittee on National Security Policy and Scientific Developments of the Committee on Foreign Affairs,* House of Representatives, 92nd Cong., 1st sess., March 23, 24, 25, 30, 31; April 1, 6, 20, 1971, 474; Lieutenant Colonel Charles F. Kraak, *Family Efforts on Behalf of United States Prisoners of War and Missing in Action in Southeast Asia* (Carlisle Barracks, Pa.: Army War College, 1975), 16, 18.
29. Russell Kirk, "Students for Victory," *National Review,* May 31, 1966, 535; Janet L. Koenigsamen, "Mobilization of a Conscience Constituency: VIVA and the POW/MIA Movement" (Ph.D. diss., Kent State University, 1987), 36, 38.
30. Ibid., 37, 77–78.
31. Clarke, *Missing Man,* 40; Koenigsamen, "Mobilization," 65, 72; telephone interview with Mike Sasek, Defense Intelligence Agency, October 9, 1990.

32. Koenigsamen, "Mobilization," 44–46; "Reminder of Vietnam Stays on Hand," *Los Angeles Times,* February 13, 1989; telephone interview with Gloria Coppin, September 23, 1990. Coppin reports that at the ball Perot refused to help finance the bracelets and even refused her plea for a loan to initiate production.

33. Koenigsamen, "Mobilization," 44–50, 78; "Unit for P.O.W.'s Has New Project," *New York Times,* February 26, 1973. Other VIVA publicity products included matchbooks, bumper stickers, "missing man" stationery, Christmas cards, T-shirts, and sweatshirts; many of these were wholesaled to other political organizations.

34. Koenigsamen, "Mobilization," 55; "Unit for P.O.W.'s Has New Project"; "Reminder of Vietnam Stays on Hand."

35. "U.S. Gives Enemy List of Missing," *New York Times,* December 31, 1969.

36. Ibid.

37. "Vietnam Unique: PWs Languish as Political Pawns," *Christian Science Monitor,* December 12, 1970; the series had begun on November 27.

38. *Public Papers of the Presidents of the United States: Richard Nixon, 1971* (Washington, D.C.: U.S. Government Printing Office, 1973), 541; Tom Wicker, "Illogic in Vietnam," *New York Times,* May 25, 1971.

39. Jonathan Schell, "The Time of Illusion IV: For the Re-election of the President," *New Yorker,* June 23, 1975, 76; reprinted in Jonathan Schell, *The Time of Illusion* (New York: Knopf, 1976), 231.

40. Telephone interview with Gloria Coppin, September 23, 1990.

41. "Agreement on Ending the War and Restoring Peace in Viet-Nam," in Gettleman et al., *Vietnam and America,* 472, 473.

42. Richard Nixon, "Remarks at a Reception for Returned Prisoners of War, May 24, 1973," in *Public Papers of the Presidents of the United States: Richard Nixon, 1973* (Washington, D.C.: U.S. Government Printing Office, 1975), 558.

43. Nixon's secret letter is reprinted in Franklin, *M.I.A. or Mythmaking in America,* 204–7.

44. Confirmation Hearings of Dr. Henry Kissinger as Secretary of State, September 7, 10, 11, and 14, 1973, as reprinted in "Americans Missing in Southeast Asia," in *Hearings before the House Select Committee on Missing Persons in Southeast Asia,"* pt. 5, June 17, 25; July 21; and September 21, 1975, 175.

45. "Long Shadow of the M.I.A.'s Still Stalks a Pentagon Official," *New York Times,* September 20, 1992.

46. Quoted in Charles J. Patterson and Colonel G. Lee Tippin, *The Heroes Who Fell from Grace: The True Story of Operation Lazarus, the Attempt to Free American POWs from Laos in 1982* (Canton, Ohio: Daring Books, 1985), 102. Patterson, who was Gritz's second in command during the first raid, published an account in *Soldier of Fortune* magazine while Gritz was still in Southeast Asia, leading to a break between the two, who had fought together in the Special Forces in Vietnam. Getting to the truth about Gritz's adventures is a formidable task, especially since each of the three participants who have written extensively about them—Gritz, Patterson, and Scott Barnes—accuses the other two of being inveterate liars.

47. "Daring Search for POWs Told," *Los Angeles Times,* January 31, 1983; "'Star-studded' Raid Fails to Free POWs," *Star-Ledger* (Newark), February 1, 1983; "Private Raid on Laos Reported," *New York Times,* February 1, 1983; Patterson and Tippin, *Heroes Who Fell from Grace,* 52. Most of the stories about the Gritz raids were broken by the *Los Angeles Times,* which received a series of oral and written messages from him in January and February 1983.

48. *Report of the Select Committee on POW/MIA Affairs, United States Senate* (Washington, D.C.: U.S. Government Printing Office, 1993), 302.

49. "Daring Search for POWs Told"; Patterson and Tippin, *Heroes Who Fell from Grace,* 50, 70, 92–107.

50. Patterson and Tippin, *Heroes Who Fell from Grace,* 146; a less theatrical version is reported in "Eastwood Told Reagan of Planned POW Raid," *Los Angeles Times,* February 25, 1983.

51. Patterson and Tippin, *Heroes Who Fell from Grace,* 128–29, 147, 176; Scott Barnes with Melva Libb, *Bohica* (Canton, Ohio: Bohica Corp., 1987), 34.

52. "Remarks at a Meeting of the National League of Families of American Prisoners and Missing in Southeast Asia, January 28, 1983," in *Public Papers of the Presidents of the United States: Ronald Reagan, 1983* (Washington, D.C.: U.S. Government Printing Office, 1984), 131.

53. *Report of the Select Committee on POW/MIA Affairs,* 155.

54. Ibid., 305–10, 334–35.

55. Ibid., 221, 276–80.

56. Review by Richard Freedman, *Star-Ledger* (Newark), December 16, 1983; Al-jean Harmetz, "2 Holiday Movies Turn into Surprise Successes," *New York Times,* February 13, 1984.

57. For an incisive analysis of the protofascist content of the POW rescue films and other movies, see J. Hoberman, "The Fascist Guns in the West: Hollywood's 'Rambo' Coalition," *Radical America* 19, no. 6 (1985), 53–61, which also appeared in a revised form in *American Film* (March 1986).

58. My analysis of the role of gender in the POW rescue movies owes a considerable debt to Susan Jeffords, *The Remasculinization of America: Gender and the Vietnam War* (Bloomington: Indiana University Press, 1989).

59. Ibid., 148.

60. See Tony Williams, "*Missing in Action:* The Vietnam Construction of the Movie Star," in *From Hanoi to Hollywood,* ed. Linda Dittmar and Gene Michaud (New Brunswick, N.J.: Rutgers University Press, 1990), 129–44, for an excellent analysis of the creation of Norris's persona in the *Missing in Action* films. Louis J. Kern in "MIAs, Myth, and Macho Magic: Post-Apocalyptic Cinematic Visions of Vietnam," in *Search and Clear: Critical Responses to Selected Literature and Films of the Vietnam War,* ed. William J. Searle (Bowling Green, Ohio: Bowling Green State University Popular Press, 1988), 37–54, offers an exceptionally insightful overview of the psychosocial significance of what he calls "the POW-MIA/Avenger subgenre," tracing its cinematic history back to Norris's 1978 (not 1977, as indicated by Kern) film *Good Guys Wear Black.* A detailed explication of *Missing in Action* is given in *M.I.A. or Mythmaking in America,* 146–50.

61. Any exploration of the role of the frontier myth in American culture owes

much to Richard Slotkin, *Regeneration through Violence: The Mythology of the American Frontier, 1600–1860* (Middletown, Conn.: Wesleyan University Press, 1973), together with Slotkin's *The Fatal Environment: The Myth of the Frontier in the Age of Industrialization, 1800–1890* (New York: Atheneum, 1985). John Hellman, *American Myth and the Legacy of Vietnam* (New York: Columbia University Press, 1986), cogently relates the frontier myth to the imagined role of the Green Berets in Vietnam. My analysis is also indebted to Gaylyn Studler and David Desser's fine essay "Never Having to Say You're Sorry: *Rambo*'s Rewriting of the Vietnam War," *Film Quarterly* 42 (Fall 1988), 9–16. Other important writings on the cultural implications and effects of *Rambo* include Don Kunz, "First Blood Redrawn," *Vietnam Generation* 1 (Winter 1989): 94–111; and Gregory A. Waller, "*Rambo:* Getting to Win This Time," in Dittmar and Michaud, *From Hanoi to Hollywood,* 113–28.

62. For a more thorough explication of *Rambo,* see Franklin, *M.I.A. or Mythmaking in America,* 150–59.

63. "Reagan Cites 'Rambo' as Next-Time Example," *Star-Ledger* (Newark), July 1, 1985; "Reagan Gets Idea from 'Rambo' for Next Time," *Los Angeles Times,* July 1, 1985.

64. " 'Machismo' on Capitol Hill," *New York Times,* July 14, 1985.

65. "Iraq Spurns 'U.S.-imposed' Council Solution; Saddam Vows Fight for Kuwait," *Star-Ledger* (Newark), December 1, 1990.

66. Jacket copy, Jack Buchanan, *M.I.A. Hunter* (New York: Jove, 1985).

67. " 'Road Map' to Renew Ties with Hanoi Could Lead to Some Trade by Year End," *Wall Street Journal,* April 15, 1991; "Concerned Citizen Newsletter," *National League of Families of American Prisoners and Missing in Southeast Asia,* May 31, 1991.

68. U.S. Senate Committee on Foreign Relations Republican Staff, *An Examination of U.S. Policy toward POW/MIAs,* May 23, 1991, 5–8.

69. Ibid., November 1991 ed., 5–8.

70. *Hearings Before the Select Committee on POW/MIA Affairs,* pt. 1 of 2, November 5, 6, 7, and 15, 1991, 443–47.

71. Poll reported in "Minor Memos," *Wall Street Journal,* August 2, 1991.

72. Telephone interview with Commander Gregg Hartung, Public Affairs Office, Department of Defense, September 23, 1991. Since then, the Lao highlander has been extensively interviewed and photographed.

73. Interview with James Bamford, the investigative reporter who led the ABC News team that exposed the fraud, February 28, 1992. Bamford played for me the extensive video tapes showing the bird sanctuary and the bird smuggler and revealing the unmasking of the scam.

74. Defense Department press conference, July 2, 1992; "U.S. Is Sure Photo of Missing Is Fake," *New York Times,* July 19, 1992.

75. "Baker Presses Vietnam on MIAs, Cambodia," *St. Louis Post Dispatch,* July 25, 1991; UPI story datelined Olney, Ill., story tag "mia-borah," July 22, 1991; *Report of the Select Committee on POW/MIA Affairs,* 319.

76. *World News with Peter Jennings,* ABC, February 11 and February 12, 1992.

77. Memorandum from H. R. Haldeman to General Hughes, April 26, 1971; and "POW/MIA Wives," memorandum from General James D. Hughes to Halde-

78. My own efforts to testify, in which I persisted from February to December
1992, were officially rebuffed not only by the committee staff and in letters
from Senator Kerry but also by Senator Kerry and Senator Grassley when I
appeared with each of them separately on national television.

79. *Report of the Select Committee on POW/MIA Affairs*, 164.

80. David Jackson, "MIAs' Kin Want Perot as President," *Dallas Morning News*,
May 19, 1992; telephone interview with David Jackson, May 18, 1992; telephone interview with John LeBoutillier, June 12, 1992; "It's Businessman
Perot and Not War Hero Bush Who Attracts a Following Among U.S. Veterans," *Wall Street Journal*, July 2, 1992.

81. "Bush Sees Gain in Vietnam Ties," *Los Angeles Times*, October 24, 1992.

82. "Corporations Ask Bush to Lift Vietnam Ban," *New York Times*, May 9, 1992;
"Vietnam: The Big Buildup Begins," *Washington Post*, December 9, 1992.

83. "Nixon Opposing U.S.-Vietnam Normalization Policy: He Could Influence
Any Move by Bush Administration to End Trade Embargo," *Los Angeles Times*,
January 9, 1993.

84. "President Clinton, Normalize Ties with Vietnam," *Wall Street Journal*, March 8,
1993.

85. "Clinton Prepares to Relax Policy on Vietnam as U.S. Business Urges Access
to New Market," *Wall Street Journal*, April 12, 1993.

86. "U.S. to Press Hanoi to Explain '72 P.O.W. Report," *New York Times*, April 13,
1993.

87. *Washington Times*, April 12, 1993; *USA Today*, April 12, 1993; *Washington Post*,
April 15, 1993; *Jersey Journal*, April 18, 1993.

88. References are to a photocopy of the English-language text sent by fax from
the Moscow Bureau of the *New York Times* to the *Times* Foreign Desk with a
cover letter referring to it as a "Sept 15, 1972 Vietnamese Top Secret report,
recently discovered in Soviet Communist Party archives — confirming that
Vietnam was holding on to far more US POWs than it had publicly [sic]
admitted." I am grateful to *Times* reporter Steven A. Holmes for this copy. For
detailed exposés of the document, see Nayan Chanda, "Research and Destroy," *Far Eastern Economic Review*, May 6, 1993, 20; and H. Bruce Franklin,
"M.I.A.sma," *The Nation*, May 10, 1993, 616.

89. "In Clinton's Words: 'Fullest Possible Accounting' of M.I.A.'s," *New York
Times*, February 4, 1994.

90. *Wall Street Journal*, April 23, 1993.

INDEX

Numerals in italics indicate illustrations.

INDEX

H. BRUCE FRANKLIN is the author or editor of seventeen previous books on culture and history. Before his academic career, he served three years as a navigator and intelligence officer in the U.S. Air Force. He is currently the John Cotton Dana Professor of English and American Studies at Rutgers University in Newark, New Jersey.